A Gringo's Journey

Cris Osborn

A Gringo's Journey

Cris Osborn

Impact Books

First published in Great Britain 1989
by Impact Books, 112 Bolingbroke Grove, London SW11 1DA

© Cris Osborn 1989

All rights reserved. No part of this publication may be
reproduced in any form or by any means without the prior
permission of Impact Books.

British Library Cataloguing in Publication Data
Osborn, Cris
    A gringo's journey.
    1. South America. Description & travel
    I. Title
    918′.0438

    ISBN .i.0–245–55066–6

Acknowledgements

Front cover photograph by
Julian and Delia Thomas

Back cover photograph by
Cris Osborn

Made and printed in Great Britain by
The Guernsey Press Co. Ltd., Guernsey, Channel Islands.

Contents

Map 7
1. Dancing naked in the moonlight (USA) 9
2. A coyote comes to dine (Mexico) 16
3. Shipwrecked in a mangrove swamp (Belize) 37
4. Bolt cutters to the rescue (Guatemala) 44
5. Hurricanes, earthquakes and volcanoes (Guatemala) 49
6. Sugar cubes and a cardboard village (El Salvador to Panama) 58
7. Death-defying gradients (Colombia) 72
8. Mudslides and guinea pigs (Ecuador) 80
9. Dodging bullets and chewing coca (Peru) 89
10. Inca ruins and lemon pie (Peru) 123
11. Tear-gassed in La Paz (Bolivia) 137
12. Blinded by the salt (Bolivia) 147
13. Out of sight, out of mind, almost out of tea (Chile) 172
14. A desert full of flowers (Chile) 185
15. Rolling south to the Useless Bay (Chile) 201
16. Trouble at the border (Peru) 215
17. Tigers in the night (Bolivia to Paraguay) 225
18. Smugglers and armadillos (Paraguay to Bolivia) 243

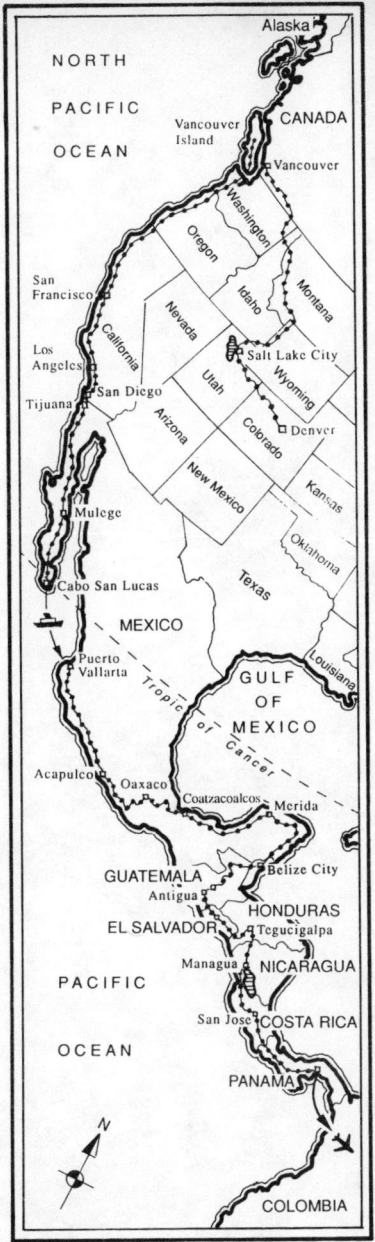

Author's Route ◆━━━□━━━□━━━□━━━◆

800 Miles

1. Dancing naked in the moonlight

It's a fine day to go to Peru. At least – it looks a fine day outside. This is my second day confined to a Greyhound bus and I am convinced that there must be a better way to go. Peru is still a long way off, and it seems overly reclusive to continue the journey imprisoned in such a fashion. A bicycle surely, would be more suitable for long distance travel.

I leave the bus in Denver, Colorado, and wander into a sporting goods supermarket downtown. Bicycles are on the fifth floor.

'What sort of bike are you looking for?' inquires the assistant.

What sort do I need to go to Peru, I wonder? My experience of bicycles is limited to the mad dash to arrive at work on time, and the occasional evening excursion to a local pub, with a group of friends whose preference for beer to bicycling fuelled an enthusiastic and sometimes foolhardy disregard for all cycling convention. A bicycle is something that you pedal and it goes.

'What sort would you recommend for touring?' I ask.

'Where are you planning on going?' she asks.

'Well, I thought I might go to Peru', I reply.

She waits for me to blurt out some other indication of jest or insanity, but I remain sensibly silent.

'Perhaps you should go to a specialist and get one made to measure', she suggests, which is clearly unnecessary, surrounded as we are by a sea of bicycles. I start looking around.

'One of these ought to do', I say, and seeing now that I am serious, she helpfully advises on technical aspects. We eventually agree on a Japanese bike – a Fuji – which satisfies both her concern with mechanical specifications and my concern with aesthetics – good looks and a nice colour.

After a trial spin around the tennis courts on the store roof, we fix on a rear rack and a set of large panniers. With a few tools and assorted accessories it is fit for the road.

'There's a ten per cent discount for registered club members', she tells me at the cash desk. I tell her about my pub-going friends in England, but as we are not included in her list of clubs I pay the full four hundred dollars. She gives me a free bell and I abandon my rucksack on the store floor.

Highway 36 west of Denver provides a formidable introduction to cycle touring. The Rocky Mountains rise up in an impressive wall. The road climbs up through flowered meadows and pine forests, and finally through bare rock where at twelve thousand feet it is the highest paved road in the U.S.A. Several sightseers admiring the view from the top remind me of this fact.

I don't get a chance to admire the view because I am too busy panting and wheezing and vowing to pack up smoking, and before I have caught my breath the pass is engulfed in thick cloud. The wind howls dramatically, and everybody climbs back into their cars as rain and sleet hammer down.

I discover a puncture. It takes me an hour to fix, crouching in the lay-by with frozen fingers, remembering fondly the days of weatherproof reclusion confined to a Greyhound bus.

Crossing the dry barren plains of Utah with clumps of sage brush and squeaking gophers, my skin is burnt red, and peels from an excess of sunshine. An appreciation of scale as well as intimacy with the climate is thrust upon the cycle tourist. Vast distances must be pedalled between towns, across shimmering silent empty regions broken only by features with such welcoming names as Starvation Lake and Dead Man's Gulch.

This is vacation season, when families take to the road in mobile homes for a quick two-week ten thousand mile tour, staying at night in the numerous campsites dotted across the country, close enough together to be reached most nights even by slow moving cyclists.

The outgoing American personality, never more pronounced than when on vacation, ensures that evenings are a whole heap of fun and geniality, with the cooking of food over the campfire, the swapping of tales and exchange of opinions, always expressed in a loud voice, and a communal appreciation of the great outdoors before retiring to the T.V. lounge of the mobile home for the late show.

If I mention my intentions of cycling beyond the borders of the U.S., stories are inevitably told of the university professor who went to Mexico and disappeared without a trace, even though investigators sent to determine his fate found the chief of police in the town he was last heard of driving around in his car, a story I hear a hundred times in varying forms and just one of the many parables of paranoia which reinforce the cozy belief that civilization ends at the national border. A belief that is of course common to all nations, because people go missing everywhere, and even when they don't there's always something else to pick on that serves equally well to arouse our fear.

After a few weeks I feel more at ease on the bike. I can plod along all day without crumpling into an exhausted heap in the evening, and, already well-practised in the arts of mending punctures, speaking in a loud voice, and keeping to the right hand side of the road, I have time to assume an air of self-confidence when, cruising down from the Wasatch range of the Rockies, banking steeply into the bends that zigzag away out of sight, whistling an arrogant little tune, I have my first accident.

Misjudging the severity of a particularly sharp bend, the road continues to curve away from me, and as I turn more acutely to meet it, the front wheel which handles lightly because of the weight carried over the rear, slips on some gravel and slides over the edge. I have a brief but tantalising view of nothing below before wrenching my feet from the toe clips, and pushing down on the bike to launch myself back onto the road.

'You stupid idiot.' I lie cursing myself, and the stupid bike too while I'm at it, but I'm relieved when I peer over the edge to see it caught on some sturdy bushes just a few feet below, close enough to haul back up. The front brake is smashed up, handlebars and front forks are a little twisted and the front wheel is badly buckled though it still wobbles its way round.

A car stops by.

'Hey feller, what happened to you? You're all covered in blood.' I do look a mess, and I'm shaking now. A woman gets out of the car with some water and a bottle of disinfectant.

'Want a ride down?' the man asks.

'No thanks, I'll ride', I say, not feeling at all like it.

At Union, the first small town on the comfortingly flat plain below, the reaction from the first person I meet is equally comforting, and typical of the welcome extended to strangers away from big cities.

'Is there anywhere around here to camp?' I ask a woman hosing down her front lawn.

'Sure, bring your bike out back, you can sleep on my trampolene. Hey, you look a bit roughed up, better come inside and take a shower.' She makes a plate of sandwiches, boils some corn fresh from the garden, and we sit and eat and watch T.V. and she tells me she's going to visit her son in hospital in nearby Salt Lake City who is still paralysed after being knocked off his motorbike six months ago by a drunk driver.

'I'm off now, and I won't be back until tomorrow. Just pull the door to when you leave in the morning', she says, and leaves me alone in the house.

Salt Lake City was founded a hundred and thirty years ago by a small group of Mormons seeking a place to practise their new found religion. The land around the Great Salt Lake was sufficiently barren and uninhabitable to be free of any constraints, and there they camped.

Today it is a modern city, the glass and concrete sky-scrapers of its thriving commercial centre can be seen from afar, sticking up from the plain into the blue desert sky, and the Mormons who live here are now sufficiently numerous and established to journey to places all over the world, encouraging religious constraints of their own.

I stay here with some distant relatives, who show me around town, and the lake that is twenty five per cent salt, warm and syrupy and leaves a sticky white crust on the skin, and who also introduce me to the delights of the thirty-two flavour ice cream parlours.

I head north east into Wyoming, through Yellowstone Park with its abundance of natural curiosities, and convoys of camper vans that shuffle along between wayside points of interest, boiling mud pools, petrified trees, fields full of hot springs and spurting geysers, pausing in long lines to photograph a bear, or allow a moose to cross the road.

Hikers and cyclists who spend the nights unprotected by mobile homes in what are denoted as 'primitive' areas of the campsites, are advised to remove all food from their tents, and to suspend it in bags from lofty branches of trees, or from the metal bars supported on poles provided specifically for the purpose, to be out of reach of the nocturnal scavengings of hungry bears, whose keen sense of smell and general lack of manners lead them to raid the tents of sleeping campers in pursuit of nourishment as unlikely as a peanut butter sandwich.

A snuffling sound awakes me during the night. I poke my head out of the tent to see a group of raccoons clambering over the bicycle, deftly unzipping panniers with their hands. One delves in and pulls out my camera for inspection, and finding it inedible, tosses it to the ground among a pile of other previously discarded objects.

'Hey, clear off !' I shout, and lob over a shoe, to no effect. I rush out of the tent to scare them away, waving my arms and shoo-shooing threateningly. They are unmoved, and greet me with growlings and hissing and an impressive array of bared teeth. Feeling vulnerable, having no clothes on, I back off, pick up a long stick and select a hefty rock from the fireplace. I advance again, with determination this time, beating the stick on the ground, brandishing the rock menacingly above my head, and for added effect improvise a little war dance. At this crucial and dramatic moment some late arrivals enter the camp in a van, the raccoons scamper off, and I am caught in the headlights, jigging foolishly with rock and stick, stark naked.

'Oh, Montana is beautiful,' people say, 'and it's just up the road', and though two months ago I thought you had to be crazy to ride six miles, now I ride sixty a day and it feels O.K. and from Montana it's just a short ride into Canada, west across the pine forests of the spectacular Cascade Mountains of British Columbia, down into Vancouver. Everything is soaked through from the steady rain that has fallen for the past four days. I'm wet and cold and my knees are aching, and I haven't seen the sun for a week. It is time to head south.

As a typically reserved and unforthcoming Englishman I find something attractive in the apparently forthright manner of the typical American. It seems as though everybody is charging around just looking for somebody in whom to confide. Anybody, and everybody, as if seeking approval. A chance acquaintance will forego pleasantries to open up their heart or pour out their troubles, and no doubt the fact that the people I meet when travelling know that they are unlikely to meet me again encourages this talkativeness, this appearance of extroversion, that is really introversion because all that they talk about revolves around themselves.

As I've caught a chill and I'm low on energy after a week in the cold and damp, I take refuge from a thunderstorm in a roadside cafe south of Seattle in the misty north of Washington State. On hearing my English accent, the man from an adjoining table comes over with his knife and fork and plate of hamburgers, skips introductory formalities and steams right in with an account of his life so far. It's not been so good just recently. Since his wife left him a year ago he's been touring the country in a pick-up truck with his five year old son, working here and there, feeling bad. I nod sympathetically, not feeling too good myself right now. He tells me his name is Jai.

'Hey you seem pretty pleased with yourself,' he says, 'what is your dream, man?' I say I'm heading for Lake Titicaca on my bicycle.

'Hey, where's that?' he asks. I draw a sketch map of South America on a paper napkin and shade in a little patch on the borders of Peru and Bolivia.

'Hey, that's far out', he says, 'Why there, man?' I tell him how the idea arose a couple of years ago, from deep in the comforting fog of intoxication which blankets much of Britain on a Saturday night and provides refuge from the dull routine of working life: save up some money and get away. But where to? As boredom was the thing to escape, it had to be somewhere I knew as little as possible about, and preferably a long way away, so that even if it turned out not to be a very interesting place, at least there'd be a chance of having an interesting and unpredictable time in getting there. Then there was a T.V. programme about South America that showed a lake high up in the Andes called Titicaca. It looked nice enough there. It even had a foreign sounding romantic sort of name. So I saved up some money and packed in my job with the bus company, and here I am, with five thousand pounds in the bank and a bicycle, and though I've already pedalled two thousand miles, Peru is still farther away than when I started.

'Everything you have, people will try to take away from you,' Jai explains to me, 'but if you get there it will always be with you' and he thumps the table for emphasis. He likes this dream. I tell him what he said may well be so but it's not the reason I'm making this journey, but because I'm sick of driving buses, and I can't think of anything better to do.

The man at the cash register by the door asks me where I'm headed as I leave.

'South', I tell him, not being particularly forthcoming now even though I know I will never meet him again, as getting back out into the rain is taking all my energy.

'How far south?' he asks, unsatisfied, 'Oregon, San Francisco, L.A.?' he adds this last with a touch of sarcasm.

'That's right', I reply, 'maybe Mexico'.

He raises his eyebrows now, the preliminary to his missing professor story and perhaps some advice about Mexicans in general, but before he can speak Jai shouts across from the middle of the cafe.

'Hey man, go to that lake in Peru.' Everybody looks at him. 'He's going to Peru on his bicycle', explains Jai to the other customers, and everybody seems to approve.

'All right!' some exclaim. 'Go for it!' encourage others and outside in the cold and wet I still can't think of anything better to do.

I join the throngs of cyclists heading down south with the strong breeze along the Pacific coast highway, through Oregon and California, and every day there are picnics in the late summer sunshine, and bonfire reunions on beach camp sites. There's Joseph and Henrike from Germany, heading for Belize, Rhyllid and Gerard and their two year old daughter from France, heading for Rio de Janeiro and an old man of sixty five, the only one heading north for home in Vancouver, who has travelled ten thousand miles on a second-hand bicycle by way of Australia.

2. A coyote comes to dine

Beyond the wire fence is Mexico. The change is sudden and complete. Shabby buildings line the streets of Tijuana, where old battered cars and buses to and fro in noisy confusion.

The road out of town leads up a long steep hill which battered old trucks ascend at a crawl, chugging out clouds of black fumes, forcing me off the road with prolonged hoots. The road is lined with shacks made of corrugated iron, polythene and cardboard boxes, and people emerge from the dark interiors to stand and watch me go by. Standing and staring is an acceptable and common pastime in Mexico, but I am new to it and find it unnerving. Yesterday I was familiar with reactions and attitudes. Today everything is different, including myself. Here I am an outsider, a foreign tourist who sticks out a mile, and I imagine hostility from people I do not understand. I climb the hill with a determination and concentration that excludes the immediate reality of a strange Mexico.

The efficient irrigation systems of southern California which make habitable much of the desert there, are non existent here. Beyond town, either side of the road is barren rocky ground, with here and there a tough bush sprouting between boulders.

A lone coyote ambles across the road up ahead, then a road-runner appears, sprinting off up the road for half a mile before disappearing up a gulley. I disappear up the gulley too, to spend the night on the flat sandy bottom, hidden from the road behind a large boulder as I'm still in the grip of 'missing professor stories'.

My ears ring in the silence, though there are many night-time noises to focus on. The scratching and scurrying of desert creatures unseen, the buzzing of an insect from behind a nearby boulder, and the barking and howling of coyotes, clear but distant. At dawn too there are sounds, as I wake to the thrumming of a vivid red and green hummingbird, hovering with wings ablurr a foot above my face.

A breeze from the ocean helps keep the morning cool, but by midday it is unbearably hot, with no shade from the overhead sun, everything shimmers in waves of rising heat. The road winds up over passes, down through long broad valleys, the lumpy asphalt often buried under dust and sand, and in places ripped completely away by last month's hurricane. A few trucks only pass on the road, the drivers, if they see me from under big sombreros, grin and wave. Others appear to be asleep. Beyond the road the desert stretches to the horizon, hot and lifeless except for cacti clustered in gullies, clinging to the sides of huge canyons, in all shapes and sizes, from miniature furry balls to gnarled giants hundreds of years old, fifty feet high, ten feet wide, with spines two feet long.

Rosario is a small village of crumbling adobe houses, dusty streets deserted in the afternoon heat. The tiny central plaza is empty too, except for the insects which hum around the enormous bright red flowers growing from an otherwise bare tree. I sit in its shade and try to put together a few words of Spanish.

'Can you give me some water please' seems like a good phrase to start with in the desert, though my phrase-book is full of less appropriate expressions like 'I want to hire the red sports car', and 'Take my suitcases to the fifth floor'.

A wizened old man emerges from a doorway, stands staring at me for a while before shuffling over, grins and speaks a few words. I say hello and grin back, shrugging my shoulders to indicate my incomprehension, then try with 'Can you give me some water please?' He beckons me to follow him into a doorway, through a single-roomed house, dark and cool, and out into a courtyard to a wooden barrel of water. He lifts the tin cover and fills my bottles from a plastic bowl. Back in the plaza, he communicates by sign language that the other building with an open door is a cafe. Inside are a couple of tables and chairs, a five year old Coca Cola calendar, and several chickens pecking around at the floor. A young girl comes through the smoky kitchen doorway and speaks a rapid stream of words which I take to be the choice of food. I ask for the only thing I can pronounce which turns out to be fried eggs and chillies with tortillas.

'How much is that?' I manage with the help of the phrase-book, though however much it is remains a mystery as I haven't learned numbers yet. I hold out a handful of coins and she takes what she wants.

It's cool enough to ride again in the late afternoon, past the few small fields that surround the village, past lemon groves, and peppers laid out to dry on roofs or on the ground in great red patches, slowly shrivelling and turning darker. The bridge that spanned the gorge just out of town has recently collapsed, and lies in chunks in the dry river bed. It fell during the hurricane, say the men levelling a route between boulders and lumps of concrete. An open-backed truck trailing a cloud of dust is trundling down the track to the river bed, the back full of men returning to Rosario after a day picking water melons. They grin and wave and call out 'Gringo', and toss me down a large ripe fruit.

For all the promises of a speedy disappearance at the hands of Mexicans, I have yet to meet one who has not been friendly and helpful, and patient in understanding my attempts to speak Spanish. Tonight I am no longer preoccupied with sleeping where I cannot be seen from the road, and bloated with watermelon, I doze off peacefully.

I am startled awake with a sharp pain where my ankle is being tightly gripped. I sit up with a fearful yell and the grip is released, though it takes a few seconds to undo the drawcord of my sleeping bag that has been done up to leave an opening just large enough for my nose to poke out, before I see my assailant. The face of a large coyote stares back at me, unafraid. He's standing just a few feet away with his mouth open, tongue lolling, sharp teeth glistening in the moonlight, looking to me like a hungry wolf. We stare at each other in mutual surprise for a few seconds. Then he lowers his head, flares his nostrils to sniff, and moves closer as if for another nibble. 'Yah! Shoo, shoo!' I shout, waving my arms in the air, and he ambles off a little way. My eyes have become accustomed to the moonlight now, and I can make out the shapes of half a dozen other coyotes, some sitting on their haunches, others standing stock-still, all watching me. I lob over a few rocks, and warn them to clear off. They trot around, whimper a little, then quietly disappear into the boulders and cacti and shadows. I lie down with penknife and a pile of rocks near to hand, and though I feel as if I am being watched, sleep undisturbed. The dawn reveals many sets of paw prints circling close to my sleeping bag.

The desert peninsula of Baja California is one of the most sparsely populated areas of Mexico. Towns are marked on the map as being sixty miles apart all the way south to the ports of La Paz and Cabo San Lucas and the ferry links with the mainland.

The town marked as Laguna ChapelIa is just a single shack in the middle of a vast plain of yellow sand. I rest in the shade of the porch. Several scrawny turkeys peck around in the dust. An old man lives here, alone in the empty desert, and he is eager to learn what I am doing out here, and all I can say is yes and no and shrug my shoulders in frustration, and ask for some water. He brings me two murky glasses which I drink thirstily, and which, down the road a few miles later, make me sick. There is no shade, and the bare rock and sand is too hot to sit on so there is nothing else but to continue, following a meandering course along the road as it winds up through stifling canyons of bare rock, out across a high plain where the hot wind is laden with sand that gets in my eyes and ears and down my throat. By evening I am too tired to think. The black dot of a vulture hanging motionless in the air high above is my only companion, and it's there in the morning when I awake, like a guardian angel, though it's much lower now, close enough for me to distinguish its features. A few seconds after I open my eyes it glides away.

I cook up the last of a packet of semolina for breakfast, though I can't keep it down. I think it's going to be a bad day.

The next town marked on my map turns out to be the remains of a wooden hut. Now there's just tumbleweed caught between the few wooden boards, and sand drifting over the floor. I sit down, sick and thirsty, wondering what the hell I'm doing here, unable to speak to anybody because there is nobody here, and even if there were they wouldn't understand me, physically and mentally unprepared for the desert that has sucked me dry, worn me down, stripped away a thin veneer of strength and independence. The unchanging landscape provides little distraction for my imagination, which runs away unchecked, digging itself deeper into a hole. Four days into Mexico and I am a wreck.

A jeep with a young couple inside pulls up by the roadside.

'Hey, do you want a ride?' I gratefully accept.

Ernie and Sue come from L.A. They're spending a couple of months touring Mexico with their two year old daughter Natalie. We speed along the road that follows the east coast of jagged brown headlands that jut out into clear turquoise sea, and camp on one of the many white sandy bays dotted with palm trees south of Mulehe. The beach is crowded with vultures that hop around, scrawny necked and not at all shy, to within a few yards of where we are setting up tents. Sue shies rocks at those close to where Natalie is playing.

Adrian and Christa spot our camp from the road, and rumble down the steep track on their B.M.W. to join us. They've come from Canada, heading down south on the first leg of a world tour. The beach is becoming crowded with gringos. There's an old man camped at the far end of the beach, cooking fish. He tells me he's called Tom, that he's sixty one, and that he spends the winter every year living on the beaches of Mexico. In the summer he teaches linguistics at a North Dakota university.

The air is full of wheeling turkey vultures, frigate birds, and groups of noisome pelicans that plunge into the sea with a tremendous splash, then bob to the surface to swallow whatever fish their enormous bills have enclosed. Fish eagles occasionally leave their perches atop cacti to swoop low over the water and with talons extended, pluck fish from just below the surface.

We decide we should eat fish too. Ernie and Sue have a selection of rods and tackle, masks and a speargun. A few feet offshore there is a wealth of fish. Shoals of tiny brightly coloured ones, and larger specimens also of striking design swim lazily to and fro, fearlessly approaching right up to our masks. It would seem unsportingly easy to kill them, though we steel ourselves in the interests of our bellies, but once armed with the speargun they seem to sense our mal-intentions and remain wisely out of range. We woo them closer with promises of goodwill, concealing the speargun behind our backs, and once within range, launch off the spear in unashamed betrayal at the fattest part of their bodies. Somehow they always dodge away unspeared, free to warn their fellows.

Empty-bellied we clamber over rocky promontories and cast lines into deep water, hopeful of hooking the big one that will fill our pot and stomachs, but all we get is sunburnt.

Evenings are spent in less energetic activities, cooking fish bought from the village, drinking cool beer, analysing our failure with speargun and line, planning how we will cook tomorrow's catch.

Ernie was born in Argentina, speaks fluent Spanish and is a devout Catholic. The village church, like many built by forced labour from the rubble of Indian temples destroyed by the conquistadores, looks more like a fortress than a place of worship, a design feature perhaps fitting for a religion that was compatible with mass slaughter and gained converts by the sword. Ernie was upset to find inside, alongside paintings and statues of Christian saints, those of Indian deities, with animals' heads, sneaked into the decor by the newly and incompletely converted when the church was built. Adrian is a confirmed atheist, and this, like most other topics of apparently no religious content, leads to lengthy discussion of theology and philosophy and other matters of great practical inconsequence long into the night. Sometimes Tom joins the party, fortified with fish he caught himself, and complicates discussions with his own ideas. He became a Buddhist in Laos where he taught English for many years after giving up spying for the U.S. government. Sometimes he digs up his stash of local grown grass and we smoke a few joints and forget our dogmas for a while.

Waiting for the ferry in the harbour of Cabo San Lucas, I bump into Joseph and Henrike again. We met briefly a month ago in California. They are heading south through Mexico towards Belize.

On deck we join several hundred other passengers, waving to the people on the dock, and causing the boat to list to one side as it leaves the harbour, nudging gently aside a lolling grey whale before chugging out to sea towards the mainland.

The ferry arrives at Puerto Vallerta, a port town nestled among palm trees and the humid green of forested mountains that surround the bay. It is a popular holiday resort for Mexicans and foreigners alike.

We bump and clatter down the narrow cobbled back streets crammed with dingy signs of hotels and bars, and take a room in a small pension which we share with cockroaches, lizards and oversized spiders.

'You must be very poor to have to travel by bicycle', sympathises the woman who runs the pension. 'There are many bad people about', she continues, 'Do you carry pistols?' I explain that we travel like this by choice, and no we don't carry pistols. This news travels. A man approaches us later to make good our deficiency, producing a gun from his pocket. Joseph inspects it.

'This weapon would be very useful to you against the desperados you will meet on the road – you can shoot them down as you are cycling along'.

The road south follows the coastline around bays and headlands in great loops and curves, cutting passage through a mass of shiny green trees on mountainsides humming with insects and brightly coloured birds.

Mid-afternoon is too hot for anything but rest. We stop at the tiny village of El Tuite and sit in the shade inside a small roadside cafe where many locals are drinking coffee or beer. Some are asleep – it's siesta time, although there is never any obligation to leave after a drink or a meal in a Mexican cafe whatever time of day it is. We eat beans and tortillas and talk as best we can with people who come and go.

When it is dark, the woman who runs the cafe with her children is happy to let us sleep in the backyard. Joseph and Henrike compete with chickens and pigs for groundspace for their tent and I tie up the hammock I bought in the U.S. It's a toy really, in comparison with the fine Mexican hammocks we see everywhere that can comfortably sleep whole families. I have not used it before and make several unsuccessful attempts to clamber in, only to fall out again, cocooned in a sleeping bag with a thud into the dust. The children watching giggle and point at my antics, Joseph and Henrike laugh loudly and offer derisive comments but eventually contain themselves to help me in. It is most uncomfortable but I'm determined to stick it out for the night without further loss of face.

The village stirs to life before dawn, with croaking frogs and birdsong mingling with the sound of people arising, banging on doors, hawking and spitting. A bus rumbles by slowly in the dark, with no lights except for a man sitting on the bonnet, shining a torch onto the road ahead. From within the cafe come the smells of fried chillies, hot tortillas, and I'm very glad to be out of the hammock and to stroll round the yard, joining the chorus of grunting pigs and clucking chickens with the creaking and cracking of cramped limbs and bones.

South of Manzanillo most traffic uses the inland highway which is in a better state of repair, and far quicker to destinations further down the coast than the meandering and incompleted coast road. No villages are marked on our map for a couple of hundred miles to Acapulco, though we pass through numerous tiny settlements of subsistence farmers, fishing communities, and clusters of huts of the workers employed by the large banana plantations.

The empty road enables Joseph to demonstrate his technique for relaxing the muscles in the back of the neck that can become stiff after long hours of riding. He simply lets his head hang down with his face to the ground. That he then cannot see where he is going seems not to concern him.

A loud bang shatters the peace. Joseph's front tube has exploded. Punctures come in batches and then don't occur for weeks. This is his third this morning, and it provides another good excuse for a rest and a brew of tea. We find some shade under a palm tree, above the roadside expanse of marsh where white herons and storks stand motionless, fishing. Joseph's already much patched tube now has an irreparable hole blown out of it so he puts in one of his new tubes from Puerto Vallerta, which turns out to be twenty seven inch size, too small for his twenty eight inch wheels. He blows a little air into it, Henrike and I lend our hands to stretch it around, but as fast as it goes on at one place it comes off at another. Joseph swears vengeance on the man who sold him the undersized tube, and retires for a cigarette.

There is a crashing and bashing behind us, then two shining machete blades appear, hacking and slashing a gap in the dense foliage, through which two campesinos eventually emerge, dressed in calf length baggy white trousers, sweat stained shirts and wide brimmed hats.

'Good morning', they greet us politely in the manner of campesinos, and take in the situation immediately.

'You have punctured?'

'Yes,' replies Joseph, 'and look here at this tube, it's too small to fit.' They roar with laughter. They work on a nearby banana plantation they tell us. We tell them we are going to Acapulco and they recommend that we take the bus. Then we all crowd around the wheel, knees and shoulders jostling, and our ten hands successfully stretch on the offending tube.

Eager for a refreshing swim, Joseph investigates a steep rocky track that leads down towards the shore. When he doesn't reappear we follow, and find him relaxing in a tiny fishing village, reclining in one of several rope hammocks hanging beneath a thatch awning, swigging at a bottle of beer. A number of other gringos are here – New Zealanders who have installed themselves under the awning that has become a restaurant. They've been here a month, surfing the huge Pacific rollers that wash up on this part of the coast.

Some fields of maize lie next to the stream that dissects the small bay, goats and pigs scratch a living too, though most of the village's hundred or so inhabitants live from fishing. The young Mexican who has turned his front yard into a restaurant spends much of the day fishing from the shore, throwing a circular net at those fish that are visible as silvery outlines in the tops of the waves, made translucent by the sun just before they break. He dives for oysters from the sea bed too. His wife cooks tortillas, eggs and rice to sell to the crowd of hungry gringos, who have the job of looking after the kids when their parents are not around. The small children from the village, even those that can hardly walk, show no fear of the huge breakers that wash up the steep beach right up to the edges of the huts, and all are proficient surfers on pieces of driftwood.

Our siesta here lasts for several days.

In the evenings some of the villagers come around and everybody drinks beer and tells stories. A few nights ago they all visited a local rodeo, and after a few beers one of the New Zealanders was inspired to take part – a brave but short-lived adventure ending in him being unceremoniously stepped on by a bull – an event which is re-enacted for our benefit. He has a broken rib and a gash in his side. One of the old women in the village applied a poultice of hot leaves and bandaged him up. He says it hurts like hell.

He's not having much luck with animals. One night he awakens everybody with cries for help, as his tent, pitched under the thatch awning, is pulled down around him. The unwitting assailant is an enormous sea turtle, digging a hole in which to lay her eggs. Apparently undisturbed by the crowd of noisy torch-shining gringos, she continues shovelling sand with spade-like flippers, lays a pile of eggs, covers them over and shambles back slowly to the sea.

The impromptu restaurant of a poor Mexican family and temporary residence of a crowd of ever hungry gringos was an unfortunate choice of nest sites, and in the morning, in shameless disregard for marine conservation, we all eat turtle egg omelettes. Such a rich source of protein are they that every one of us buzzes around all morning with an excess of energy. Joseph, Henrike and I are even motivated to end our three-day siesta, load up our junk, push it up the steep track and head off down the road.

We stop at a deserted crossroads an hour or so before dark, thinking about where we might stay for the night. Large tarantulas are crossing the road here, striding out on long hairy legs, strikingly marked in bright orange, pink and black. We follow the rough track that we think should lead to the sea but which peters out after a few miles in a dusty village where we are immediately surrounded by children.

'What do you want?' they ask. We ask if it is far to the sea.

'It's a long way. Through there', they say, indicating a thin sandy track overgrown with bushes that we cannot possibly venture down with the bikes. A group of older youths have gathered too now, agressive in manner of speech and posture they demand of us what it is we want here, why we have come, working themselves into a state of considerable excitement, not listening at all to our explanations. An old white-haired man appears and everybody falls silent. He says he is the chief of the village, and asks us what we want here, waving a short stick dramatically in the air. We get no chance to reply as everybody else immediately volunteers their own particular explanation of our presence, clearly indicating with shouts and gestures our bad intentions. Finally the chief has heard enough and raises his baton in the air. Everybody shuts up.

'You are not welcome here', he pronounces, 'Get out of town.' The wall of bodies parts enough for us to make our exit from the only place during three months in Mexico where we are not made welcome with great generosity and kindness.

Back at the crossroads we take a different route which leads to another small village. An old woman is standing outside the doorway of her house, sweeping leaves from the road into a bonfire. We ask if there is anywhere we might stay for the night.

'Yes of course', she says, and directs us to the restaurant. We become lost in the maze of narrow alleyways that in the gathering darkness all look alike, and end up back where we started, with an entourage of children accumulated on the way. The old woman scolds the children for not showing us the way and they lead us shrieking and laughing to the restaurant – a small hut built like the others with walls of bamboo poles and a roof of banana leaves supported on a rickety framework of thicker poles.

The woman who lives here with two young children, alerted by the commotion outside, invites us in, insisting that we bring the bikes too. She doesn't have many gringo customers she tells us, mostly they speed by on the road to Acapulco in their buses. We ask if there is anything to eat, and if we can stay for the night, and she says yes of course, you're welcome, and brings us plates of eggs, rice and beans and a pile of tortillas.

The candle lit restaurant is primarily a bar. Several villagers come in for a drink as we are eating, and join us when we have finished. They find it amusing that gringos should travel on bicycles for pleasure when they can afford to take buses, strange too that they should want to leave home for any length of time in the first place. In common with many Latin Americans, they express high regard for the life-styles enjoyed in Europe and North America.

'People in England have good lives and are wealthy. One day I will go there to live and work, or to the United States and then I will be happy!' says one. I tell him that though people in England are wealthy, they seem not to be any happier than people in Mexico, that as soon as they no longer have to worry over their poverty, they find other things to worry about to equally distress them.

'In Mexico I earn twenty dollars for six days' work in the fields. How much do you earn in England?' he asks. I say I earn a hundred and fifty dollars for five days.

'Ha!' he exclaims, 'With a hundred and fifty dollars a week I would have no worries.'

When I try to order some beers he will not allow it.

'Here, I buy the beer', he states, 'In Mexico, you are my guests.'

The woman of the restaurant provides us with large hammocks in which to sleep, and from somewhere in the village a fold-up camp bed has been found for Henrike. In the morning she adamantly refuses payment for last night's meal, or the breakfast she has pressed upon us.

'Go', she says, 'Go well. It's a long way still to Acapulco.'

This generosity when first encountered is overwhelming and embarrassing, but it gives great offence not to accept. To give food and shelter to strangers with no thought of repayment may seem to us an alien concept, but we find it a widespread custom throughout Mexico, as it is common among the poor all over Latin America, and it makes no difference if you happen to be a gringo from a wealthy nation who earns a hundred and fifty dollars for a five-day week.

In Acapulco the tall buildings of banks and offices of the business quarter, and the modern hotels that stand shoulder to shoulder along the seafront overlooking the bay, provide a facade of prosperity, monuments to inequality that rise out of the squalor of the surrounding shanty towns spilling over the tops of the enclosing hills.

Many of those living in the shanties are families displaced from the land through the increasing mechanisation of agriculture. They come because they have nowhere else to live. Others come from the poverty of rural life through choice, drawn by the hope of a job and a better future that the flaunted wealth and affluence of the city seem to promise, and though they often find themselves worse off than before, they remain. In the city there are at least plenty of doorways to sleep in, plenty of people to beg from, plenty of fat wallets to lift, plenty of garbage heaps to pick scraps from with the dogs and the vultures.

We swoop down past shanties to the seafront and the private marinas with high fences and armed guards where luxury ocean going yachts and cruisers lie tightly berthed, and pop into one of the tourist kiosks that dot the tidily swept concrete quayside. A tubby man from the Ministry of Tourism who has been to London welcomes the opportunity to practise his English.

'It's good to see young people travelling so far', he says, 'but why are you so dirty?' It is true that our appearance, while conforming to the practical and environmental dictates of rural Mexico, is not in keeping with the less liberal, socially dictated standards of downtown Acapulco.

I explain about travelling by bicycle, being on the road for many days away from hotels and showers and such things, but he is unimpressed.

'People will say, "Here's a nice young man from England but why is he so dirty?" Perhaps you are friendly with the walker from Canada? He passed through here a few days ago, pulling a handcart to South America. He was dirty too.'

In the maze of narrow winding cobbled streets of the old part of town we find a hotel suited to our budget and appearance in which to make ourselves sufficiently presentable to walk the streets without fear of further criticism.

We leave the Pacific coast at Puerto Escondido and rise into cooler climes of the central highlands.

Oaxaca lies in a broad fertile valley at the crossroads of ancient trade routes. It is still a thriving market town, overlooked by relics of its distant past. During the Olmec civilization nearly three thousand years ago, local labour was directed to artificially flatten the summit of the nearby mountain – Monte Alban – which rises a thousand feet above the surrounding valley, in order to provide a lofty position from which the realm could be governed.

Successive civilizations have utilized this vantage point, adding their own characteristic architecture. Much remaining is of Zapotec origin from around 500 A.D., huge stone blocks piled into pyramids and temples, sturdy constructions built to withstand earthquakes and popular uprisings.

In common with other nations in our current civilization, the government of today does not rely upon physical elevation to maintain surveillance of its realm, though its level of detachment and remoteness from the lives of the people under its administration might well have been envied by those early governors perched upon their mountaintop.

Saturday is market day. Before dawn people start arriving from surrounding villages, goods packed in sacks on their backs, on the backs of donkeys, piled high on the roofs of buses and trucks.

The market spreads over a wide area, a seething mass of colourful confusion: fruit and vegetables still wet with dew; chicken and turkeys, legs bound with string; pigs and goats tethered to stakes; mounds of wool; hides of leather; tin cans and buckets; clay pots of every size from an egg cup to a cauldron; painted ceramics; handwoven textiles; reed matting; bundles of bamboo;

wood carvings, stone carvings; second-hand glass bottles; sacks of grain; bright plastic containers, and all the time the hustle and bustle of bargaining, shouted invitations to buy, try, feel the quality, sniff a little, taste a little, stay a little and haggle awhile.

To show the slightest interest in any article for sale provokes immediate hard sell tactics. Joseph picks up a pair of sandals for inspection and is bombarded with praise for the workmanship and assurances of quality from half a dozen men and women sitting on crates at the back of the stall, chatting and laughing and drinking home-brewed mescal from tiny cups. Joseph feigns disinterest, walks away, is called back to consider a better offer, and though his bargaining position is weakened by the protrusion of one of his toes from the end of his shoe, a price is agreed that satisfies everybody, and business over we are invited to sit on the crates and share a drink.

As comparatively wealthy gringos this knocking down of prices is not essential, but it is important to enter into the spirit of negotiation.

Fortified with a little mescal we buy some hammocks which prove invaluable. Hammocks are a common alternative to beds throughout Mexico and Central America, being cooler to lie in during the heat of the day as air can circulate around the whole body. They can be suspended out of doors in a breeze, inaccessible to insects that crawl up onto beds, reducing molestation to merely the flyers, jumpers and extremely tenacious. Whole families sleep quite comfortably in large hammocks, and once we become accustomed to it, we do too, suspended beneath trees, and from the hooks to be found everywhere, incorporated into the walls of the adobe huts of campesinos, restaurants, municipal buildings, churches, police stations, and welded onto the sides of trucks.

The main road south out of Oaxaca is busy with local traffic. A line of parked cars reduces the width, and the door of one opens directly in front of me as I'm speeding downhill. I swerve out to avoid hitting it head on, but the rear rack and pannier smash into it, bringing the bike to a dead stop.

I keep right on going, over the handlebars, bumping and scraping uncomfortably before coming to rest in the middle of the road. Joseph and Henrike, following close behind, manage to dodge around me, and other vehicles skid to a halt in disarray. No bones broken, I sit up, a little dazed. The nearest drivers, seeing that I'm alive, honk their horns that I might swiftly remove the obstruction of my person from their path. Joseph waves his arms and shouts at them which quiets their impatience, and helps gather me up to the side of the road. The collision has broken some spokes and buckled the rear wheel, and we postpone our departure after such an inauspicious start to the day. The man who opened the car door seems oblivious to the palaver caused, and is concentrating on getting his key into the door to lock it up. He is completely drunk, and my remonstrations and gesticulations provoke no response. He just staggers away shrugging his shoulders.

In order to replace spokes in the rear wheel it is first necessary to remove the cluster of sprockets – the freewheel – and I return to the little shop where I bought a new tyre a few days ago. The young lad here is keen to prove that he can remove the freewheel with a spanner, and I have to physically restrain him from continuing for fear of permanent damage being done to the freewheel tool by the force of his enthusiasm. Out in the backyard is a bench vice. With the freewheel tool held securely in the vice, the whole wheel can be used to lever off the freewheel. My repair book claims that once broken spokes are replaced, a buckled wheel can be straightened by adjusting the tension of spokes to draw the rim to one side or other, and after following its advice for an hour or so, the wheel is serviceably round again.

We leave the valley of the central highlands at the village of El Tule, locally famous for its enormous tree which stands forty metres high and an incredible forty metres in girth. Reputed to be over three thousand years old, the trunk alone is as big as the adjacent church.

Descending the mountains towards the plains that border the Gulf of Mexico, the air becomes thick and warm, rich with the smell of flowers and decay.

Several large industrial towns have sprung up along the gulf coast, serving the interests of the petro-chemical industries which boomed in the last decade. Heavy rain has fallen for the last few days, and in Coaztacoalcos the road has turned to a sea of mud. Much of the traffic is heavy trucks and tankers, which plough through the slush that lies a foot deep, creating hidden ruts into which we stumble and judder, all the time being sprayed with a coating of liquid mud. We are black from head to foot, and it is not until several miles on where the road rises out of the quagmire that we actually see its surface again.

It is a recently asphalted highway, the main route to the Yucatan peninsula, busy and important enough to have a hard shoulder alongside. The shoulder is several inches lower than the road and it is necessary to constantly ride up and down the kerb. Up, to avoid the potholes, mountains of broken glass, dead animals and mangled wrecks of burnt out cars, and down to avoid the trucks and buses that make it clear that cyclists either ride on the shoulder or die. It can be a tricky manoeuvre in the wet and mud, and in one emergency avoidance Joseph and his bike flip right over.

'Scheisse', he swears, and we know he's alright, but one of his crank arms is so bent that the pedals don't turn round. Between us we lack the tool to take it off in order to straighten it. We make our way towards a mountain of scrap metal that rises above the trees a short way down a side road, a sight that normally indicates the location of a garage.

In the yard, several men sit under a polythene canopy around a fire in an old oil drum. A more weatherproof corrugated iron shack in a corner is home to several families. The yard is strewn with bits of engines, rusting wrecks and mangy dogs. Some children are enjoying target practice, throwing stones at tethered armadillos.

They don't have the appropriate tool here either, but tell us proudly that Mexican mechanics do not rely on having the right tools to make repairs.

Joseph's bike is passed around, looked at from different angles, and after some lively discussion, laid ceremoniously on a large wooden block. A crowbar is produced, precisely placed, then heftily whacked several times with a sledge hammer. The crank arm is straightened with no apparent destruction to any other parts. These are repairs 'a la mexicana', the men tell us.

We follow the quiet side road, bordered by thick swamp plants – trumpet-shaped flowers a foot across, huge lily pads and palm trees. Herons and storks wade in the water, parrots and vultures rest in the treetops, and every now and then from out of the green sea rise huge valves and pipes five feet in diameter with PEMEX painted on.

Pemex is the Mexican petrol company that has refineries around Coaztacoalcos and drilling rigs offshore.

Normally when we ride we wander apart and straddle the width of the road according to our own pace and abstraction, but darkness approaches, and not wishing to ride the potholed roads without lights, we ride in single file which we find useful when confronted with a strong headwind or wanting to make good time. With practice we have become confident to follow each other at a distance of a few inches, taking full advantage of the windbreak effect. On level ground the third in line need not pedal at all for long distances but simply gets dragged along in the slipstream.

It is dark when we arrive at the fishing village of Sanchez Magellanes. A group of children lead us to the bar on the beach where a merry crowd is gathering for a fiesta.

The bar owner invites us to spend the night here and we provide further merriment in clambering on each other's shoulders to secure our hammocks to the poles of the roof, which seems prudent, as in addition to herring, the local fishermen catch crocodiles that live in the brackish waters of the lagoon, and several gaping-mouthed specimens are kept here in the bar in flimsy cages of rusty wire.

The fiesta focuses on a group of dancers. Five women in colourful blouses and long skirts dance around an old man, each linked to him by coloured streamers attached to his hat. The hat is shaped like a large top hat, wound around with streamers, and stuck to it are packets of cigarettes, cakes and Coca Cola bottles.

The small brass band plays slightly out of tune on dull and rusty instruments – trumpets, horns and drums – two distinct rhythms: one to accompany the organised movements in the play being acted by the dancers, played with a concerted effort to synchronise timing and remain in the same key; and another faster rhythm which signals the group to move on, played with emphasis on individual expression with little regard to orchestral convention, each musician playing whatever he feels like, stopping to swig from one of the bottles proffered by the crowd, some in their engrossment wandering off in completely different directions.

We do not know the reason for the fiesta, nor the significance of the curious masks and hats, and cannot make much sense of the varying interpretations we receive when we inquire, but after a while, jigging with the crowd as it wends an unpredictable course through the streets, any meaning beyond the simple participation in the spirit of festivity ceases to be important.

There is not much to see either side of the straight flat roads of the Yucatan except a wall of green. A bend or a hill is something to savour. Big blue and red lizards with tails two feet long sun themselves on the hot roads. At midday, the asphalt becomes soft and flows away at the edges in waves and folds, dotted with nuts and bolts and other pieces of metal that have become embedded.

The air is alive with insects, particularly around the carcasses of dead animals – dogs, snakes, rats, and the occasional donkey or horse. Crows and vultures feast on the larger fresher bodies.

The Yucatan peninsula is littered with physical remains of the Maya civilization which came to an end in the early sixteenth century with the Spanish Conquest. In common with many of the Indians of Belize, Guatemala and Honduras, a language descended from the Maya is used in villages. Sites of Maya temples and cities, always known of, and long ignored by the local population, have been rediscovered by archaeologists. Hundreds of thousands of visitors flock annually to the Yucatan specifically to go 'ruining'.

The ruins at Uxmal are some of the most visited. There is no village here, but a couple of tourist hotels and a restaurant have recently been built, clean, modern and expensive, and though we recognise the importance of tourism to the Mexican economy, we sling up our hammocks in the trees across the road.

Chichen Itza is another much visited site, extending over many acres of cleared land. Walls and halls, columns, temples and pyramids of stone thrust themselves into the sky; once centres of culture, science and religion, these mighty ceremonial props are now redundant, slowly crumbling back to the earth, home to nesting swallows, bats, and big lizards that heave their cold bodies out of cracks to warm themselves in the sunshine.

An archaeology student from Mexico City joins us as we picnic by the edge of a pit. The pit is a hundred feet deep, two hundred feet across, with a murky lake at the bottom. The student explains that from the relics brought up from the bottom of the lake – mainly skeletons of young children – it is supposed that this is where sacrificial victims were tossed to please Chac, the Maya rain god. The student is concerned that we should not misjudge this ancient barbarity.

'Mostly it was a highly sophisticated society in which religion was integrated into daily life. They had a calendar based upon a great knowledge of astronomy, and a highly evolved system of mathematics, though they had no use for the wheel. You must remember that it was an agriculture based society, the success of crops was vital, and therefore the sacrifice of human life to ensure rain was considered acceptable. It was a kind of insurance premium.' Joseph assures him that we understand, and points out parallels today.

A party of Mexican tourists stops by at the pit. Their guide talks about sacrifice too. Then he turns our attention to more pleasant modern-day aspects of the site – the new car parking facilities, toilet and refreshment areas, and he points out restoration work being done on the ruins. To confirm this, a loud explosion rings out and we all get showered with small pieces of debris from where restoration workers are blasting with dynamite. Restorations 'a la mexicana' obviously.

Coba, in its isolation is most impressive. Only recently discovered by archaeologists, much of the site which extends over many miles is still being uncovered from trees and bushes that grow high all around, with passages and tracks cut through the undergrowth between points of interest. We climb an enormously high pyramid that rises clear above the canopy of trees, and with ancient stones vibrating beneath our feet, and the Yucatan spread out green and soft in all directions to the horizon, it is easy to imagine ourselves in a Mayan observatory. It also seems equally possible that such a pyramid was built for no other reason than to reach up out of the humidity below into the cool breeze.

The streets of Merida, capital of the Yucatan, in the days before Christmas, strain and bulge with people and festive bustle. We leave the city on Christmas Day, heading south again towards Belize, passing through many tiny villages unusually crowded. Everybody is at home today, and increasingly as the day goes on, drunk.

It's dark when we stop in the village of Hoctum. The main street is full of people staggering home.

'What are you doing?' asks one old man among a crowd of people who gather around us, between swigs on a bottle.

'We've come from Merida and we're looking for a place to stay.'

'Well you can't stay here,' the old man slurs.

'Don't be so mean,' says a younger man slapping him roughly on his back, then turning to us says 'Welcome to our village. You can stay anywhere you like.' He makes a sweeping gesture with his arm.

The old man turns his back and pisses onto the road, scattering younger boys who have been standing there, and thus encouraged, take the opportunity of emptying their own bladders.

We pass by the church as the priest is coming out, and ask if we can camp in the churchyard.

'I am not of this village', he replies. 'Why don't you ask the president if you can sleep in the palace?' and he points across the plaza to the municipal building. We climb the steps and knock on a big wooden door. A man steps out in pyjamas and slippers.

'Good evening, what can I do for you?' he asks politely.

'We are looking for a place to spend the night and the priest suggested we ask here.'

'You'll have to ask the president, and he isn't back yet. I'm only the caretaker', he says, and disappears back inside.

We sit on the steps and cook up some tea, play some cards under the light of the street lamp. The village becomes quiet with just a few people stumbling by. A man falls down next to us and sings for a while, rolls around, dribbles and paws over us, shouts and gesticulates. Henrike talks to him but he doesn't understand, works himself into a rage and shouts some more. Henrike shouts back at him in German, and then a young boy appears who says he is his brother, and solves the problem of our misunderstanding by picking up one of the drunken man's legs and dragging him away down the steps.

The palace porch seems a fine place to sleep, and I bang on the door and tell the pyjama'd caretaker that we are going to sleep here. He invites us inside, leads us through several long halls with high ceilings, walls hung with municipal scrolls, certificates, faded portraits of past mayors and heroes of the Mexican revolution, then outside into a concrete square surrounded by high walls. It's the prison yard.

'You will be safe here', he assures us.

We lay out our sleeping bags under the stars, but don't sleep because there is a groaning coming from the far end of the yard. We feel our way through the gloom to a couple of cages. An old man crouches inside one, clinging to the bars. He moans pitifully. The cage stinks. His blank eyes stare out from an expressionless face, and though they rest on us, he seems unaware of our presence. We speak to him and he seems not to hear. We can offer no comfort. Joseph gives him a cigarette.

Later the heavy doors burst open and several smartly dressed men come over. It's the village president and some local dignitaries back from a Christmas feast in a neighbouring village. We exchange cutomary pleasantries. Joseph smokes one of the president's cigarettes, and asks who the man in the cage is.

'Oh him', says the president, as if just remembering him, 'Bad man, bad man.' He repeats it several times, dismissively, like a formula.

'He is in a wretched condition', says Joseph.

'The man has broken the law', replies the president.

'There is nothing else to do with him. I am bound to keep him in the cage. It is my duty and not my choice. I have no choice in the matter.'

The law is the law even on Christmas Day, and the man in the cage has no choice in the matter either. He lies amid his own shit and piss, groaning and spitting all night.

3. Shipwrecked in a mangrove swamp

A former British colony, Belize gained independence in 1981, and many characteristics and attitudes acquired under British colonial rule clearly remain. Two thousand British troops remain too, training the Belize Defence Corps in matters of national security. Neighbouring Guatemala claims Belize as part of its national territory – its maps show Belize as one of its provinces, a disagreement over sovereignty that led to the breaking of diplomatic relations between Britain and Guatemala. The Guatemalan army receives training and finance from the United States, whose influence over foreign policy makes a military invasion of Belize unlikely, but the perceived threat to its independence makes the majority of Belizians who have no wish to become part of Guatemala, grateful for the continued presence of the British army.

We stop by a broad mud-coloured river, to swim and wash off some grime. Reggae music booms out of a number of wood plank houses raised on stilts above the swampy ground.

A white-haired man emerges from the shell of a bus, set up off the ground on blocks, where he lives with his family. He invites us to camp here. He speaks both English and Spanish fluently like most Belizians, and tells us how he makes a living fixing cars and fishing. His three canoes, each fashioned from a single tree trunk, lie upturned on the bank.

The spot is a popular car wash. People come along in the evening to drive vehicles down to the river, wash them, swim, talk, listen to music, smoke a few joints, drink a few beers. A relaxed atmosphere prevails in Belize.

Belize City has a Caribbean feel. It revolves around the quays of the central canal, bustling with life in the morning, quiet in the heat of the afternoon. Its dusty streets are lined with rickety wooden houses, mostly raised on stilts above small yards thick with weeds and junk. We lounge around contentedly in a guest house run by two old ex-pats from Kent, musing over where we shall go and what we will do next.

Joseph has run out of funds and is trying to decide where he can go to make some money, whether to return to Germany. I dig out the Bartholomew's map of South America confidently bought back in England. After six months' journeying I'm still pathetically far from even its northernmost boundaries. Fortunately, among the collection of books at the guest house is a complete set of volumes of the Encyclopaedia Britannica which contains several maps of Central America which we pore over.

Joseph has been unusually tired for a couple of days, and one morning he wakes up yellow. We suspect hepatitis. We look it up in the Encyclopaedia Britannica, which confirms our suspicions. Hepatitis is a disease which affects the liver, particularly its function of cleaning the blood and in the breakdown of fats. The cure is a long rest and a careful diet. It leaves Joseph little choice but to return home right away.

Twenty miles off the coast of Belize is a coral reef. It stretches for a hundred and fifty miles and is cause for some national pride, featuring on the back of one of the bank notes with the legend 'The second longest coral reef in the world'.

Henrike and I take a boat out to Caye Cauker, one of the many small islands that lie near the reef. Half a dozen other gringos are camping on the beach and we find vacant palm trunks from which to sling our hammocks. This northern part of the island is just a few miles across, inhabited by lobster fishermen and ex-pirates. Coconut palms and stout bushes cover the flat sand. The southern end of the island is inhabited only by snakes and crocodiles, being an impenetrable mangrove swamp. Some years ago an attempt was made to build an airstrip there. Tons of sand and gravel were dredged up from the shore and plonked down over the mangroves which promptly grew up through it, and the project was abandoned due to lack of funds and the difficulty in attracting labour to such intolerable working conditions. Today small boats ferry supplies and people to and from the mainland. One magnificent yacht also lies moored against the dilapidated wooden jetty, owned by a Captain Ray who is looking for a fare paying crew to sail to Honduras.

The inhabitants of the island number a few hundred. A wooden shack serves as bar and cafe for islanders and tourists alike, bread can be bought at the police station – a wooden hut on stilts – and fruit and vegetables from the tiny post office which doesn't sell stamps.

Most people come here to visit the reef. Everybody has their own idea of the best way to get out there. Pete and Bob have been paddling out in a rented dugout canoe. The reef is about a mile out, and today they capsized and had a rough time of it. Motor boats can be hired from the islanders also. Dan, a plump shrimp fisherman from Florida, sets his heart on sailing out in Captain Ray's yacht, but after speaking with him decides he is no true sailor and far too smooth-talking besides. Fireside discussions are interrupted by Martin who announces that a scorpion has just stung his big toe. A frenzied hunt and general excitement ensues, and the offending beast is eventually cornered, and killed with a hefty whack from a boot. Post mortem reveals it to be a medium-sized black scorpion. Popular opinion is that these are not very poisonous, and a jab on the big toe is certainly nothing to worry about. Martin is not wholly convinced and lies down for a while.

'I've found a sailboat we can take to the reef!' says Dan excitedly the following morning, 'And you can be my crew.' Henrike and I are less enthusiastic when we see the thing – an old wooden dinghy lying at an angle half full of water.

'It was my husband's before he went away', explains the woman who lives in the hut next to the boat. 'It hasn't been used for several years, but you are welcome to borrow it.'

The mainsail is in disrepair, ripped and rotten, patched with cotton and nylon sacks. Dan hunts around the island and comes back with a bundle of sacks which we stitch crudely over the worst of the holes. It takes a while to bail out the water with a bucket, and secure the remains of a rudder to the stern with some of the frayed and rotten rope.

The main mast looks fairly firm, and the pulley at the top, though rusty, is serviceable.

'Hoist sail!' cries Dan. We pull on the appropriate rope and the sail gets half way up the mast before the rope snaps. We knot the rope together and it holds on the second attempt. Several bits and pieces of rope and pulleys are left over, but Dan assures us they are extra, so heaving aboard a large rock for an anchor, and armed with masks and snorkel, we cast off for the reef.

The wind whistles through the gaps and tears in the patchwork sails, but enough is trapped to propel the boat forward, gently out to sea.

Dan is ecstatic with pleasure, dons a skipper's cap, and positions himself by the tiller. He emits joyful gurgles and whoops between instructing us in the fundamentals of sailing. He says it is perfectly normal for a sailboat to creak and groan, and leak a little through undiscovered holes in the hull.

Below us the water is light blue and clear, the sandy bottom never more than twenty feet down is dotted with colourful clumps of coral.

After an hour the wind dies right down, bringing our sedate progress to a halt. The reef is still a way off, which doesn't matter because here too we can swim down among strange and intricate coral formations, alive with the darting of hundreds of vividly coloured fish.

Clouds accumulate during the still afternoon, and towards evening darker clouds indicate an approaching storm.

A breeze blows us slowly shorewards between calms when the sails hang idle and we can only wait. The island seems a long way off.

Captain Ray motors by in his yacht, returning from fishing in the deeper waters beyond the reef. He offers us a tow back. He was one of the sceptical onlookers to our earlier preparations, and Dan, rightly proud of our workmanship, and to maintain our nautical integrity, signals that this is unnecessary. We are clearly in for a good dousing.

The wind and rain arrive soon after dark, in a gale that billows out the sails which tear a little here and there under the strain, and push the creaking craft along at a cracking pace. In darkness we near the island several hundred yards downwind from the little jetty. Dan explains that the true sailor does not beach his craft willy nilly on the shore just because of a little wind and rain, but heads back out a short way in order to return on the correct tack. We head back to sea. Just as we prepare to 'come about', a manoeuvre Dan has patiently been teaching us, an untimely conspiracy of wind and waves that have increasingly been buffeting the boat, causes the boom of the front jib sail to come away from the mast, snapping the rope that holds it up in the process. There is panic among the crew as they are shrouded in flapping sail. The boom swings about menacingly. Dan tries to maintain discipline and order, shouting over the noise of the storm unintelligible nautical terms like 'splice the mainbrace!' and 'shiver me timbers!', and bravely throws his considerable weight on the waywardly wavering boom.

The lights of the island recede as we drift out into open water. Waves whipped up by the wind break over the boat. Without the jib sail we are unable to turn around, so I clamber on to Dan's shoulders to reaffix it with a knotted rope to the top of the mast. The task proves impossible in the high wind as the boat swings violently from side to side, and spins around aimlessly. Imminent capsize is only averted by drastic stabilising measures – Dan and I tumble down on top of Henrike in the bottom of the boat, now awash with water that has sloshed over the sides, as well as entering through the still undiscovered hole in the hull.

The mainsail finally shreds itself into useless rags and we bob up and down in a heavy sea, driven only by cold wind and rain. There are two lights on the horizon, one directly in front and one directly behind us, and though we differ in our opinions as to which one we should be heading toward, it matters not, our course is set and any land would be welcome.

We miss the land by half a mile, but do become sheltered from the wind, and fired with desperation, one of us paddling, one using the long pole to punt, and the other continuously bailing out water that is entering now at an alarming rate, we reach the shore at a place clear of the tangled roots of mangroves, the abandoned site of the incompleted airstrip. The silhouette of a metal crane rises above the swamp.

Our joy at reaching land is short-lived as we are immediately besieged by swarms of mosquitos. Dan being the most scantily clad in just a pair of shorts is most eager to get out of here, and leads off into the swamp.

The swamp is a tangled maze of living roots, full of sucking and popping noises, and strange calls of creatures unseen that crawl from our path. Some rush away noisily, startled, others slide away slowly, unconcerned, or watch us with luminous eyes.

Each step is an effort, extracting a foot from its entanglement, lifting it over hidden slimy obstacles, feeling for somewhere firm to set it down, mostly squelching into oozing softness, then following with the arms, searching for a passage through which the body might twist and squeeze, mostly finding no passage at all, and having to twist and squeeze back to a place where it is possible to stand and rest in a comparatively uncontorted posture, and all the time mosquitos humming and buzzing and whining, biting the face, burrowing into ears and droning up nostrils. After ten minutes of struggling and cursing and face slapping we have come perhaps ten yards from where we started.

'What about following the edge of the swamp', Henrike suggests sensibly. We wade into the water, but the tide is in and we find ourselves having to swim. It seems the sort of place where crocodiles and sea snakes might lurk, and open to the wanderings of the sharks that come through the break in the reef at night to feed.

'I'll go ahead and try to find a way through', says Dan, 'I'll stop and whistle if I find a good route', and off he clambers, oozing and squelching into the murk. We call to each other a few times, and then we hear no more. Back at the crane we find a rusty platform, which though strewn with jagged metal and glass, is at least a solid place to spend the night.

In the morning the sailboat lies full of water. The mosquitos disappear with the rising sun. An osprey has made a nest atop the jib of the crane, and a chick peeps over the side and squawks.

Where is Dan? Did he survive a night in the swamp?

A motor boat full of people passes by in the distance. Henrike and I wave our arms and call out. They wave back and pass by. Another boat passes later. We wave and shout out, with the urgency appropriate to shipwrecked sailors. The boat comes alongside with two fishermen aboard.

'What are you doing here?' one asks.

'We want to get out of here. Our boat sank', Henrike explains. They take us to the jetty at the other end of the island. We ask around about Dan. Somebody saw him early this morning.

'He's gone looking for you.' We go looking for him. Along a sandy track we bump into each other. We are all swollen and red from mosquito bites. Dan is covered in scratches and sores. He tells us his tale of the trek through the mangrove swamp, how he went around in circles a few times, lost all sense of direction, climbed palm trees to gain a view of the stars, and got lost again as soon as he descended, flung off snakes, shouted at crocodiles, and graphically illustrates his account with twisting and crawling actions, and contortions of his face. We all have a good laugh. It took him about seven hours to travel three miles.

With the help of an old lobster fisherman we tow the sailboat back to its owner.

'Oh, you've brought it back', she says with surprise, 'I'm glad to see you're all right.'

The fisherman is blind in one eye, and his other is failing. He says he can't fish much now because he can't see his pots. We help him locate them, twenty feet down on the sandy seabed, and collect a sack full of lobsters and two enormous stone crabs.

In the bar we buy him some beers and he tells us how he lost most of his family and all of his houses in the hurricanes, how he survived the last one by roping himself to the top of a palm tree, and swung in the wind while the island sloshed around below. He gives us a couple of lobsters which we boil up for dinner, with fried breadfruit and bananas, and coconuts roasted in the fire.

There are no mosquitos at this end of the island tonight as a plane flew over earlier spraying D.D.T., leaving a fine dust on everything. The tiny sandflies have developed a D.D.T. resistance, but the strong wind keeps them at bay, and the only concern as we lie in our hammocks tonight is the threat of being hit on the head by the falling coconuts which thud occasionally into the sand.

4. Bolt cutters to the rescue

Three days along the west road out of Belize City brings us
to the river Belize, that marks the border with Guatemala. Belize
and Guatemala border posts face each other from opposite ends of
a long bridge. Small boats ply across the river between huts hidden
in dense vegetation – border control is limited to the road-bound
minority.

'NO COUNTRY IS AN ISLAND' proclaims a huge billboard by
the Guatemala immigration building, next to another huge board
depicting Belize, bristling with Union Jacks and guns, floating
unsociably away from Central America into the Caribbean.

Young boys with machine guns as large as themselves follow
us into the building. The chief immigration officer shoos them out
and with sweeping gestures welcomes us to his country. I have no
entry visa and I don't know if I will be permitted to enter. Henrike
requires no visa and hands over her passport, and the immigration
chief, assuming that we are both German, busies himself with filling
out forms. On discovering that I am British, he charges me one U.S.
dollar, and stamps a lengthy note in my passport which I don't
understand, but the general idea is that I must present myself to the
immigration control in Guatemala City within thirty days.

The chief goes on to tell us about the country, and advises
us to take care in this region as the road to Peten is not only in
bad repair, but made unsafe for travellers by communist guerrillas
who are attempting to undermine the authority of the government
with violence. He assures us though, that the government is 'taking
steps to restore the peace.' We take this as reference to the recent
military campaign in the low lying jungles of the north east, peace
restoration steps which involve the wiping out of villages suspected

of harbouring support or holding sympathies for the guerrilla movement. Over the last two months this has resulted in over a hundred
thousand campesinos fleeing their homes to the refugee camps that
have sprung up in the southern Mexican state of Chiapas.

We heave our bikes up among the bundles of belongings piled
high on the roof-rack of an already overloaded bus, which trundles
around the border village of Melchor for half an hour, touting for
more passengers and luggage before leaving. It takes the conductor
half an hour to work his way through to the rear of the bus, where
he exits through a back window and returns to the front by way of
the roof.

The bus is stopped at an army checkpoint – a concrete hut and a
barricade of sandbags around a mounted machine gun. A wooden
pole bars the way, and high ridges of earth are banked over the
road to slow vehicles to a crawl. Everybody is ordered outside to
line up alongside the bus while soldiers search inside, and through
the belongings on the roof. Passengers are searched too, with legs
spread and hands against the side of the bus.

Two men have no documents. They are called to stand forward a
few paces and questioned, shouted at. Two other passengers speak
up in support of what they are saying and are told to shut up.
Everybody else stands silent, not catching the eye of any soldier, or
making any move to make themselves be noticed.

The two men are allowed back into the line with a kick, and we
all file back onto the bus, checked and searched once more as we
board.

There is some question of the validity of the identity papers of
the old man in front of me. An argument ensues, and in view of
the unnecessarily disrespectful shouting and pushing by the young
soldier I cannot help but raise an eyebrow reproachfully. The soldier
regards this unsolicited expression of support for the old man as
an unacceptable personal attack, a doubting of the unquestionable
rightness of his position, and perhaps even more intolerably, a threat
to his authority. He reacts, of course, according to the wisdom of
his military education, shouting, pointing his gun in our faces, and
shoving us roughly up against the side of the bus. A superior
intervenes, and we are allowed to reboard.

The bus toots into the market place of Peten, bustling with
people and animals scurrying from its path. Our bikes are passed

down from the roof amid a crowd of curious Indians, grinning, laughing, pointing, asking what we are doing. The campesinos in their daily lives, away from the repressive influence of the military, show a great openness and joy. Despite the poverty and hardship, despite the fearful machinery of oppression which dominates their lives, in individual relationships they refuse to abandon those things which all about them have been pushed aside – dignity, integrity, compassion.

Presenting different aspects of oneself according to the demands of the circumstances, is, among the campesinos, a necessity, because the circumstances are so extreme. The principle is of course the same for everybody everywhere, though not always so clearly defined. This detachment, this apparent withdrawal and passive obedience, used as a defence when confronted by the army, is often viewed as contributary to continuing oppression. From far away it may seem a simple truth. Close at hand there is no doubt as to its expedience. Before arriving at Peten, we passed through several checkpoints similar to the first, and though far from perfecting the expressionless mask adopted by the campesinos, I had at least learned to suppress any subversive inclinations of my eyebrows. Fear is simple and everybody understands it. The principle is the same everywhere. Here it is obvious because it is used overtly. Those that overcome their fear and commit themselves to reform are required to become outlaws, because the law simply does not permit it. Political enlightenment of the masses and encouragement of alternative systems of government is done on the run by people with guns slung over their shoulders, for they are hunted down like animals.

Lake Peten Itza has risen over two metres in the last five years. The old town of Flores lies on a small circular island reached by a narrow causeway lined with sunken houses. The streets are arranged in concentric circles, with a church at the top. Compared with bustling Peten, Flores is a ghost town. We meet one person on our tour round the island. He owns the hotel, and eagerly leads us there.

'Not many tourists come here now', he admits.

The ground floor of the hotel was never completed as the lake rose during its construction. It remains a concrete shell, two feet underwater. We pass through on wooden planks, balanced above the water on piles of bricks. Fish and frogs swim in and out of doorways. A heron, its fishing disturbed, flaps its wings twice, and with just an inch of clearance either side, disappears through a space in the wall once intended as a window.

The hotel manager loans us his dugout canoe and we paddle around the lake. It's ten miles across. Bulrushes, lilies, and tall yellow reeds cover large areas, criss-crossed by paths of open water cut by local fishermen. Small trees remain standing, drowned and slimy beneath the surface. Abandoned houses dot the shore, with just the thatch roofs still visible.

The croaking chorus of frogs and toads commences in the early evening and continues until dawn. One night Henrike is disturbed by another sound, and wakes to see a man crawling along the floor. He leaps to his feet at her startled cry, and flees into the darkness. Wakened by the commotion the manager appears, machete in hand, and makes a search of the empty rooms. He finds no one. We persuade the manager that the affair is not serious enough to bring to the attention of the authorities, whose efforts in restoring peace and order we have no wish to encourage. Henrike's purse containing a few coins and her penknife is all that was taken.

Attached to the penknife was the key to Henrike's padlock. The padlock is locked to the cable around my bicycle.

Flores is less deserted of people in the early morning. I tour the town with the bike over my shoulder in search of a hack saw. A small crowd gathers in the hardware store where the proprietor and I take turns to saw away, ineffectively, at the cable which is proving to be particularly resistant.

The story goes around as to why we are engaged in such energetic early morning activity, and the Guatemalans, proud of their honesty, join in condemning the actions of the night thief. A variety of instruments are produced – pliers, hammers, machetes, axes – and pitted eagerly, separately and in combination, against the unyielding cable which is finally sliced through with a set of bolt cutters.

The road is paved once more at Rio Dulce, and joins the main highway that links the capital in the western highlands to the east coast port of Puerto Barrios. Huge trucks thunder along hauling Sea-Land and Hapag Lloyd containers, bound for the U.S. and Europe.

The ride is smooth but it is uncomfortably hot in the afternoon. Palms and banana trees shimmer in the heat by the roadside.

We reach a small railway town in the evening, feeling tired and weak. Henrike has a fever and no appetite. In the morning there is a yellow tint in her eyes.

We board the daily train for Guatemala City, an ancient engine pulling open-ended wooden carriages slowly out of the lush lowlands, through dry hillsides of stunted bushes and cactus, into the mountains and volcanoes of the western highlands. It takes twelve hours to cover the hundred miles, with numerous stops at tiny trackside villages where people board with bundles and animals, and sell fruit and vegetables, and maize cakes baked in banana leaves. The food smells good but we are not hungry. We both have hepatitis.

5. Hurricanes, earthquakes and volcanoes

The city of Antigua lies in a valley twenty miles from Guatemala City, surrounded by mountains and volcanoes and, being off the main north–south highway, retains an unhurried pace of life.

The cobbled streets are mostly lined with single-storey adobe houses, whitewashed, or painted in light oranges and browns. The roofs are a patchwork of red tiles and shiny tin.

Until the devastating earthquake of 1773, the city was the Spanish colonial capital. Successive earthquakes have rendered many old buildings unsafe, churches stand amid huge chunks of fallen masonry, though the architecture of the central plaza remains largely colonial – the cathedral, government and municipal buildings. Cafes, shops and a cinema peep out from between the pillars of the sidewalk arcades.

The largest and oldest of the trees in the plaza, that shade the stone benches and fountains, is said to be over five hundred years old, and a witness of the Spanish invasion. Numerous other plants grow within the depressions of its gnarled boughs.

The symmetric cone of volcano Agua, twelve thousand feet high and ten miles to the west, towers over the town. The town itself is four thousand feet high, and refreshingly cool at night.

We find a room in a small pension in which to recover our health. I visit the hospital. The waiting room is so full of people in such obvious and great need of attention that I leave right away, intending to return the following day. The following day I am physically incapable of doing so.

For several days we have neither the energy nor inclination to get out of bed. In time we become more active – making trips to the shower, to open a window, or brew tea – but for a week just getting out of bed in the morning feels like a hard day's work and we have to rest all day sitting in a chair to summon the strength to get back to bed at night.

Henrike visits a local doctor who speaks some English.

'Hepatitis is not so serious', he tells her. 'Just don't drink too much beer, and wash your hands before and after meals.' She hasn't eaten a proper meal in two weeks. He sells her some pills too.

Much of the gringo population in town seems to have had experience of hepatitis at some time. Everyone has their own pet remedy based on the varied and often contradictory advice of doctors, though there is a general agreement on the virtues of boiled rice, fruit and vegetables, and a long rest.

Antigua is well supplied with vegetables, being the market centre for surrounding villages in the fertile valley. A trip there in our sloth-like state is a major expedition that must be broken into manageable distances, with many rests in shady doorways, or simply in the gutter when dizziness threatens. Sitting down to rest in the gutter is a common practice in Guatemala.

We steel ourselves for the journey to Guatemala City to extend our visas, a fifty minute bus ride over the mountains, down into the smog of the sprawling capital. Arbitrary checks are carried out on vehicles entering and leaving the city. Half the vehicles are stopped and searched, the passengers lined up and frisked at gunpoint.

The building of the immigration department is thick and noisy with people and bureaucratic confusion. It takes some hours to locate the correct forms and queues before handing over our passports and visa applications for processing.

'Come back in the afternoon', we are told.

The parks and plazas are crowded with city workers lunching at the numerous food stands. Shoe-shine boys scurry around for business, barbers ply their trade in the shade of large umbrellas. People hawk round all manner of things to sell.

A crowd has gathered around a man expounding the virtues of some sticks of wood.

'Use them as a detergent', he announces, sloshing a stick around in a bucket of water, creating a froth of bubbles.

'This wood comes from the eastern jungles. It has many medicinal properties', he claims. 'Chop it into a powder,' he says, doing so, then scrapes the powder into a glass of

water, 'and drink it to cure constipation.' He downs the glass
in one.

'Use it to relieve asthma, bronchial complaints, and to unblock
the nasal passages. Smell some', he urges, offering the stick around
the attentive circle of faces. Everybody sniffs. It has no smell, but
immediately clears the nose, making breathing astonishingly sharp
and clear. This is the first effect. The second effect is that those who
first smelt it start to sneeze. Everybody laughs at them. But soon
everybody is at it, sneezing uncontrollably, hawking and spitting.
A larger crowd is drawn, amused by the sight of so many people
alternately sneezing and laughing, pointing at one another. Some
military police are attracted by the gathering – they are never very
far away – and barge through into the circle, to see what subversion
can be sniffed out. People stop laughing and disperse, still sneezing
and spitting, throughout the plaza.

Henrike collects her passport in the afternoon, stamped valid for
a further sixty days. I am handed a scrap of cardboard covered in
illegible scrawl and told that for *Britanicos* the application takes a
little longer – 'come back in two weeks.'

We squeeze onto a bus for the return journey. There is some
kind of regulation regarding the number of passengers permitted.
It seems that as long as everyone is seated it's O.K., but anyone
standing is too many. Every time a policeman is spotted, or a
military checkpoint passed, which is quite often, the driver's mate
shouts, 'Down, everybody sit down.' People stand tightly packed in
the aisle, so simply allow gravity to take over, though this is not
always enough, and those whose feet were not touching the floor
in the first place are pulled down by their neighbours into at least
a crouch.

Back in Antigua our sedentary life continues apace. A marimba
band practising nearby provides welcome musical accompaniment
to our immobile activities: watching sunsets; taking siestas; following the courses of hummingbirds between the small trees and
hanging plants; anticipating the arrival of a large black bumble
bee which makes a regular mid-afternoon tour of the courtyard,
brief and clumsy, blundering into walls before disappearing up a
favourite piece of drainpipe.

Joseph writes to us from his sickbed in Germany, and
thoughtfully sends us hefty Steinbeck tomes in both German and

English. The kindly staff at the pension accept us as permanent fixtures.

Martin burst into the courtyard one morning, none the worse for his scorpion sting on Caye Cauker. Like other gringos in town he is taking a course at one of the Spanish schools. He knows an American doctor who is training staff at the hospital, and encourages us to go along for blood tests. The American doctor oversees our blood tests, which suggest that our livers are now functioning more or less normally. He recommends that we eat no fats and do no strenuous activity for a few months, and drink no alcohol for a year!

Encouraged by this medical pronouncement of fitness we visit colourful rural market villages with colourful names – Huehuetenango, Chichicastenango and Panajachel, also known as Gringotenango, on the shores of Lake Atitlan. The setting here is idyllic. The still clear lake lies below massive volcanoes. Two of the volcanoes at present provide refuge for guerrillas from government 'peace restoration' efforts.

Henrike takes a boat to the far side of the lake, seeking a quiet spot for some serious relaxation and recuperation. I take a two-week course in Spanish at one of the schools in Antigua. It's not a big school – a single-storey house with whitewashed adobe walls surrounding a small courtyard. There are three other students here. Billy, a German psychologist, and Tim and Slim, two rather nervous young Americans, never seen out without a copy of *Time* or *Newsweek* magazines tucked securely under an arm, a link with home and the wider world that only serves to increase their unease, filled as they are with reports on new areas of Latin America gripped by civil war, declaring martial law, and always a few colourful photos showing mounds of dead bodies.

We sit in the shade of a mandarin tree learning Spanish. Our tutor is one of the few Guatemalans who doesn't shy away from speaking of politics. He says things are getting better, outlines the country's electoral system, and says there is nothing for the law-abiding Guatemalan to fear. The pieces of paper on which he has written a few innocuous political outlines he tears into shreds and places in an ashtray.

'Stay off the streets this afternoon', our tutor warns one day. 'Today is the Day of The Poor and hundreds of people will be marching.' It is an annual event. Hundreds of campesinos from the surrounding villages converge on Antigua to protest at the lack of rural development since the promises of last year. The government demonstrates its concern for their grievances by lining the streets with soldiers and riot police.

The day of the visit of the Pope to Guatemala is declared a national holiday. In Antigua, Pope banners hang from every window, Pope badges and stickers are sold on every street corner. Children hold Pope balloons. The appearance of the man himself – a hand waved from the window of the bullet proof Pope helicopter that hovers over town – is greeted with wild cheering and waving of Pope flags.

'Stay at home tonight', warns our tutor a few days later, 'The radio warns of a hurricane coming.' The wind increases in strength all day, filling the air with dust and litter, and during the night it rises to a furious roaring. I take a look outside. A large sheet of corrugated iron, once the roof of the house next door, comes hurtling through the air, twisting and turning like a leaf, along with other objects that shouldn't really leave the ground, like flower pots, planks of wood; and rocks that should hold down the tin on roofs rattle and roll along like pebbles.

Inside, the noise is deafening as airborne bits and pieces crash into the walls and windows, or bounce off the tin roof. The door bursts open under a particularly heavy bombardment, and in the few shrieking seconds before I can close it, and push the bed in front of it, the room is filled with dust and leaves and somebody's laundry.

By morning the wind has moderated to a gale. The sky remains a sickly yellow all day, and though not cloudy, the sun never appears through the dust laden air. The streets are full of debris. Telegraph poles lie across the roads. Some wooden houses have been blown right over. The woods on the surrounding hillsides have been blown down like a field of corn.

The central plaza is almost unrecognisable. The big old tree has crashed to the ground, uprooting stone benches and huge sections of pavement. A small army of local people are scrambling over the fallen giant, filling the air with the sound of chipping machetes as they hack off branches for firewood, and dislodge carefully the small plants living in its boughs, to be borne away to new homes.

People get sick in the wake of the hurricane. Some bug has been blown in, so the popular story goes, and the homeopathy stalls in the market do a roaring trade in roots and powders. The staff at the pension all get a fever.

Dean returns from a month hiking in the eastern lowlands to find the entire gringo population that usually can be found gathered late into the evenings in dingy cafes discussing gringo matters, confined to their beds, shivering and sweating with what seems to be a particularly virulent strain of flu.

He is eager to test some cure – all medicinal herbs he picked up in his travels from some jungle *brujo*, and one evening bullies us into leaving our sick beds to gather in his room 'for a brew up'.

We sit around wrapped up in blankets, sniffling and shivering, watching feverishly as Dean boils up a broth of leaves and stems in a huge pot. A bitter smell fills the room. Dean crouches over the concoction, poking and stirring it authoritatively, adding leaves and other unidentifiable ingredients at appropriate times, telling tall tales of guerrillas and jungle herb lore.

When it is deemed to be ready, no one volunteers to be the first to taste what even Dean admits is an evil looking brew. We suggest Dean should try it as he made it, but he declines, saying he did his part in collecting the ingredients, and anyway, he's not ill. We all find equally valid excuses.

Dean says to quit fooling around and drink the stuff because it works best when it's hot. We resort to a democratic decision. Being a cyclist, and therefore sufficiently foolhardy, I am considered most suitable as a guinea pig. I dip a cup into the pot, and down the dark brown murky liquid in one. Urgh! What a foul tasting brew it is. I grimace and hold down the desire to vomit. 'It's horrible!' I announce, at which everybody is curious to try some too. We polish off the whole potful in no time at all and retire to our beds to await results. In a couple of days we are all out and about and feeling fine.

Easter in Antigua is celebrated with much pomp and ceremony, with religious plays, processions and general festivities lasting for three days.

The preceding week is a time of preparation – private houses set themselves up as hotels to accommodate thousands of visitors who come from all over the country, bazaars and markets spring up in the small plazas, traders from the capital set up stalls on vacant lots and any available pavement space. Gangs of shoe-shine boys invade town, and fight for territory with the local lads. Prices double for the duration.

All night long, people work by lamp light in the cobbled streets, laying down carpets of flowers, coloured sand and sawdust in intricate designs, all destined to be destroyed in a few minutes the following day by the shuffling feet of fifty or sixty men bearing the enormous wooden floats with statues of Christ crucified, the weeping Virgin, and other biblical celebrities.

There is hardly room to move in the crowded streets as people line the route of the procession, and follow along behind the floats to one or other of the many churches where services are held, then on through the night, with lamps and candles and brass bands in attendance.

It seems an opportune moment to make a trip to volcano Agua whose distant peak alone remains aloof from the storm of celebration.

The little man in the office of the Ministry of Tourism, dressed for the weekend in smart black suit and tie, assures me that the volcano is easy to climb – there being a track right up to the T.V. relay station at the top.

'When I was a young man I used to climb many volcanoes', he tells me. 'I was a very athletic young man and I loved sport. My favourite two sports were football and climbing volcanoes.'

Santa Rosa is the village at the base of volcano Agua, lying amid intensely farmed land – fields of tomatoes and aubergines, orange, mandarin and avocado trees, irrigated by streams diverted down the mountainside. Paths criss-cross the fields.

'Which is the track up the volcano?' I ask two young children. They run away. I ask a woman pulling up onions, piling them onto a blanket. She points vaguely upwards.

'That way', she says, 'Just follow the path up.'

The track winds up through a shady coniferous forest, soft with fallen needles, smelling of pine and wild flowers, then zigzags out above the tree line where the wind blows cold and hard and whistles through the tough grass that clings to the steep incline, and around the rocks and boulders strewn around from recent rockfalls.

The top is shrouded in thick cloud. It's twelve thousand feet high and the air is cold and thin. The crater floor is the size of a football pitch and perfectly flat, surrounded by the crater walls which rise almost vertically to a sharp ridge several hundred feet above.

I scramble up towards a light coming from one of the wooden huts perched on top of the circular ridge. Several large masts lie broken on the ground nearby.

Three men are sitting around a fire inside the hut.

'Come in gringo. Sit down.'

They make room for me around the fire, and brew some coffee. The wind howls outside. They tell me they are engineers, up here to repair the T.V. masts that were blown down by the hurricane. Two of them are stationed here by the government for six months at a time. The visiting engineer tells me that the remoteness and altitude have turned them crazy, and they all laugh. I laugh too but I don't find it funny. Certainly two of them act a little strange at times, whispering and giggling together, and rolling their eyes around. The third engineer goes off to sleep in another hut, and warns me half jokingly on the way out to watch out as these two are a couple of thieves. We all laugh again.

I am woken in the morning by a shuffling noise, as one of the men goes through my bag. He removes the two oranges that are all it contains. I pretend not to see.

Outside it is a clear frosty morning, the sky is ablaze with the colours of sunrise.

The shadow of volcano Agua is cast clear and sharp across the land far below, onto the distant volcanoes of Acatenango and Fuego, smoking gently twenty miles away. The landscape is spread out like a map. I sit and watch, spellbound, as clouds float across below, casting moving shadows over towns and villages, swirling around other volcanoes, then breaking free and floating away.

By midday the land is completely hidden by a vast sea of cloud, several thousand feet below where I'm still sitting, with just the peaks of volcanoes, poking up like islands into the blue sky. The soft white fluffy cloudtops, spread like a covering of fresh snow, appear solid enough to stand on. I feel I could walk right out, stride across to neighbouring volcanoes, and beyond to mountain-tops unseen, and descend to find myself in South America, or back in England. It wouldn't really matter where.

A few mountains of litter are all that remain of the Easter celebrations when I get back to town. It feels like coming back home.

'A whole gang of cyclists from France passed through yesterday', one of the girls at the pension tells me. 'They were going to South America.'

I take a few short rides out to nearby villages on the unladen bike, and return exhausted, feeling ill. One way or another I must leave the country soon as my three-month visa extension expires.

One night I am woken by a loud regular knocking coming from somewhere inside the room. I reach for the light but it doesn't work. The noise is coming from the bedstead, banging violently against the wall. The mattress starts moving up and down, as if someone is underneath it, and I suspect that somebody has sneaked into the room to play a joke. But then the door and windows on the far side of the room start opening and slamming shut, apparently of their own accord, and in the pitch darkness I accept with some fright that the disruption has a supernatural origin. But then small pieces of masonry start falling from the ceiling, and I become aware of a low rumbling noise coming from outside, and know it must be an earthquake. I bury my head under the blankets, relieved at such a natural explanation, and wonder if I should go outside for safety, but no one else seems to be moving around so I stay put too.

6. Sugar cubes and a cardboard village

On a fine spring morning we leave Antigua, its courtyards and dusty streets now colourful with lilac and bougainvillaea blossom. Henrike is heading north for Mexico, and then home to Germany. I'm heading south for Salvador and I'm sad to say goodbye. But travelling demands attention to the present and precludes the indulgence of melancholy.

'Where is your exit visa?' inquires a Guatemalan immigration officer at the border.

'My what?'

'*Britanicos* cannot leave the country without an exit visa. You must return to Guatemala City.'

The exit visa takes a further three days to acquire, and joins eight full pages of Guatemalan stamps in my passport.

El Salvador is the smallest country in Central America, and with eight million people is comparatively densely populated. It has been devastated by the civil war in which tens of thousands have been killed. Hundreds of thousands of refugees have fled to neighbouring Honduras and Guatemala. Literally millions have been forcibly uprooted by the army, from their homes in rural mountain areas, and relocated to areas where the government forces can maintain military control, in an attempt to remove the popular campesino base from which the guerrilla organisations draw support, and to create a free-fire zone. Nobody is unaffected by the war.

San Salvador is smoggy and crowded and sombre. Open-back trucks full of soldiers patrol the streets. Buildings are shabby, neglected, the most prosperous seem to be the funeral parlours which are numerous, and flash out their services in neon lights. 'Funeral Parlour Misfortune' glares one.

No one approaches me on the street, indeed, people noticeably avoid bumping into me or holding my gaze. But some people are following me around the streets at a distance, not just idly curious – trying not to be noticed. Perhaps obviously trying not to be noticed. I take refuge in one of the dingy looking hotels near the bus station which also double as brothels.

The manager and some of the girls are learning to speak English through a taped course.

'Ah! An Englishman. Welcome, welcome!' I'm just the man they were waiting for to help explain the accompanying textbooks.

'When we can speak English, we can go to the United States. This is why it is important to us', the manager explains, and in appreciation of my services he waives payment on the room for the night. This is not financially crippling to him, as judging by the noise that continues through the night, the brothel part of the business is thriving.

One of the prostitutes learning English tells me how she came to the city two years ago from a small village east of Santa Ana, a region that was alternately occupied by the army and by guerrilla forces.

'Life became impossible in all the villages in the war zone', she says. 'The electricity and water supply was blown up by the guerrillas when the army was in control and the crops and livestock were destroyed by government bombing when the guerrillas were in control. People died in every raid. Everybody is tired of the fighting. Everybody has a close relative who has been killed. Everybody wants the violence to end. Is that so much? The government will not give way to the demands for reform. The campesinos are caught in the middle and forced to take sides. They fight because they have lost everything and there is nothing else for them to do.'

There is currently fighting along part of the Pan American highway under guerrilla control in the south of the country, so I enquire about buses to Honduras at the office of Tica Bus, the main company that operates international routes throughout Central America.

'That service doesn't run anymore', the man at the desk explains, 'Part of the route is under control of the F.M.L.N. and sometimes they take our buses. No company runs a service to the border for fear of losing buses. If you want to go to Honduras you will first have to return to Guatemala.'

Having left Guatemala I cannot re-enter for one week, and the prospect of remaining in San Salvador with the possibility of being followed around the streets is not attractive.

I hunt around the local bus stands in the market and find a small battered bus that the driver assures me is going to the Honduran border. I tie the bike onto the roof-rack and take a seat inside. The bus is full, though compared with the buses that are bringing people into the city, it is spacious and comfortable. It is the morning rush hour. Incoming buses are packed full inside with city workers from the suburbs. The roof-racks are also fully occupied – thirty or so people sit, kneel or stand, businessmen in dark suits, market traders in rags, clutching onto bundles and briefcases and each other for support, and at least another twenty people on every bus are spread out around the outside – hanging out of doors, clinging to window frames and balancing on the bumpers. One bus has so many people standing on the front bumper, holding onto wing mirrors and windscreen wipers, that the driver is standing up in his seat to see out.

At every small bridge and every bend in the road there are earth ramps to slow vehicles, and checkpoints where soldiers – mostly young boys – crouch behind barricades of sandbags, in trenches dug into the ground, and large mounted guns are positioned either side of the road. Checks are carried out seriously, fearfully, with no show of the casual arrogance that was common in Guatemala.

The vegetation for a hundred metres either side of the road has been burnt or cleared. It is the end of the dry season, and the wind whips up the exposed earth, carries it in the air in a fine dust which settles on everything and everybody, permeates all luggage.

Many passengers wear scarves and handkerchiefs over their mouths and noses. None attempts any conversation with me. Perhaps my own nervousness discourages them, though nobody is speaking much anyway.

The bus is almost empty when it rolls into the small town of San Miguel. Everybody gets out. I assume it's a toilet stop but the driver is on the roof untying my bike.

'Terminal', he calls down, 'We don't go any further.'

'I thought we were going to the border.'

'Not today. It's too dangerous.'

'Which way is it to Honduras?' I ask him.

'That way,' he points, 'but it's not safe for a gringo on a bicycle. The F.M.L.N. will kill you.'

I load the panniers onto the bike and the bus driver offers advice.

'Just keep going straight. Don't turn off the road, go as fast as you can and don't stop. There are guerrillas on the road and they will shoot you.'

It's thirty kilometres – a couple of hours' ride to the border, and I fill up with water at a bar, not stopping to think or consider an alternative route, because I know I'll only get scared, or frustrated about having to take a week-long detour.

Just out of town is a little adobe house by the road. A man sitting outside on a bench leaves his automatic rifle against the wall and stands in the road as I approach.

'Hi there, where are you going?' he asks.

'Honduras.'

'Good, good', he says. 'It's the safest part of the country here because there are no soldiers.'

He admires the bike and we talk about cycling. I mention that people warned me against coming this way. He says not to worry.

The road beyond is strangely quiet. There are no houses, no soldiers, no people, no sound except for the chirping of insects, nothing to see but the scorched earth and distant wooded mountainsides shimmering in the afternoon heat.

I make an effort to appear uncurious about the surroundings, casual, looking ahead, riding unhurriedly, though I'm all tensed up inside, acutely aware of every little sound or movement I think I see. I stop in the shade of a dead tree, to rest and drink some water, though I don't feel tired or thirsty with so much adrenalin pumping around my head. The quiet is unnerving.

I am conscious of playing the role of a cyclist. It's a disguise, a passport, a declaration of intent to travel slowly. It offers no threat. Everybody recognises it, it's easily understood.

My fear makes my cap and shorts feel like a suit of armour. A number pinned to my T-shirt, and a placard reading 'Keep Politics out of Sport' might complete the ridiculous costume.

I see not a soul during the ride to the border, though I feel I have been watched the whole time.

Across the bridge in Honduras, small boys gather around offering to guide me through the long open-ended, barn-shaped customs and immigration building. A soldier hands me a long blank strip of pink paper.

'What's this?' I ask.

'You've got to get it filled up with stamps', he says.

I enter the first of the tiny offices that line either side of the building, and pay one dollar to officially declare my intention to enter the country. For this I get a stamp. The quantity of stamps is not the only consideration here, the order in which they must be obtained is also important, and bears no relation to the order of offices. I enlist the help of a small boy.

The second office to be visited involves a declaration of the amount of local currency being brought into the country.

'How much do you have?' asks the fat official, slouching behind a wooden desk, empty except for an ink pad and a collection of stamps. I have changed a few unspent Salvador notes.

'Three *lempiras*', I declare.

'That'll do, give it to me', he says, and so I get the general idea.

I reach the end of the building and try to leave. A soldier inspects my pink strip, not quite full.

'Go back and fill it up', he says, waving it in the air.

There are forms to be filled out in the office concerned with registering bicycles, the same forms used for all vehicles. The vehicle registrar tut-tuts at the blank spaces for 'engine type', 'length of trailer' and a number of others, though the blank space for the number plate is most problematic.

'All bicycles in Honduras have a number plate', he scolds. 'Seven Frenchmen came through a week ago and they all had number plates. Some were the same but they all had one.' He makes it clear that he is doing me a personal favour by admitting me to the country in an unregistered vehicle.

The hilly countryside of Honduras is green with plantations of bananas, coffee and cotton. People stop to talk, without the suspicion and division so apparent in Salvador.

The capital Tegucigalpa is hot and crowded and noisy. I am herded with the evening traffic to the central market, and watch with fascination from the safety of a market drinks stall as a line of buses nose their way, bumper to bumper at a snail's pace through the pot-holed streets, all blowing out clouds of black diesel exhaust and honking their horns, amid a sea of people, traders trying to sell a few last goods, as beggars on crutches and trolleys hobble and scoot from their path, and babies crawl around, perilously hidden along with the dogs and pigs snuffling through the cardboard boxes, rotten fruit and vegetables and accumulated market debris that lies knee deep over the road.

I take a room in a nearby hotel that boasts cold showers, clean rooms, and even has new mosquito netting over the windows which effectively prevents the mosquitos already inside the room from leaving.

I am woken by a scratching noise that sounds like the rats that woke me last night, gnawing at the headboard. But no, here it is again, a loud rapping at the door. Unmistakably human.

I open the door to find two large smartly dressed men who I sleepily assume will ask me if I want to change some dollars, which is a common occurrence, and I prepare to launch into the customary negotiations. Then I notice one holds a pistol so I keep my mouth shut. They produce from inside their jackets, cards identifying themselves as undercover policemen, and stroll past me into the room. One of them immediately goes through my things.

'You come from El Salvador', says the other. It's not a question. 'Passport', he says. I hand it over. He asks a few simple questions while the other man rummages through the contents of the panniers he has tipped out on the bed. When he has finished ransacking my things, he shakes his head and pulls a disappointed face. I take this as a good sign.

'What's this?' the man with my passport asks, pointing at the bicycle.

'It's my bicycle.' Men with guns get simple, sincere sounding answers. He furrows his brows a second, perhaps trying to identify a facetious inflection to my Spanish, then lets it go – I'm a foreigner after all.

'What are you doing with a bicycle in Honduras?'

'I'm a tourist passing through. I travel by bicycle.'

He inspects the bike himself, feels the hardness of the tyres, tings the bell, and apparently satisfied, goes to leave. I ask why they have come.

'We are undercover police. It is our job to know things.'

The city streets descend steeply down to the river – at present just a trickle, but the gorge it has carved when in flood is broad and deep. Rickety slums perch along the crumbling cliff edges. Cows and goats graze on the few tufts of grass growing on the dry river bed, which also serves as a football pitch and city dump. Pigs and chickens scratch for food among the heaps of sludge and rubbish that in a month's time will be washed away by the summer rains.

Strolling around in search of the Nicaraguan consulate I become lost in the maze of backstreets where people eke out a living in rough shelters made of canvas, tin, cardboard boxes and polythene. People sit outside, mending clothes, fashioning articles from scrap metal, weaving cane baskets and matting. Prostitution is common too. In one alleyway every other makeshift building is a brothel.

An old man sitting on a packing case calls out – 'Hey, gringo. You like my daughter? She's only twelve years old.' A young girl stands beside him. He pulls up a stool that I might sit and consider his offer.

'No thank you, I'm looking for the consulate of Nicaragua.' A gringo is a rare sight down here, good cause for general teasing and merriment, and my answer provokes incredulous hilarity. Word goes down the alley that the gringo has come to look for the Nicaraguan consulate, people gather around, to grin and stare, and practise saying 'gringo'. I'm a huge joke, obviously a wealthy one too, and I find myself surrounded by a gang of women, grabbing me by the arm, pouting their lips, bearing thighs and breasts, urging me to accompany them to one or other of the dilapidated shacks. Everybody else is shouting and laughing and making obscene gestures. Clearly it is the moment to increase the general merriment by adopting the sort of stiff upper lip detachment from base street humour expected of the British abroad, by walking calmly away. The pose is destroyed by one of the women with a particularly keen sense of humour, who in one deft movement, pulls my trousers down around my ankles, and leads me along in a most undignified manner.

Riotous laughter ensues. Old men fall off their chairs, women screech with delight, and I have to laugh myself, before breaking free and making a dash down the street, to the whistles of appreciation at having provided such amusing entertainment.

In the evening I have a visit from a man with a card which
identifies him as an immigration officer. He searches my things, and
asks a string of questions, though he seems uneasy to be alone in the
room with me, and keeps interrupting his search to check on what
I'm doing. I show him my pink strip of paper filled with stamps to
put him at ease but he only frowns and asks where I got it.

I ask him why visitors to his country are subject to such official
interest. He explains that the government is worried by the movement of arms between El Salvador and Nicaragua. I expect a lot
of international arms traffickers use bicycles.

The man and woman at the hotel desk stop talking now when I
come and go, and call me sir. I leave for Nicaragua.

'You are not permitted to enter Nicaragua with materials that
may be of use to the Sandinista army', says a Honduran soldier at
the border, confiscating my penknife.

'But it's for my personal use. I need it', I complain, and offer to
buy it back.

'It's my property now', the soldier says, gazing into the distance
as if the episode is finished and forgotten. 'I'm in charge here, and
I've got all day.'

The cathedral was one of the few large buildings in Managua
to survive the earthquake of 1972. From its front today hangs a
colossal banner of General Sandino, the 1920's revolutionary from
whom the Sandinistas take their name. The millions of dollars of
international relief that arrived following the disaster to help repair
the devastation was alas largely redirected into the coffers of the
private business empire of the then dictator Somoza.

The site of the old city remains largely a wasteland, vast
areas overgrown with weeds and scrub from which protrude the
remains of buildings – piles of concrete and rusty metal. Present-day
Managua has been rebuilt as several separate centres, spread over
several miles, mostly since the popular overthrow of the Somoza
dictatorship in 1979.

The whole city swelters in the afternoon heat. Nobody stirs from
the shade until the relative cool of the evening, when residents bring
rocking chairs out into the streets, to sit, and talk, and knit, and
relax. It's still very hot. A casual atmosphere pervades.

Politics is the favourite topic of conversation, and is discussed quite openly and passionately in public. Nobody lowers their voice if a policeman or soldier happens along. It is refreshing to see after the fear and mutual distrust that is noticeable between the civilian population and army in other Central American countries. Here it is not apparent because the nation has been united by the outside threat to its integrity.

Government troops are fighting a guerrilla war in the north east of the country against U.S.-financed 'Contra' forces, whose ranks include many of the exiled soldiers of the former Somoza regime, and a number of indigenous Misquito Indians from the Mosquito coast, whose genuine and much publicised grievance over loss of land rights lends a degree of political legitimacy to the Contras' otherwise apparently purely mercenary cause.

The war in general, and the U.S. in particular, is seen as the main obstacle to the success of the revolution. The continued success that is. Everybody in Managua can quote figures for the remarkable progress in the development of an education and public health system that was formerly virtually non-existent, despite the colossal drain of finance and resources needed to fight a war.

The U.S. dollar is welcomed however, providing the hard currency required to buy imported consumer goods. Tight government control on its exchange ensures a flourishing black market.

'The government wants all the dollars it can get,' explains the street changer who offers me five times the bank exchange rate, 'and why does it need so many dollars? To buy arms to fight the U.S.'

Twenty dollars is exchanged for instant wealth. I have just a week to spend it so I go for a meal in the restaurant of the Hotel Intercontinental. Deep-pile carpets brush the mud from my boots as I stroll in air-conditioned coolness along the buffet counters that occupy one side of the room.

Silver trays of bacon, ham, eggs, rice and beans keep warm over gentle flames. Cold meats and salad vegetables surround piles of hot bread rolls and dishes of decoratively shaped individual portions of butter. Cut glass bowls of melons, mangos, pineapples and grapefruit and jugs of fruit juice line up next to coffee pots, tea pots, jugs of milk, jugs of cream, dishes of sugar, brown, white, speckled and cubed. Shiny cutlery rolled in serviettes gleams cleanly from one end, suggesting civilized table manners to befit such a spread. And this is only breakfast.

Hotel guests enter, dressed for breakfast in carefully tailored suits, long dresses, polished black leather shoes, high heels, smoking cigarettes, cigars, clutching briefcases, handbags, speaking in English, German, American, Japanese, of markets, sales, purpose, direction, and completely immersed in the perfume of deodorant and success.

I eat my fill in this enclave of the western world from which I come, to which I belong, but it feels strange, offensively decadent, a little obscene, because I have become accustomed to living with the poverty that lies right outside these tinted plate-glass windows, and the contrast is shocking. I am confused. Out there has begun to feel like home. Coming in here feels like a betrayal of allegiance, and it highlights my hypocrisy, exposes the decadence and obscenity of my hidden bank account which supports my own travels, reveals my pretentions to concern as no more than the mere feelings and opinions of a privileged voyeur.

Morally indigested, I pedal out of Managua.

Lake Nicaragua lies south of Managua, a hundred miles long, like a sea, with a volcano or two sometimes visible beyond the far shore. South of Rivas a rural school building stands amid the dry grassland and parched fields of the plain. The class is being held outside today, benches arranged beneath a large tree. Thin goats and cows browse on the sparse brown grass, and stretch up to reach the withered leaves of stunted trees that line the dried up watercourses.

The children shout, wave and rush into the road as I approach. The headmaster is here too.

'You must give us a lesson about the countries you have visited', he insists. This gives me a lesson in Spanish.

'What do people think in Honduras?' 'What do people eat in Salvador?' 'What do people do in the U.S.?' 'How many punctures have you had?' The children shout and giggle and listen.

Their enthusiasm and curiosity is unflagging.

'You are welcome to stay. We are all most grateful', the headmaster tells me when I become hoarse with speaking. I say it has been my pleasure. Now I feel good again.

The girl at the vehicle exit desk at the border post of Penas Blancas refuses to stamp my passport, for failing to produce the appropriate vehicle papers. I argue that I was never issued with any such papers when I entered the country. She says I'll have to return to Managua. I tell her it's a long ride and far too hot besides, and go outside to sit under a tree.

Another young official approaches, asks for my passport, and disappears back inside. Half an hour later I am called back too. A group stands around the vehicle exit desk, discussing technicalities, and the case for my being made to return to Managua is eventually overridden. The girl types out the relevant form reluctantly, muttering that I should really ride back to Managua no matter how hot it is.

The man in charge of the Ministry of Sanitation disinfectant hose is accustomed to spraying truck tyres, and thoroughly douses both me and the bike before I leave the country.

Clean and germ free I enter Costa Rica – itself clean and germ free by Central American standards. It is a time of oppressive heat and humidity that precedes the rainy season. By mid morning anybody without pressing duties is sitting outside in the shade, sweating.

The rain finally arrives, not falling as drops, but in thick continuous streams, as if poured from buckets. At a pass in the central highlands where it is said both Atlantic and Pacific oceans can be seen, visibility is down to a few feet – beyond is a curtain of water.

Everything becomes damp, even my passport and money, wrapped in polythene bags placed in the remotest part of my panniers become sodden. Waterproof clothing is no proof against such rain. I ride in just hat and shorts.

Birds stand dejectedly in trees, splodges of red and yellow feathers ruffled and blurred on a background of grey. Bright green frogs and big brown toads squat at the roadside, and lie squashed the size of dinner plates in the road. Vultures sit hunch-shouldered in treetops.

The rivers become brown and swollen torrents that carry away trees and all manner of floating debris. Huge boulders become dislodged and roll down to block the road. The road itself becomes dislodged in places, and slides down towards the rivers.

Muddy streams of gurgling water run down the narrow streets of Neilly. Most of the inhabitants seem to have congregated in the large store-cafe-bar, or sit on the verandah outside, watching the rain.

'Hey! Americano, come and have a drink.'

Ten different people offer to buy me a coffee, a beer, a meal.

'You Americanos, you make some problems here in Latin America, with your interference', says one, continuing the conversation that was in course before I arrived. 'We are all tied to your purse strings, financially, economically. There is no political independence without economic independence. You should leave us alone.' They're having a little anti-gringo get-together.

I say I'm from England.

'Ah, England. There is a democratic country! There is the famous Margaret Thatcher who made war on the Malvinas!' The conversation continues now as it always does when I mention England, which at present is synonymous with the Falklands war, an event which, unusually, united much of Latin America in condemnation of the powerful war-mongering imperialists from overseas, and paradoxically, following the subsequent downfall of the Argentine military junta headed by General Galtieri and the election of a civilian government, united it in support of the kind of democratic rule which those same imperialist nations are seen here to represent.

Everyone is sick and tired of something – the government, U.S. interference, corruption, commodity prices – we all have a good gripe. I gripe about the rain.

An empty storehouse is offered to me as shelter for the night – the rain does not dampen the hospitality extended to passing travellers, even those from war-mongering imperialist nations overseas. In heaving the bike upstairs without the required care – it weighs fifty kilos or so laden – I pull a muscle in my back and have to lie down on the floor. There's nothing to be done about it – no one is likely to come by, or even hear me if I call out, because of the deafening roar of rain on the roof – so I may just as well fall asleep.

I wake in the morning with a feeling of pins and needles. I'm covered in ants, crawling hither and thither, stopping occasionally to bite. It's just the incentive I need to overcome the pain in my back. I stand up and take vengeance on the fat ants.

For a while this morning it rains insects. Large orange and black hornets fall from the sky in showers, landing on the road with loud thwacks, where they lie unable to take off again. Most fall facing upwards, legs trailing in the air. Others desperately try to remain airborne and spiral down, ineffectively moving their wings, and after impact with the road, describe small circles. Once on the ground there is no hope. Some, perhaps in an attempt to become revitalized, eat the bodies of their dead and dying fellows who lie in their thousands. The dry popping and crunching of their bodies, crushed unavoidably beneath my wheels, accompanies me to Panama.

The clouds that have made their daily descent from the mountains in the east are about to give everything the benefit of another deluge as I clear customs. A bus destined for Panama City has just completed its formalities too, and sits with its luggage doors open, displaying a gaping bicycle-sized space. I take the opportunity to avoid my daily dousing, and catch the bus.

Everything imaginable is for sale on the streets of Panama City, brought in on the cargo and container ships that can be seen lining up with oil tankers anchored offshore, awaiting passage through the canal.

The construction of a road south of Panama City has remained a proposition for many years, and the overland link with Colombia is a trek along a hundred miles of muddy trails, and through the swamps of the Darien jungle traversable only by canoe. It is a regular route for hardy gringos. I don't feel hardy enough to try it with a bicycle, and instead hunt around for a large cardboard box in which to pack up the bike for an airplane ride.

The offices of Lloyds Bank where I collect the money I've had transferred from England is one of many tall buildings that back onto waste ground where people live in houses built of other people's trash.

Barefoot boys in rags dart in and out of the rush hour traffic, hawking facecloths to drivers and bus passengers in the queues at traffic lights, sweating in the smoggy humid afternoon. There's a large cardboard box in a bar. I offer to buy it.

'That's not a box, it's my bar!'

Another box, by a pavement jewellers. I ask if it is for sale.

'That's not for sale. It's my shop.'

I eventually obtain one, free, from the yard of an importer of Japanese refrigerators, that is burning them, almost brand new ones too, in large numbers. Once you've started seeing boxes it's hard to stop. I've already got one, but dragging it back to the hotel I keep spotting more. One here, another there, and across the road, a whole village of them. But you don't need one, so don't ask. And anyway, you know what they'll say – 'That's not a cardboard box. It's my house.'

7. Death-defying gradients

The Colombian customs men, unshaven and wearing dark glasses despite the gloom of the terminal building of Medellin airport, seem disappointed that the metal objects inside the pockets of my anorak, revealed on their X-ray machine, turn out to be spanners, derailleurs, chains, and other assorted small heavy pieces of bicycle, carried as hand luggage to avoid paying excess baggage fees.

Cycling is a national sport in Colombia. This weekend hundreds of competitors are converging on the city for an international event. I haul my cardboard box outside, and quite a crowd gathers to see what will emerge, and disperses quickly when it becomes obvious that it's just another bicycle. Medellin has the dubious distinction of being the cocaine exporting capital of the world – eighty per cent of South American cocaine is said to pass through here – so perhaps they were expecting something more exciting.

One man introduces himself as a sportsman, and invites me to stay with the other competing cyclists at an address he writes on a piece of paper.

Between thunderstorms that roll down from the surrounding mountains, I ride the five miles into the city centre, by which time I have lost the scrap of paper and address, so simply follow the main road, which narrows and narrows and ends in a maze of market stalls and a solid mass of people, slipping and sliding on wet cobble stones. I dismount, and have to jostle my way along like everybody else, bombarded by shouts to buy these apples, grapes, melons, bananas which sit piled up, glistening with rain on wooden carts.

I have no Colombian money, and inquire of a kerbside pineapple vendor the possibility of changing some dollars on a Sunday morning. Suddenly there is a squeal of tyres, and a taxi comes into view, skidding sideways down the middle of an adjoining road. The driver's face is set in concentration, trying to bring the vehicle under control, and this he finally achieves – the car moves forward in a straight line. Unfortunately he's now pointing in the direction of the market area, and is still travelling at some speed when he hits the kerb. Startled pedestrians flee as the car takes a flying leap, continues airborne for several yards, and lands with a series of bounces a few yards from the pineapple barrow.

There follows a moment's hush as a collective sigh of relief is breathed. Then the crowd closes in around the car, peering in at the driver who sits in a state of shock, his hands still gripping the steering wheel, offering sympathy to the passengers in the back who also appear shaken, and the tension of a potential disaster is released in shouting and laughter. Even those people who seconds before were running for their lives now smile reassuringly at one another, and demonstrate with elaborate gestures to anyone who may not have witnessed the event, what actually happened, how they ran. There is loud debate among the mechanically minded as to the cause of the accident, an impromptu inspection of the car, kicking of tyres and fingering of dents, ten heads peer under the bonnet, and several men crawl beneath the chassis.

The pineapple vendor spits in appreciation of such amusing Sunday morning activity, and consults with a couple of bystanders about money changing. Another man standing near volunteers to lead me to a building where he thinks it might be arranged. It turns out to be closed, but undaunted he enlists the help of other pedestrians who take up my cause, and six people eventually escort me to a large hotel, and remain outside on the steps to guard my bike while the uniformed doorman accompanies me inside and directs the receptionist to change me some dollars at a reasonable rate.

Factories line the valley floor for many miles south of Medellin before the gradient becomes too steep. On the map the road follows the river Cauca, but in real life it frequently leaves the unstable ground near the river to wind up enormous mountainsides into mist and cloud and cold rain, tops high passes and plunges down into the hot green steamy valleys to join it again. On the opposite river bank the remains of the railway that was mostly washed away by floods ten years ago can be seen.

The hills are tough going, but I am continually encouraged and accompanied by groups of cyclists out training. Road racing has a big following and traffic does not toot or try to force cyclists off the road.

Small children follow me through villages where my progress is slow, shouting 'gringo', holding onto the panniers, or playfully pushing sticks between my spokes, sometimes as far as the next village where a fresh gang will appear and help me along with their own favourite games.

Ascending particularly steep climbs need not be strenuous. A truck hauling coal, moving not much faster than I am, stops a little way ahead. The driver indicates that I should hang on to the rear. This turns out to be a popular method of ascent. Several trucks pass this one, each with a number of cyclists in tow. The trick is to speed up as a truck goes by, spurt into its slipstream and grab hold of any suitable projection. Really proficient cyclists can hop from truck to truck for an increasingly fast ride, or simply to be sociable.

Near Buga the valley is broad and flat. Fields of wheat and cotton extend to the distant valley sides. Farmers drive donkeys laden with produce, and small flocks of goats and pigs along the wide grassy verge. Also on the verge is a gringo, sitting by a handcart, busy patching up a blister on his foot, in the same manner of practised ease and engrossment that I repair punctures.

I stop and say hello. It's the same Canadian guy I heard about six months ago in Mexico. He shakes my hand with a vice-like grip. His cart with all his junk weighs over a hundred kilos he tells me. We sit and talk. Mostly he talks – a continuous stream of outrageous experiences and philosophy, though I manage to slip in a few tales and theories of my own, and we laugh in delight at being able to share feelings and thoughts.

'In Colombia we have many fine cities', says the motorcycle policeman who rides alongside me approaching Cali, 'and Cali is the finest.'

In the last village I stopped at, a gang of policemen surrounded me demanding money. 'A present', they said. This one only wants to talk.

'There are many things to see and do in Cali', he says, and goes on talking, perhaps describing the fine things to see and do, long after I can no longer hear him because of the constant beeping of the traffic that is building up behind, impatient to pass. He refuses to move from his position in the middle of the road, and seems oblivious to the cacophony, continuing his monologue with now and then a flowery gesture of a hand. I nod in agreement and occasionally show surprise at what I guess to be appropriate times. To everybody's relief he departs at the turn off to that fine city, and seems disappointed that after showing such interest I ride straight on. The traffic queue roars by. I move onto the gravel verge. The verge is blocked by a group of vultures, pecking and ripping at the carcass of a dead horse. I ride into their midst, and only at the last second do they hop clear. Some beat their huge wings just once, enough to let me duck under their claws before dropping back to the feast.

The valley of the River Cauca narrows as it winds higher into the Andes. Dry rocky cayons plunge down thousands of feet, and rise almost vertically up out of sight among the clouds. At best the road clings precariously to the mountainside. Often it undulates like a roller coaster where the ground beneath has been undermined by the recent heavy rain. In places the road has been washed away in rivers of mud. Tortuous detours plough through the mire.

Plants, animals, people and houses cling to whatever piece of land will safely support their weight. Small patches of maize and huts of stone and thatch perch at incredible angles, accessible only by foot, by paths that wind like stairways up rocky cliffs.

The Colombian government, like most Latin American governments, does not always have the cash to hand to maintain service payments on the foreign debt. Sometimes it needs to borrow more money to make these interest payments. Some of the development schemes initiated with money borrowed from abroad prove too expensive to continue, being unsuited to economies that are not highly industrialised. Often there is pressure put on debtor nations to adopt programmes of economic reform in accordance with policies suggested by the creditor organisations, the implementation of which are requirements for further loans. These policies are primarily concerned with cost effectiveness, with the raising of profit that can then be paid back to creditors. In agriculture this means the restructuring away from the traditional labour intensive multicrop small farms, geared to supplying the internal market, towards the more profitable and highly mechanised cultivation of cash crops for export. This is good for the markets of Europe and the U.S. which are assured of plentiful and cheap bananas, coffee, and cotton, good for the Western banking organisations who reap any profit, good for the Colombian government and those involved in development schemes assured of further loans, good for the economies of industrialised nations that can continue to sell expensive and unsuitable technology. Everybody is making a fast buck except the vast majority of the population within the developing nations, which governments and lending organisations claim to be concerned about. Peasant farmers – campesinos – displaced from workable land now given over to cash crops are forced onto ever more inaccessible unproductive land ill able to support their basic needs. They live a hand to mouth existence. Trees cut for fuel are not replaced and the thin soil is washed away in the first heavy rains.

A woman and two small children sit outside a house built on a flat piece of land by the road, shelling peas into a bowl, tossing the shells to a goat. It's the first house I've passed all day and I stop to ask for some water.

'Hello gringo!' the woman calls out, 'Sit down and rest.' I mention the huts that can be seen across the valley, perched half way up the mountainside.

'My sister lives over there', she tells me. 'Her husband was thrown off the land down the valley by the big farmers. They buy tractors to do the work and they don't need people. Many people have to move. Up here they can't work with tractors.'

'Is it hard to work?'

'Yes it's hard. They are hungry and their children are sick. It's hard.'

She invites me to eat here and stay for the night.

In the yard out back are herbs. Baby goats, chickens, dogs and cats grub around, pecking and sniffing for scraps. Two young lads are working on a rusty truck engine. I wash under the shower – a pipe at head height fed by a drum of water on the top of the wall in a corner of the yard. The children stand around and giggle.

A cloud of moths and other insects flutter around the kerosene lamp that lights the wooden tressel-table around which the whole family eats the evening meal – rice, peas and maize soup.

'What do you do in England, gringo?' the eldest man asks me.

'I drive buses.'

'What do you do here?'

'I've come to travel, to see what Colombia is like.'

'But you don't travel like other gringos. Why not, no money?'

'You can see more on a bicycle.'

'That's true', says a younger man, the old man's son, 'You have stopped here, you get to take a shower in our yard.' Everybody laughs.

The talk is of farming. What are farms like in England? I say they are big tractor farms.

'But what do the people do?'

'There is much industry too. Most people have jobs.'

'You don't have poor people.'

'Yes, but not as poor as here. In England there is a social security system. People with no jobs can get money from the government to live on.'

'Holy shit!' says the old man.

'Yes it's true', says his son. 'It's like that all over Europe, right gringo? You have good governments there?'

'They have good points. But there is much dissatisfaction too. Not everybody is happy.'

'That's right', says the son, 'it's all relative. People without jobs want as much as everybody else.'

'In Colombia the government takes our land, it takes our money, and when we are hungry they give us nothing', says the old man. 'If they gave me money to buy food for my children, for clothes and medicine, then I would be satisfied.'

'Yes, but people like to feel that they are doing something too', I say.

'There are always things to do', says the old man. 'That has nothing to do with the government.'

He looks to me to justify the criticism of a government that gives money to its people, which under the circumstances I cannot do.

'It's different there', is all I can say, and he nods his head in agreement that it must indeed be different.

I am given the bedroom to sleep in. There are two large beds against the walls. They are the only beds in the house. I say I can sleep comfortably in my sleeping bag outside on the ground.

'No, you sleep here', says the woman. 'I invited you.' I sleep in the bedroom on one of the beds and the rest of the family sleeps in the kitchen on the floor.

Popayan lies high up near the head of the Rio Cauca valley. Three months ago an earthquake struck. The town is in ruins. Every building is cracked. Some are just piles of rubble. Some appear to have survived with minor damage in whole rows, but looking through the windows and doors, the interior walls and roofs can be seen caved in, leaving just a front, like a movie set street.

Many streets are impassable after three months, all have piles of rubble, broken lamp posts and telegraph poles and lengths of twisted wire cables heaped to one side. Three mechanical diggers are at work, scooping up the debris into the backs of trucks that take it away and dump it in the river gorge.

The epicentre of the earthquake was directly under the town. During the first rumblings many people were praying in the cathedral. All were buried under tons of rubble when the roof collapsed on them.

Few people live in the town now, but makeshift offices have been set up. A bank, some shops and cafes are open. Most of those remaining now live in the hastily built camps on the hills just outside town, in shacks with shiny tin roofs that shine in the sun alongside the dull tin roofs of the shanties that were there before, which seem to be the only structures not irreparably damaged. It's a sad town. I eat in a cafe, and sleep in a back room under a cracked and drooping ceiling supported by walls that lean and bulge at improbable angles.

Between Popayan and Pasto the road finally climbs out of the Rio Cauca valley, up over high barren passes, cold and bright. Frequent army patrols and checkpoints ensure that this section of the Pan-American highway – the main road link with Ecuador to the south – remains under government control. The surrounding area of remote and roadless mountains, by virtue of its inaccessibility, is suitably ungovernable to provide a secure base and refuge for the M-19 guerrilla movement that enjoys popular and widespread support around here.

The driver of an articulated truck – one of the few vehicles travelling on this road – stops and offers me a lift up the hill into Pasto. He's hauling thirty tons of imported fertilizer from the Caribbean port of Barranquilla to Ecuador.

He tells me the M-19 guerrillas are thoroughly respectable.

'Even the politicians like them because they just make war on the army. They're not supported by cocaine money like the other guerrilla organisations are, like the army is, like the government is.'

He has no firearm licence for the pistol he carries in the cab, and though he hides it in a different place at each checkpoint, it is always discovered. We are delayed a number of times before reaching Pasto, where he insists on dropping me off in the centre, effectively blocking off the busy narrow mainstreet.

8. Mudslides and guinea pigs

The high mountain valleys of Ecuador seem greener and softer than those in Colombia a few miles back – a softness that suffuses the people too. Police checkpoints are not compulsory for cyclists. When I am stopped, it is to test the hardness of my tyres and ting the bell rather than to examine my documents or pannier contents. This does not make me any more inclined to stop. Wherever possible I ride straight by. Not catching the eye of any official on duty is helpful, or timing it so as to pass when attention is taken with a vehicle, or simply ignoring the whistle that is the customary indication that a check is required. The best trick of all is to whizz by so fast that I am not seen at all. This is not always possible as a barrier or chain, or ramps of earth, often bar the way.

A bus has been stopped at a small checkpoint outside the town of Otavalo and a policeman is standing on its roof, making repairs to his stop sign with a piece of wire. The barrier is up and I hope to pass by unseen. There is nothing unpleasant about a check – it just becomes tiresome to be subject to the same questions that are asked more to relieve boredom than out of interest. I speed down the hill. The bus passengers and groups of people who gather around checkpoints to sell food and drinks to those passing through, grin and point as they see me approach. I see the ramps when I am a few yards away, and only have time to grip tight the handlebars and assume the crouching posture that is helpful in reducing shock and increasing balance. The bike hits the ramp at speed and takes off, causing some concern to those nearby who feel they may be in the flight path and hastily abandon their positions by pails of hot corn cakes, braziers of barbecued guinea pigs, and jugs of lemon squash. The clanking of the bike and general jangling of jarred pannier contents when I land, accompanied by the screams of delight at such a spectacle by those onlookers in no danger of injury, alerts the sign repairing policeman to my presence. I hear his frantic whistling from the roof of the bus, but the adrenalin now pumping around my system is sufficient to put me beyond his jurisdiction.

The narrow cobbled streets of Otavalo are busy with people making their way to and from the market, bundles of goods wrapped in brightly coloured cloth on their backs – men in pigtails and wide white trousers, clean and pressed, women in shawls and voluminous skirts and Panama hats.

Market stalls of woollen goods abound: blankets, ponchos and all manner of clothing. I buy gloves and two hats – a woollen one and a floppy felt one. This is not excessive. Many people, particularly high up in the mountains, wear two hats at the same time – one to provide shade from the strong rays of high altitude tropical sunshine, and one underneath for warmth, because out of direct sunlight, beneath the shelter of a sunhat for example, the air is cold.

On my map, the line representing the equator is hard to pin-point, as Ecuador is only two inches across. On the ground, a few miles south of Cayembe is a small roadsign reading 0′ 00″, and a spherical metal framework depicting the earth, with outlines of the continents, the equator, and other key lines of latitude.

An old man sits sleeping on the bench that more usefully marks the spot, with his chin resting on his chest and his legs stretched out among the weeds, one bare foot in each hemisphere.

Small farms and patches of corn dot the green damp valley floor, overlooked by the wooded hillsides that rise up into the cloud, up to the snows that cover the high slopes of volcano Cayembe.

The rainy season has lasted already two months longer than usual. Downpours occur daily.

The capital city of Quito, lying on a plateau nine thousand feet high, shrouded in mist and drizzle, feels long soaked. People trudge through the muddy puddles and streams in the old part of town where long ago the drainage system ceased to cope. They seem not to notice the rain, or to have forgotten what it is to be dry. The hustle and bustle of street trade goes on regardless of the damp. Hot food is cooked and sold on the pavements, doled out from big black pots set up over kerosene stoves, every kind of food, boiled, baked, grilled and fried, roasted, toasted, stirred and sampled, ladled out and gobbled up in the rain.

I bump into Leo, one of the gang of French cyclists I last heard about heading through Salvador. He's recovering from hepatitis at the moment, as are several of the others, in various places. The healthy ones are spread out in smaller groups now, he's not exactly sure where – some as far south as Peru, others last seen disappearing into the Darien jungle of Panama.

Leo is planning to move south for a while by train, though services at present are sporadic because of flood damage. The prolonged rainy season this year has coincided with a weather phenomenon known locally as El Nino which occurs every five to seven years, brought about by a warm water coastal current and abnormal atmospheric conditions over the Pacific Ocean that combine to bring violent storms to the coasts of Ecuador and northern Peru.

Many villages along the coast have been destroyed by flood, and in the wake of the disaster more people are dying in epidemics of cholera, typhoid and outbreaks of yellow fever and bubonic plague.

In the capital, students and trade unionists lead a demonstration and university professors are on hunger strike to bring public attention to the plight of those made homeless, and to protest against the government's failure to alleviate the suffering of those affected by the floods. Thousands of people block off the main street out of the city, with banners and piles of burning tyres. Trucks and buses reverse and U-turn through the central park. The riot squad also turns up.

The road through the central highlands of Ecuador is known as the Avenue of Volcanoes, winding its way between towering cones – Cotopaxi, Chimborazo and Sangay.

The sky clears for the first time in weeks as I'm slowly ascending a quiet side road up the gorge of the river Chambo towards Riobamba, revealing snowy peaks, glistening like dollops of melting ice cream.

A steep slope rises on one side of the road, the river gorge falls away thousands of feet on the other. I weave around rocks and boulders strewn in random fashion across the road, and though such peculiarities in road conditions normally provide me with hours of mental diversion in speculating about their origin and nature, I am so engrossed in the beauty of the scenery that I pay no attention.

A gentle swishing noise takes me by surprise. High up the steep slope a sheet of stones is moving. Quite a large sheet, both ahead and behind. I stop to watch and listen. It's quite beautiful too, and

sounds like waves on a distant shore. It's a few seconds before
I realize that though they look like stones they are in fact large
boulders and rocks of a similar size to those already on the road.
Idiot! Back down the way I've come seems the most expedient escape
route, and I'm pedalling off, dodging around the boulders already
in the road as the first of the falling rocks bound down. Most hit
the road at a terrific speed and bounce just once before flying out
into the gorge below. Some of them hum. Some land with a heavy
thwack and split into fragments that scatter in all directions.

The fragments whistle and ting and ping through my spokes,
twang off the frame which vibrates and clacks. I take just one hefty
whack on the foot – a dull unmusical thud.

A swollen foot is reason enough to linger a few days in Riobamba,
to pass time wandering around town, to loiter around the market
stalls amid the traders who converge here from the surrounding
valleys, bringing vegetables, livestock, leather goods and blankets
and their quite separate culture and sense of time, and to sit on the
roof of a three-storey adobe hotel with its chickens and curly-haired
pigs and its breeze and sunshine and view of the mountains, and
to watch in the evenings the traffic below toot and beep in flowing
motion, and bump itself into parking spaces with gentle nudges of
neighbouring vehicles, and later when the town power supply is cut,
to enjoy the undimmed flashes of electric storms light up the clouds
and ice of distant mountains, red, pink and gold.

The new road out of Riobamba, marked by a dotted line as
incompleted on my map, is reportedly impassable, but rises
invitingly up a long gentle valley into the sunshine, bordered by
tiny wild flowers trembling in a wind blowing so favourably from
behind that I cannot resist following it.

Young children with dogs herd groups of animals – goats,
black curly-haired pigs and a donkey or two – from one patch of
grass to the next. Small settlements nestle against the steeply rising
mountains at the edges of the valley.

The valley narrows into tight gorges that constrict the river into
fast flowing torrents. Waterfalls roar and echo between towering
cliffs.

On a bridge that spans the river by a group of houses I am
surrounded by a group of young children.

'There's no way through!' they shout excitedly. 'There's a landslide ahead, you have to go back!'

I camp on the flat grassy banks of the river a little way upstream where the valley broadens. This is the first time out of its bag for the tent I bought in Quito, to replace the one that, along with other items not required in the warmth of Central America, I parcelled up and posted from Mexico, and which not totally unexpectedly, never arrived in Ecuador.

The tent is made in Taiwan. There are no clues as to the manner of its erection, so I stand awhile puzzling over the intended design. The children who have accompanied me prefer the more direct method of trial and error to solve the problem, grabbing poles and pegs, sticking them right in the ground, hoisting and stretching complaining nylon to conform to their own design.

We stand around admiring the small and curiously shaped structure, irregular and flimsy, and flapping in the wind.

'It's a beautiful tent, mister', the children all agree.

'But you can't sleep here – there are thieves about.'

A group of men are returning down the valley, wrapped in ponchos, barefooted, leading donkeys laden with firewood that fart furiously with the strain of scrambling across the stream bed, which delights the children who throw stones and clods of earth to encourage them to further effort.

The men tell me that the road ahead is buried for many miles under mud.

'People can walk across, and two weeks ago another gringo came by on a bicycle – Señor Don from North America. He went out there and he didn't come back so you should be able to get through.'

Some of the women from the houses come over as it gets dark, bringing candles, and invite me to sleep in the houses. I decline, explaining that the tent is quite adequate, hoping I'm not being too offensive. I know that some family would end up sleeping on the floor, and I'm quite settled here now.

'But there are thieves and bad types about at night', the women tell me.

'Have you seen them?' I ask.

'Oh no, but they live in the next valley.'

In time I have come to ignore these reports of thieves and robbers that everybody warns me of wherever I go. They are variations of the 'missing professor' stories I heard in the U.S. That thieves and robbers exist there is no doubt, though largely it seems they exist in our imaginations, and those real ones are equally likely to be encountered in this spot as the next, this valley as that, in a hotel, a police station, a house or a tent.

Sleeping in a different and unknown place every night, it becomes impossible to sustain a fear based on a belief that time after time is proved baseless. In the mountains the fear is of robbers from the next village, the next valley. In other places these robbers inhabit the next country, the next state, the next culture, the next continent, and when we journey to that next village, that valley, that next continent, we find exactly the same fears expressed about the places from which we have just come. I try to explain this when confronted with rumour, because it seems important. It is enough for me that I become afraid when I hear a strange sound outside the tent at night. It seems unnecessary to fill one's head with the fears of other people's imaginations as well.

A short way up the valley, the mountainside saturated with rain has slipped away. The road disappears under a thirty foot wall of mud and rock. I scramble up. A sea of mud covers the mountain, with a slight levelling indicating where the road is buried. There is no chance of pushing the bike along – the surface is uneven as a ploughed field and the wheels sink right in. I hoist it onto my shoulder and try walking, but under the weight I sink up to my thighs in soft sludge. To reduce the weight I take off the panniers, and sinking and stumbling, carry the bike for a hundred yards, then return for the panniers. Progress is slow and exhausting.

The firm road comes into view after an hour or so, but only for a few hundred yards before disappearing under another wall of mud.

Here and there a tree that has been swept away sticks up to break the monotony. Mostly there is just mud. The cloud which has been descending all morning finally engulfs everything. I carry the bike ten yards or so, until the pile of panniers is just visible – they are covered in mud like everything else – then return for them, trudge forward, dump them down and return for the bike, back and forth through the soft grey gloom of cloud that muffles all sound, squelching and panting, sinking into the sludge with every step, all sense of time and slowly covered distance becomes lost in the mist and mire. It is not unpleasant – the soft enclosed world has a dream-like quality – there is a whiff of unreality about it and I cannot help but laugh out loud when I sit down to rest at the absurdity of being here at all. There is even a deep low thrumming sound that seems to be coming out of the ground, though this is no natural resonance, and turns out to be the hum of the engines of a road crew, who with bulldozers and diggers are yard by yard removing tons of mud, scooping it up and shovelling it down the mountainside. They tell me they have been working for three weeks and have come perhaps one kilometre. They say that it was fortunate that the mudslide occurred just here because there are no villages.

Just beyond where the mud wall ends there is a village. I am covered from head to foot in mud. The bike too is a uniform grey – horribly sickly grinding noises come from the chain as it slides over muddy sprockets. Though the road is rideable I have to stop frequently to free the mud that collects between the mudguards and brakes that effectively stops the wheels turning, and everything is drenched in the spray of liquid mud that lies an inch deep over the road.

'How muddy you are, gringo!' remarks an old woman from the doorway of her house which is made of dried mud bricks.

I put up the tent on the first piece of dry flat land, on a ledge overlooking the valley. The cloud has cleared now, and the chunk of displaced mountainside appears from here as just a small scar, which though clearly recent, will soon be populated with plants, and become indistinguishable from other longer established features of the valley, themselves formed by similarly monumental landslides. On the timescale of mountains, chunks of earth are continually being released from the tension of improbable gravity defying formations, to tumble like a house of cards with a roaring geological sigh.

Luckily we flit and buzz around the earth, putting up our tents and building cities, cocooned reassuringly in our own fleeting timescale where the proportion of people swept away in landslides is sufficiently small, and the ground beneath sufficiently firm to give an impression of permanence necessary for a good night's sleep.

I'm still swathed in mud when I arrive in Cuenca, Ecuador's third largest city. Despite my appearance, two girls invite me to their house – a hardware store in the centre of town – where the whole family welcomes me with typical Latino effusiveness. Berta and her sister are on holiday from school, show me around town in their father's flat bed truck, and take me to the local hot spring pools.

Roast guinea pigs are the main course in the evening meal, cooked whole, splayed out on their backs with legs spread-eagled. It's popular fare in Ecuador.

'We're having them tonight because you are here', Berta's mother tells me. 'They are a speciality.'

Politeness requires that I put aside a tendency to vegetarianism and memories of a childhood pet, and rip the little animal limb from limb in the customary manner with my fingers. It is in fact very tasty.

'Have another one, gringo!' encourages Berta's father. He never calls me anything but gringo, even at the dinner table.

The road through the highlands to Peru is reportedly impassable, so I backtrack north to the junction where a road plunges down out of the mountains along the valley carved by the river Naranjal. It's tough going today. My body is not functioning properly. I think it must be flu. My visa expires in three days' time, and it's three hundred miles to the border so I wrap up in all my clothes and waterproofs and keep going.

Nearly a hundred miles is downhill. Steep downhill – from twelve thousand feet to near sea level. Beneath the cloud base half way down, the mountainsides can be seen dropping down to the coastal plain below, dissected by silvery lines of rivers. Thick tropical plants grow right up to the road, the air becomes thick with insects and buzzing sounds, the smell of earth and decay. Houses are built of comparatively insubstantial bamboo and thatch and nobody is wearing ponchos or Panama hats. It seems a different, warmer, gentler world down here. I don't need to breathe in great lungfuls of air, my one airtight water bottle becomes crushed with the increase in pressure, but despite the warmth I still feel damp and cold and feverish, freewheeling down to the plains. The Andes have spat me out.

The pills I buy in a pharmacy in La Troncal succeed in dulling the fever for a while, but they numb my body as well. For two days I continue as if asleep.

Between Machala and the border, the normally arid semi-desert is flooded, swathed in a blanket of green vines and creepers that cover the cactus and thorny scrub, masking features like a covering of green snow.

Only my legs seem to know what they are doing, continuing mechanically, detached, as if no part of me. I entrust myself to their care while my head busies itself with feverish argument and division, as warring factions shout each other down, in a succession of disagreements that at times becomes so hectic that I have to shout out loud to maintain some kind of order, and sometimes get caught up in it all, and shout the odd word of support, or deride a particularly ridiculous opinion. In this slightly delirious and schizophrenic manner, we all make our way across the border into Peru.

9. Dodging bullets and chewing coca

The two-mile strip of road between the first and last border controls of Peru and Ecuador is seething with market stalls, traders and money changers, and the constant ringing of bells of the tricycle barrows which taxi goods and people back and forth.

Money changers hang around in groups, easily identified by their briefcases, pocket calculators, and the way in which they run in a jostling gang towards any prospective customer. The first to arrive steams in with his offer and is quicky followed by a second and third, who make good their athletic deficiency by offering a better rate of exchange, and all providing good reasons for changing money with them.

'All the banks to Lima have been destroyed!' they tell me.

The recent heavy rains brought by El Nino have made dramatic changes to the land here – the northernmost part of the Atacama desert which stretches out for two thousand miles south along the coast. The fifteen miles from the border to the first Peruvian town of Tumbes is barely passable. All the bridges over the gullies and wadis have been washed away, the track winds up and down the sides, fording the small trickles of water that remain. Many new gullies have been created by the floods, slicing across the road as if it had not been there.

The streets of Tumbes are muddy trenches and deep pools. The poorest inhabitants of the town were the worst hit. Hundreds of families living in the shanty towns along the banks of the river were swept away by a wall of mud and water. With much of the Pan-American Highway washed away into the Pacific Ocean, road links with the rest of the country to the south are completely severed, but an airstrip and the road to Ecuador in the north ensure the provision of essential supplies, and though inconvenienced by the lack of electricity, and a water supply for just two hours a day, the townsfolk are well aware that in comparison with their neighbours in the remote highland villages to the west, they are well-off indeed. In the mountains whole regions are completely cut off, the only way in or out is by foot or helicopter. Villages have been destroyed by swollen rivers and flash floods that washed away crops, livestock, food supplies and homes. People are dying of starvation and disease, unable to leave.

The army has a large permanent base in Tumbes and is much in evidence in the town, patrolling through the slush of the streets in trucks, arousing some resentment among the civilian population who believe it would be more usefully engaged in tackling the problems affecting those in the mountains.

I share a table in the candle lit interior of a cafe with a man waiting for a flight to the capital.

'The government has announced a state of emergency in several areas', he says. 'Not because of the disaster here in the north, but in response to the activities of the Sendero Luminoso guerrillas in the south who in the current climate of general public dissatisfaction with the government, have stepped up their campaigns of bombing in the capital and insurgency in the mountains of the south.'

The darkness of the cafe is increased by the black covering of flies on the walls and ceiling, tables and chairs. They swarm over my plate of fish and I give up trying to keep them away and concentrate on preventing them from entering my mouth with the food on my fork.

'Does the army not have helicopters to fly supplies into the areas cut off by floods?' I ask him.

'Sure, the army has plenty of helicopters. They use them around the capital, and to search for guerrillas in the mountains of the south. Here we are a long way from Lima.'

The bus depot on the outskirts of town is packed out with long distance buses, optimistically showing Lima on their destination boards. Outside, a man lounges on a wooden bench in the shade, waving flies from his face with a Toyota cap. I ask him how the road to Lima is.

'There is no road', he replies. 'It's destroyed. If you want to go to Lima you must fly.'

'When do you think the road will be open?'

'Oh, quite soon, maybe a few weeks.'

'Do you think a bicycle can get through?'

'No, I don't think so. The road is all washed away, and it's all desert, but who knows? If you can get to Chiclayo, they say the road is open from there.'

'How far is Chiclayo?'

'It's five hundred kilometres, more or less.'

I set off early in the morning, and struggle all day through thick mud that clogs up the wheels, clings to my boots where I have to trudge through on foot, across gullies and wadis, vaguely following the sandstone cliffs where the track is completely obscured, and travel perhaps ten kilometres. I return exhausted to Tumbes.

'It's only a small plane', the airline booking agent warns me, 'You'll have to pay extra for the bicycle.'

'How much?'

'How much does it weigh?'

'I don't know.'

He steps outside the office with clipboard in hand, finds he cannot pick it up off the ground and hold the clipboard, so lifts first one end, then the other.

'Twenty dollars', he decides.

The daily flight is always overbooked, so as soon as the plane is sighted coming in to land, passengers shove and jostle and squeeze their way through the barriers onto the tarmac.

Lima is shrouded in sea mist at this time of the year, which adds to the permanent industrial smog. The city centre is fifteen miles from the airport, and it takes me all day to find it, spending many hours lost in the gloom, touring industrial areas and cruising on exitless, fenced off bicycle–prohibited multilane highways which inevitably lead to one or other of the outlying suburbs that in turn peter out into the shanty towns that cling to the steep hillsides all around the city, where millions live in labyrinths of lean-tos and shacks made of tin and polythene and wooden packing crates.

Finally arriving in the city centre, I take a room in an ancient and decrepit boarding house. Many families live here in tiny rooms with crumbling walls that are damp and covered with moss. Ancient crumbling Alsatian dogs roam the corridors searching for scraps, or sleep on the stairs, and leave piles of dogshit which one of the ancient employees roams the building sweeping up. The corridors echo with the sound of children playing, crying, running among the washing slung over lines and draped over banisters to dry in the damp air that always smells of cooking and dogshit.

I bump into Leo again, wheeling his bike along one of the modern shopping precincts. He travelled from Tumbes to Chiclayo with Rudi, a Swiss cyclist, in a small fishing vessel – two days sheltering from the sun and sea spray, lying on fishing nets under sheets of canvas. Their bikes lay exposed and quickly developed a layer of rust, and he's searching for a bike shop with the tools to separate the sprocket rings of his freewheel which has seized up, in order to clean it.

He arrived in Lima a week ago on the bus from Chiclayo, still weak from hepatitis, and met up with Max and Jean-Louis, two more of the gang of seven French cyclists. Rudi is still in the desert, battling his way against the headwind.

We pop into the tourist office to find out where road maps can be bought, and to inquire about the travel restrictions in the area of Ayacucho, currently under martial law because of insurrection by Sendero Luminoso guerrillas.

'Tourists are prohibited from this region', we are told, which differs from what other travellers have told us, but tourism being a major source of much needed foreign currency, the government Ministry of Tourism is keen not to adversely affect the tourist trade – particularly now at the height of the season when thousands of visitors flock to the tourist meccas of Machu Picchu and Cusco.

'By road you should follow the coast road south to Nazca and head east into the mountains by Abancay. Most people prefer to fly. The roads are very bad.'

The Peruvian Geographical Society has reasonably detailed maps of the country, and back in Leo's room that is full of his bike, the bikes and bit of bikes of Jean-Louis and Max, we pore over the winding coloured lines that traverse the brown shadings, impressed with the nine different classifications of dirt roads, the large stretches with red scribbles marked '*Destruido*' (destroyed). Whatever route is taken there are sixteen thousand feet passes all along the way.

Jean-Louis and Max are heading off south in a couple of days and Leo intends to follow with Rudi when he arrives. They all have similar brand new knives – a present from Gérard, another

French cyclist who headed off east up into the mountains a week ago.

'Gérard is a fanatic', says Leo. 'He's very fast. He contacts the media wherever he goes. He bullied his way onto T.V. whilst he was in Lima.'

Gérard also writes articles for magazines and newspapers, and to anyone who might be remotely interested in international cycle touring. He wrote to a cutlery manufacturer in France, and they sent him a consignment of culinary knives.

I visit the consulate of Argentina to find out if I can get a visa. They say yes, but it could take six weeks, so I remove the remains of the front mudguard, damaged beyond repair during the excitement at Tumbes airport, and head out of the city, east along the road that follows the valley of the river Rimac up into the Andes.

Up above the coastal mist the overhead sun at midday casts no shadow, and glares back from grey towering rocks that rise almost vertically up out of sight on either side of the valley.

There is a small store open in the tiny plaza of a small village. I stop for a drink and to sit in some shade. The shop interior is full of sacks of grain, flour, potatoes, with a few shelves of cans of fish and bottles of fizzy drinks.

The man in the shop seems not to hear my asking for a bottle of drink and instead steps outside to examine the bicycle. He asks me where I come from and where I am going and how long it has taken me to get here. Normally people ask how many days it has taken to get here and are amazed at any length of time more than a week. I tell him ten months, but he just nods sagely. His wife steps outside and he tells her it has taken me ten months to come from England.

'Ten months! From England?' she shouts with incredulity to some neighbours who have gathered round the bike, and they discuss with amusement the idea of travelling on a bicycle for so long. I sit down on a wooden bench and think about a cool drink.

The shop owner is now pointing out features of the bike and explaining some of its complexities to the crowd of friends and neighbours and small children. The drop handlebars, the brakes, the gears all come in for inspection. He demonstrates the hardness of the tyres – the thin tyres – and tries out the horn. I bought the horn two days ago in Lima, an enormous four-trumpet contraption with a large rubber bulb that produces a loud discordant blare, to supplement the ineffective clicking sound which is all that comes from the small racing bell that came free with the bike and is kept for sentimental rather than practical reasons. A horn in South America is one of the most important parts of a vehicle. Drivers will set out on long journeys without lights or water in the radiator, with faulty brakes and shredded tyres, but if the horn is not working they don't leave till it's fixed.

After battling through a strong headwind full of sand and grit earlier this morning, the new horn has refused to make even a squeak.

'It doesn't work', the shop owner calls out, obviously disappointed. I tell him it's only two days old and we all have a good laugh.

'May I ride around the village?' he asks.

'Go ahead', I say and he wobbles away, zigzagging across the plaza, pursued by a crowd of children.

Normally I am wary of letting strangers ride the bike. It carries all my worldly goods, my passport and two thousand dollars secreted about its panniers. It is my home, my past, my roots, my way of life.

I acquired a knowledge of Spanish so slowly that for many months I was forced to rely on tone of voice, mannerisms and body language to interpret meaning. This has proved to be a useful exercise, for now people sometimes ask to ride the bike and though I understand what they say, I refuse because of a contradiction between words and posture. Their mouths say one thing, their whole body says another.

In many small villages, though the bike may be crowded with onlookers, I leave it to go into a shop, a cafe, for a walk around, and I know that nothing will be touched. It is a useful ploy at times to leave it somewhere and walk away just to distract attention from myself, to enjoy some privacy. If I show no concern about guarding the bike, people think there is nothing worth stealing. In the cities, and in villages where I don't feel at ease, I never let it out of my sight. The man in this village just wants a ride round. He reappears, still wobbling, still pursued by the children.

'What can I do by way of return?' he asks, pleased at the ride. I say he can sell me a bottle of fizzy pop.

It takes two days to climb to the pass – first gear all the way, from sea level to nearly sixteen thousand feet in eighty miles.

In places near the top there is no room for the railway lines which follow the same valley, and the track is supported on a scaffold of steel girders like a fairground roller coaster which does everything but loop the loop.

The air is thin and cool, and the towering canyon walls in places overhang, showering the road with small stones.

A few miles from the top a truck passes, hauling steel poles that overhang the trailer by ten feet or so. It's not moving much faster than me so I grab hold and get a tow. Just hanging on is hard work at this altitude. I force lungfuls of air in and out, puffing like a steam train without seeming to gain my breath.

The driver stops at the top to get out and chat. A bitter wind whistles around a billboard advertising Selva ice cream, and states that the pass is 4818 metres high. Snow and ice lie around unmelting in the bright sunshine.

The driver tells me that a lot of stuff is being hauled up by road to La Oroya – the mining town down the other side of the pass – though this is the only truck to have passed me all morning.

'The Senderistas blew up a railway bridge and part of a train last week', he says. I ask him why.

'They are revolutionaries, Maoists. They want to bring down the government by destroying the economy.'

'What do you think of them?' I ask.

'I think they're too violent. I think they're crazy.'

La Oroya is a bleak and windswept mining town. Early morning sunshine sparkles in the frosted slush of the main street, in the clouds of condensation breathed out by the men wrapped in ponchos and blankets and woolly balaclavas on their way to work.

A man comes out of the house opposite a roadside coffee stall and comes over to where I sit on the pavement, drinking coffee and thawing out the hypothermia of last night's high camp. He produces a week-old copy of a newspaper – The Huancayo News – and shows me a photograph of Gérard sitting astride his loaded bicycle.

'He stayed at my house for the night. He was a Frenchman and he gave me a knife. Are you racing him? Shall I contact the newspaper for you?'

I tell him I'm not racing, that in fact I've never met him, which he finds hard to believe. Two gringos on bicycles must surely be brothers or cousins, or at least know each other.

'If you ride fast you will catch him, but after Huancayo the road is very bad and you will have to walk.'

Despite the directions he gives me out of town, I end up following a new concrete road to the entrance of a mine. Two armed security guards re-direct me. They think it likely that I will be held up by bandits or guerrillas, and beyond Huancayo, where the road is very bad and there is no law, because I have no gun I will certainly be robbed and killed and tossed into a river.

It is usually people who carry arms themselves that are alarmed or surprised that I don't have a gun. Perhaps the belief in the necessity of arms is generated by their possession. Or perhaps the belief comes first. Probably most people don't think about it one way or the other – arms are part of making a living. Carrying a gun would not make me feel any safer. It would be just another barrier to overcome. And it seems like an admission of defeat.

The road follows the high valley of the river Mantaro which flows four thousand miles from here into the Atlantic Ocean. The Pacific Ocean is just a hundred miles to the west.

The air is so clear that small objects on distant hillsides are seen sharply defined. A bend in the road ahead, or a bridge or village appear quite close, but take a long time to reach.

Packs of large woolly dogs with shiny red eyes bound down to greet me from some of the villages. The road is flat so I am able to speed past, waving my pump defensively to keep them at bay.

In Lima, a man who had visited the U.S. remarked to me how he was surprised to find dog hairdressers, psychologists and dog cemeteries. 'They treat dogs better than humans', he said. 'In Peru it is different. Here a dog is something you kick and it goes away.'

No aggression is tolerated from dogs. If one comes at me and the owner is nearby, they shout, or throw a rock or two to discourage it, but it is expected of the passer-by to defend himself. Throwing rocks and stones is acceptable behaviour, though it seems to me at first to be unnecessarily cruel, and I am regarded with surprise when I merely shout or wave a bicycle pump. One is supposed to get on with the business of throwing rocks rather than waste time and energy becoming angry.

The valley broadens near Huancayo and, sheltered from the wind by surrounding mountains, it becomes warm in the afternoon sunshine. Oats and barley are being harvested, cut by hand and piled up to be threshed by donkeys driven round in a circle, then tossed into the air to separate the chaff from grain. The cleared fields are being turned with hand hoes by lines of men and women bent double, though a few bullocks and donkeys are harnessed to small ploughs.

In the evening, the central plaza of Huancayo is crowded with people watching two groups of street performers. Many such groups tour the cities of Peru, making a living swallowing swords, breathing fire, clowning and doing acrobatics.

One group is playing folk music, with Pan-pipes, flutes, *charangos* and a drum, to which two young children barely old enough to walk are dancing.

The other group is performing a play – a fairy tale with a modern theme, politically satirical – involving audience participation in playing bit parts of presidents and government officials, which goes down well, given the tendency of most Peruvians, particularly the campesinos, to regard the workings of government with complete indifference or cynicism.

As the crow flies, the distance from Huancayo to Cusco is about four hundred kilometers. By winding mountain dirt road it is over nine hundred. Reports on the road condition vary from very bad to impassable, which, together with reports of routine robberies, guerrilla activities and the propensity of large dogs to molest travellers, makes me doubt the wisdom of embarking on this part of the route.

The road rises steeply, through quiet hamlets, past dusty fields and patches of maize and gurgling streams. Dogs seem uninterested in giving chase because I'm moving so slowly.

Passing through Cullhaus I am almost pulled from my bike by a couple of girls from the cafe. They ply me with coffee and bread rolls, and one of them pulls down a postcard of the Eiffel Tower from the wall.

'Your friend stayed here three days ago,' one girl says.

'He was a nice boy. He ate three big meals and slept on the floor and he gave us a knife from France.'

The road continues to rise, beyond houses and fields into a land of rock and tough grass and bleak windswept passes covered in cloud, cold and grey with rain and snow, then down steeply, out of the cloud into the valley of Pampas.

The soldiers at the roadblock at the entrance to town are reluctant to let me pass.

'This is a military zone under a state of emergency', they tell me, 'Tourists are prohibited.' I am left standing in the rain.

A sergeant appears who seems more open to persuasion. I say I'm a cyclist not a tourist.

'That's what your friend said a few days ago. He was famous though. He showed us many newspaper items, and he's been on television.' He allows me to pass, even though I'm not famous.

With Gérard blazing a trail of goodwill and fame ahead I feel I can't go far wrong.

The road soon leaves the flat valley floor to climb up the mountainside in a series of zigzags that disappear out of sight among the clouds far above.

A few houses of adobe and stone perch on flat pieces of ground, amid small vegetable plots irrigated by carefully directed channels of water.

It is thirsty work. I fill water bottles with water that trickles from a roadside spout fashioned from a piece of bamboo. It looks clear enough, and it's the same stuff that the locals keep in drums in their houses. The road recrosses the same stream a little higher up. Pigs are wallowing in it, women are washing clothes in it, and in the adjoining field a man is spraying pesticide on potato plants from a cylinder strapped to his back.

Houses become infrequent higher up where the land is barren, capable of supporting only hardy animals – small groups of llamas and goats wander from one patch of coarse grass to another.

Only in the lowest gear can I make progress up the steep rocky gradient, always riding around the less steep outside of bends, and over the steepest parts, zigzagging from side to side in an effort to keep up momentum, for when I stop it is to hard to start off again, and sometimes only possible by rolling off downhill and doing a U-turn once mounted.

There is little traffic. One vehicle an hour – usually a battered open-backed truck piled high with people and bundles, pouring out clouds of diesel fumes and trailing a cloud of dust. I have to hold my breath when a vehicle comes by, which means stopping. I'm unaccustomed to the thin air, so breathe like a set of bellows to suck in enough oxygen, sometimes taking four deep breaths for every revolution of the pedals in first gear.

The clouds that were clinging to the tops of the mountains have dispersed when I reach the top of the valley in late afternoon. Range after range of sharply defined mountain ridges are revealed, one behind another far into the distance.

The road is a narrow rocky ledge that offers spectacular views over valleys that lead off in all directions, plunge away to depths too hazy for anything to be seen.

On a bend overlooking one bottomless chasm a group of men is standing outside a small stone hut. I stop because it seems polite in the middle of nowhere to say hello. I ask if it is far to the next village. The men just look at me.

'What are you doing on a bicycle, gringo? Where are you going?'

'Just riding. I go this way', I reply pointing ahead, trying to appear casual and confident because there is hostility in their manner and I feel uneasy.

'It's a long way, gringo, to the next village. Are you alone?'

'No, my friends are coming', I say, and I'm about to leave, but then another man emerges from the hut and rushes over to stand in front of me. He has a stick in his hand. Dark green coca juice dribbles down his chin as he speaks, half shouts, a rapid stream of words that I cannot understand. I'm scared now but try not to show it, and as slowly and calmly as I can, playing for time and hoping that a means of extricating myself quietly from the situation will present itself, I ask him if he can speak more slowly as I cannot understand what he is saying. He speaks faster and more aggressively than before, pointing at my panniers, scowling. I understand the word 'money' and am fearful now of being robbed and tossed into the river as promised.

I make to ride off but he prevents me, dropping his stick and grabbing the handlebars and holding the front wheel between his knees. He reaches down and opens one of the front panniers. Things are out of control. Time slows down. I shout at him in English, angry

at such a blatant act of robbery, angry at having been made to feel
so scared. He looks up, surprised perhaps at hearing English, and
as he straightens up I shove him back and dismount, aware of the
scene as if from distance, not afraid anymore, expecting to be set
upon, resigned to a brawl.

My outburst of energy has taken us all by surprise. The man I
shoved is sitting in the road. The other three are standing nearby,
undecided about what to do. I quickly remount and pedal off down
the road.

Though I am soon far from the place, the episode repeats itself
over and over in my mind. I try to put it in perspective. Did I grossly
misread the situation?

I am shocked and angry. Angry that the shield I imagined
my vulnerability offered should prove so ineffective. Angry at
the humiliation. Shocked that I lost control and so automatically
resorted to violence in a location so remote and potentially dangerous. And for what? – A few meagre possessions? Or in defence of
something more obscure, according to some underlying dictate of
pride, to restore self-esteem.

The jagged lines of the sierras, darkening now against the
evening sky, offer a wide perspective but no moral support, or
condemnation, or reason to pronounce judgement.

The road descends from the high spur to join another that
comes along an adjoining ridge. A group of houses face each other
across the junction. A girl sits on a bench outside one of the houses,
spoon-feeding a small child a bowl of soup.

I stop to ask if I can pitch my tent in the shelter of the house.

'A tent? No, you sleep inside with us', she replies. She hands
me the child and brings out a cup of coffee, and tells me that
she has recently finished school in Huancayo, and finding no work
there now lives back up here with her family, helping look after
the children, the animals, and cooking food for the travellers who
stop by.

'This is a restaurant too', she says proudly, 'Restaurant La
Esperanza.'

Inside the house the rest of the family is sitting at a long
wooden table. The small windows in the thick walls are already
shuttered and the room is lit by the warm flickering glow of the
fire, hissing and crackling inside its mud oven. A large black pot

sits on top. The girl's mother ladles me out a bowl of potato and noodle stew.

The family was speaking Quechua when I entered. Now they speak Spanish. One of their goats went missing today and they discuss where it might be.

Shadows dance around the walls, on the sacks of flour and grain, on the carcasses of meat which hang from the wooden beams. The cosiness is overwhelming.

Three men enter – a road crew based in Huancayo. They spend several days at a time up in the mountains, filling in holes and subsidences, shoring up crumbling cliffs, sleeping in roadhouses and being picked up a few days later in a corporation jeep.

They clomp their hard hats and tin lunch pans down on the table and warm themselves around the fire. A kerosene lamp is lit. The girl relates to them my tale of attempted highway robbery. They whistle and demand I tell it again.

'You have to be careful up here', they warn me. 'The police and the soldiers stay down in the towns. They are afraid to come into the mountains because of the Senderistas. People take advantage of this to rob.'

'Are there many Senderistas around here?' I ask.

'Yes, plenty.'

'What do they do?'

'They fight against the army. Many people join from the poor villages in the mountains. They are Maoist revolutionaries who want to bring down the government.'

'But they don't do such good things', argues another. 'Nobody likes the government. I don't like the government. My brother doesn't like the government. The Senderistas try to make him fight. He works all day just to feed his children. He has no time to fight. They take food from his house and he can do nothing. Sometimes campesinos who refuse to help are killed.'

The family and the road crew discuss the Senderistas and the state of the country in general, long into the evening. Wrapped in blankets and ponchos, they seem not to notice the cold.

The children busy themselves clambering over me as I lie fully clothed inside my sleeping bag. Draughts of cold air whistle up through cracks in the wooden floor from the animal pen burrowed beneath the house. Shuffles and grunts waft up too.

The old man does not believe that a sleeping bag can possibly keep me warm. He's right too, and I'm grateful when he brings me a pile of sacks to lie on and use as blankets. Frost sparkles on the wooden beams.

Outside in the morning the sun bursts over the jagged ridges of the horizon. Small yellow finches and swallows swoop out across the chasms. Birds of prey coast on the weak early morning thermals.

The girl points in all directions and tells me the names of the mountains and the villages that lie hidden in the valleys below. With a stick she draws the route to Ayacucho in the dirt.

I ask her if another gringo on a bicycle has passed recently, for Gérard would surely have stopped by for something to eat, but she says no.

She presses bread rolls and an orange on me, fills my water bottles with sweet coca tea, and is offended when I offer payment for the food and lodgings I have received. I give her the four-trumpet horn that doesn't work because she likes it anyway.

The road follows the top of a ridge where llamas graze on clumps of tough grass, and wander casually across the road. They stop their munching when I approach, hold back their heads and peer down their long noses, inquisitively sniffing with nostrils that open and close independently of one another. Then they run away. The bolder ones stroll aside slowly, and the largest ones more brazen still, refuse to budge, and make me move around them.

The road begins a curving descent into the valley. A side track veers off and climbs steeply up over the ridge. In the distance the bright colours of the skirts of women who shepherd small mixed herds of animals stand out against the brown and grey of the mountainside.

I wonder which is the Ayacucho road and sit down to wait for a vehicle. After a while I'm not waiting any more. In air so clear and sunshine so crisp amid scenery of such grandeur it is enough just to sit.

After a while a truck comes by. The driver confirms that the steep track is the road to Ayacucho, and like most drivers who pass, he offers me a lift.

I push the bike up the steep incline to the ridge, beyond which the road sweeps down into a wide greener valley, then steeply up again to a rise from where a vast and magnificent desert valley can be seen, red and yellow and dusty brown that merges with the haze of a far distant horizon.

A small village overlooks the view – Churcampa – and I eat rice and eggs in the cafe.

'Stay here with us and play football', say the children kicking a bundle of sacking around the yard. 'It's hot down there and there's lots of flies.'

Of the nine different categories of dirt road distinguished on the map, the route from Churcampa down the head wall of the valley is shown as the least passable. It is little more than a boulder strewn dry watercourse, broken by stretches of deep sand. The bumping and jolting shakes loose a number of screws, and further down the left front pannier collapses and drops right off. I mend it, like the other one, with wire and string. Increasingly the bike is held together with pieces of wire and string.

Mayocc lies at the bottom of the steep descent, dry and dusty, all doors and windows of the bleached adobe houses are closed. The streets are deserted except for the flies which buzz exhaustedly in the intense heat.

The soldiers stationed by the bridge that spans the river a little further on search my panniers, ask questions, and warn me to hurry to reach Huanta before the ten o'clock curfew.

It is twenty miles to Huanta, along the sandy flat valley floor, and darkness falls long before I reach town – a darkness so complete that the road cannot be seen except as a vague line in the distance. I feel my way along over the bumps, allowing the front wheel to find its own course of least resistance.

I am exhausted after the day's ride, and have no strength left to dispel a paranoia that takes over my imagination in the dark. The sound of leaves rustled by the wind and the occasional faint glint of starlight reflected off a smooth boulder makes me jump. I should stop and camp but I'm too tired to think.

The lights of Huanta are a welcome sight. I'm even happy to go through the routine of questions at the checkpoint before town, the searching of panniers, the testing of the hardness of my tyres and tinging of the bell is all harmless fun.

Soon after the ten o'clock curfew the walls of my room in the pension are rocked by an explosion which is followed by bursts of machine gun fire. In the morning I am woken by a policeman and a man from the immigration department.

'What is your business in Huanta? Have you come to work?' I say I am a tourist passing through.

'The area of Ayacucho is under a state of emergency. Every stranger must be investigated', explains the immigration man apologetically. 'Terrorists are active in this area and no one is free of suspicion. Last night the post office was blown up in the main square.'

'Yes, I heard.'

'Perhaps you have seen something suspicious in your travels?'

'No, nothing extraordinary.'

Numerous streams dissect the hills of cacti and spiky flowering bushes south of Huanta. Bridges are tricky to cross, sometimes no more than two sets of planks – often cracked and filled with protruding nails – wide enough for the wheels of vehicles but too narrow to walk alongside a bicycle.

Descending into the Ayacucho valley, army checkpoints become numerous. Columns of trucks full of soldiers patrol the roads, armoured jeeps with guns mounted in the back lead off up secondary tracks into the mountains. Helicopters – sometimes in convoys of six or more – swoop low over the ground, huge guns poke out of the side doors. They can be heard constantly overhead, and seen as dots in the distance, scouring hillsides inaccessible by road.

Slogans denouncing government oppression and urging revolution are daubed in big red letters on prominent roadside boulders, painted on cloth hung as flags over telegraph wires.

I pass through at least ten checkpoints before reaching Ayacucho. The soldiers at the last one are more casual. They want to see my passport, travellers cheques, search my panniers, swap boots, exchange guns for the bike, give me an orange and then let me through.

The town has narrow cobbled streets, many lined with balconies of Spanish style colonial buildings. Flowering plants climb up crumbling walls. A huge military base lies outside town, built on a flat-topped rise above the valley. The base and the valley are overlooked by mountains.

From these mountains in 1980 the Sendero Luminoso guerrilla movement launched its insurgency campaign under the leadership of the former university professor Abimael Guzman. In 1982 it took control of the town and released two hundred and fifty political prisoners. It was a hit and run coup. From obscure rural beginnings it has spread its influence to the cities where it now carries out bombings and assassinations. To the politicians and press that speculate about its motivation and direction it remains something of an enigma.

The hotel down one of the streets that lead off the central plaza is large and empty, a colonial house with three floors, and a courtyard with trees and a fountain and pool overgrown with weeds.

'There were many foreigners and tourists visiting Ayacucho before the trouble', the woman who lives here tells me. 'Now just a few traders pass through.'

She leads me to a room on the third floor, with flaking whitewashed walls, a sagging bed and a little desk so perforated with woodworm that it barely stands up amid a pile of its own sawdust.

Tourists are uncommon in town. Many people approach me as I walk around, welcome me, inquire as to the purpose of my visit.

I buy a pair of sandals in the market.

'There was another gringo in town two days ago,' the sandal maker informs me. A Frenchman on a bicycle. He left yesterday.'

It seems I am always a few days behind Gérard. If I left today I might catch him but I have to stay awhile to rest my knees which are proving the most reluctant components of the cycling machine. When food is poured into the stomach, the leg muscles work without complaint, even for hours on end up steep hills, standing out of the saddle. The lungs have become accustomed to pumping air in and out at high altitude, the composition of the blood has no doubt changed accordingly. The machine adapts itself to the demands put on it – involuntarily, automatically, because it is alive – but within certain physiological parameters. It works fine if it is left to itself, but it is driven too often by a psychological machine that conforms to different laws, within different sets of parameters. So there is conflict and it makes itself felt to me as pain in the knees. I try to reduce this by following advice given to me when it first occurred back in Canada – to stay in low gears and keep the knees warm – but the only cure is a few days' rest. They always click afterwards, but I tell them this is a healthy mechanical ticking over. They tell me I'm a fanatic.

Returning from the market I spy a French-made bicycle leaning up outside a chemist shop, the front rack loaded down with gear. Inside the shop is a gringo in a pair of shorts. I wait for him to come out and accost him. 'You are Gérard!'

He left town yesterday but had to return when his bike collapsed. Tremendous strain is put on the bike when throwing it from side to side in climbing hills. His frame snapped near the rear wheel drop-outs where the rear rack is attached.

Gérard is taking two years unpaid leave from the French telephone company. He takes every opportunity to write articles that help support his trip. He writes to French cycling magazines, and to component manufacturers who send him spare parts. The company who sent him a T-shirt with their name emblazoned across the front give him a hundred dollars for every published photograph of him wearing it, which accounts in part for his enthusiasm for contacting the press. He still hasn't managed to give away the consignment of culinary knives.

We both worry about the tales of violence. Gérard thinks the local people fear the army more than the guerrillas. He does too. When he arrived in Ayacucho the Senderistas had bombed the leader of the local Communist Party, destroying most of his house, and in taking a photo of the pile of rubble, Gérard aroused the wrath of a drunken soldier who pointed his pistol in his face.

Before the eight o'clock curfew the central plaza is busy with people returning home from the market, and families out for an evening stroll. A student of engineering from the local college sits and tells me about himself and his view of the country.

'Ayacucho is one of the poorest regions of Peru, and the natural home of left wing politics. The roads are very bad because of the mountains. It's a long way from Lima and everything comes slowly. Development and reform come slowly. Investment and money comes slowly or not at all, and when it does it all goes to combat the guerrillas. The guerrillas say they are fighting for the campesinos, that they just hate the government because it is unfair to the poor. But they hate other people too. They kill those who refuse them support, they exploit the campesino cooperatives, they blew up the leader of the Communist Party. Their violence is met with army violence. It's a dirty war. The government is seeking a military solution to the uprising but it is only political change that can remove the discontent that started it. Everybody wants reform but the government believes that everybody in Ayacucho is a radical or a revolutionary. Students who graduate from the university of Ayacucho cannot get jobs in the civil service.'

Suddenly there is an enormous explosion, and from the corner of the plaza the air is filled with dust and small pieces of falling debris. Then another explosion louder than the first, and the town is plunged into darkness.

'Go! Go!' cries the student, pulling me to my feet, and off he runs.

An army truck full of soldiers enters the plaza at high speed with its headlights blazing. Shots ring out from several different directions and the soldiers return the fire with their machine guns, though except for the beam of the headlights it is so dark they surely cannot see what they are firing at.

People are screaming and running in all directions. I run too, across the road and up the steps onto the pavement that borders the plaza where many people are standing behind the big stone pillars – people with bundles on their backs going home from the market, mothers hugging small children, women with babies, popcorn and candy vendors, the lamps of their abandoned trolleys still throwing out a faint glow.

Between the bursts of shooting when the plaza is filled with the sound of bullets pinging off stone, I run like everybody else, crouching down, from pillar to pillar, not so fast as to be mistaken for a fleeing terrorist, or so slow as to be left behind, trying to exude innocent civilian fear because everybody looks the same in the dark – soldiers, Senderistas, Indians, gringos.

There is no one else running down the road to my hotel. It seems endlessly long. A jeep enters from the other end, blinding me with its headlights. There are a few single shots from behind me and I flatten myself into the nearest doorway and hold my breath. The jeep races by with its engine screaming, the soldiers in the back firing away willy nilly.

I reach the hotel and hammer on the door. Bang bang bang goes my heart.

'Who?' demands a voice from inside.

'The gringo', I shout.

Bolts are drawn and a man peers out, then pulls me inside and bars the door behind.

The lady of the hotel brings a candle up to my room.

'Are you all right?' she asks.

'Yes thank you', I reply, though I can't stop shaking and I feel like I'm going to be sick.

'Good for your heart, good for your lungs', the woman selling coca leaves in the market calls out.

I buy a couple of ounces.

'What do you think of our town, gringo?' she asks. I say I think it's nice but I don't like the shooting.

'Och, it happens every evening after the curfew', she sympathises. 'Always the same. The soldiers and the terrorists chase each other around the plaza, around the empty streets and try to kill each other. People here are used to their stupidity and let them get on with it. They stand on their balconies and watch. Do you have a bag?' I say I don't and she pulls a thin polythene bag from a roll.

'That's fifty *soles* more for the bag.'

I make sure I am inside the hotel well before curfew this night, but I don't stand on the balcony to watch when soon after eight o'clock there is the sound of gunfire and vehicles and motorbikes tearing around. The desire to leave town spurs my knees to a hasty recovery.

Not much will grow in the dry desert valleys around Ayacucho. The coca plant copes better than most in the harsh conditions of barren high altitude hillsides, where daytime temperatures soar under continuous sunshine, and plummet well below freezing at night.

The road climbs steeply through a landscape of brown and yellow rock, dotted with coca green. Houses have a bush or two outside, and larger patches are grown commercially for sale in local markets.

In the more inaccessible east of Peru where the Andes join the jungles bordering Brazil, vast areas of coca are grown for conversion into cocaine paste, and furthur refinement into powder for export. Locally the plants are grown for the leaves, to be brewed as tea, or more commonly, chewed with *lejia* – an alkali mixture of ash and vegetable pulp of variable composition.

The use of coca as a mild stimulant like tea or coffee, is widespread among campesinos throughout Peru and Bolivia. By slightly increasing the rate of metabolism it aids circulation and respiration at high altitude, and it also provides trace elements commonly lacking in the diet of peasant farmers. Its traditional importance dates back to use in ceremonies of pre-Inca religion. Physically it can help ease aches and pains, and in reducing feelings of hunger and cold it helps to alleviate the harsh conditions under which much of the rural Andean population lives. This is well known and may be a contributing factor in the apparent reluctance of government to comply with international pressure to stamp out coca growing in an effort to remove the source that provides most of the world's ever increasing demand for cocaine. Social discontent is already high because of economic austerity measures implemented as conditions for rescheduling interest payments on the foreign debt, and a degree of popular support is required for the continuance of civilian rule which can be a fragile thing at the best of times in South America.

The colossal cost of financing an eradication programme is also a factor of some importance to a bankrupt nation, and the loss of earnings from export sales that trickle obscurely back to the government cannot be ignored either, although cocaine dollars tend to be taken out of the country, or used to finance mechanisms of corruption, construction of mansions and the formation of private armies rather than being made available for investment in economic developments of a more generally beneficial nature.

So coca continues to be grown, and the governments of the developed countries continue to fret over the annual billions of dollars of revenue lost to cocaine that might otherwise be spent on taxable commodities by their citizens in search of amusement.

A truck coming down the mountain stops. Inside is Gérard. In the back is his bicycle. He's heading back to Ayacucho to get his bike welded together again where it broke in a different place.

At the top of the pass is a house. An old woman with a face of wrinkles lives here with her son. They are herding thirty or forty goats into the backyard for the night.

She invites me to spend the night here. As soon as the sun sets she boards up the door and the tiny windows, and beckons me into the back room which is windowless, and murky with smoke from the fire. A large pan sits among the embers.

She indicates that I should find myself a space – there are no tables or chairs, or anything resembling furniture, though the floor is strewn with bits of sacking, old boxes, blankets and assorted belongings.

The old woman has a terrible wracking cough. All evening she coughs up lumps of phlegm and spits them out onto the floor, or into the fire.

She speaks a little with her son in Quechua. I make an effort at conversation, but she seems unable to speak much Spanish.

'Don't worry, gringo. You sleep safely here', she says.

She ladles out the stew between the three of us – potatoes and lumps of goat – and the sound of our munching is broken only by the howling of the bitter wind through the cracks in the ceiling, and the occasional hawking and spitting.

I wake in the morning stiff with cold, despite having kept all my clothes and my boots on and lying in my sleeping bag next to the fire, to the familiar sound of the thud of gob on the floor. The woman stokes up the fire to boil a pot of water. Her son splits wood. I sit wrapped up in my sleeping bag, drinking sweet coca tea. The old woman sits wrapped up in blankets, her face occasionally cracking into a grin as she looks at me.

How can I thank her for her hospitality?

I say thank you. She spits on the floor, fills my bottles with tea and presses two hard bread rolls on me.

'You're my guest', she says, as if being one requires no gratitude.

The road is up or down, never level, always steep. Ascents are made in first gear, slowly. Arms and legs and lungs and heart find their own rhythm. There is no hurry.

On the lip of a huge valley the village of Ocros is visible below. It seems close enough to toss a pebble onto but it takes many hours to zigzag down. Descents can be thrilling. The bottom of the furrows worn into the dirt road by the wheels of trucks and buses is filled with rocks and stones, but the sides are smoother, made of finer dirt and grit over which it is possible to move quickly without risk of puncture. The risk is of plunging over the edge around tight bends where in order to remain on the smooth soft side of the furrows – worn deeper to form high banks – it is necessary to be moving quite fast and to lean at an acute angle.

Half a dozen soldiers are lounging around at the military transit checkpoint at Ocros.

'Where are you going?' they want to know.

I say I'm going to the village for something to eat.

'Eat here', they say.

Around the back of the adobe building that serves as a barracks is a small yard. Two girls from the village are cooking under the thatch shelter in one corner. They giggle at the sight of a gringo in a pair of shorts. A space is cleared of machine guns on the wooden tressel table, and a large plate of rice and fried bananas and potatoes is put in front of me. Everybody watches me eat. The soldiers crowd around, shouting and laughing, high-spirited like schoolboys. The girls titter over the fire. I feel like a zoo attraction.

The conscripts are not enjoying their military service. They have been stationed in Ocros for four months, mostly in this building, checking traffic for arms, and they welcome the distraction I bring to their boredom. They come from all over Peru – the jungle, the northern desert, the cities – and look forward to returning to civilian life. But they all agree that the army has good points – as much food as they can eat and a set of clothes. The soldiering goes with it – the guns and the haircut and the routine – accepted as unavoidable, but they make no pretence of accepting the military ideology behind what they do, and though they speak in the presence of officers, they express understanding of the cause of the guerrillas against whom they are fighting.

'Peru is a poor country', one soldier explains, 'and every Peruvian loves his country – wants to change it for the better. The government wants to change it one way, the Senderistas want to change it another way. If you are rich you can pay not to do military service. If you are poor, you have no choice but to join the army. You can join the guerrillas but either way you have to fight. Both sides fight against each other and nothing changes, nothing gets better, nothing gets done except that the valleys get filled with corpses.'

'Sometimes at night the Senderistas fire rockets at this post', another soldier tells me. 'But you need not fear them. If they stop you on the road they would only want to talk.'

I am offered a bed for the night, assured that the post does not often come under siege.

Beyond Ocros the track continues its steep winding descent to the river Pampamarca, a wide rushing ribbon of blue and white that dissects a bare red rocky desert canyon that marks the boundary between the areas of Ayacucho and Apurimac.

The long steel girder bridge across the torrent shows signs of hasty repair. It has been blown up twice in the past three weeks.

It takes me an hour to cross. because I have to unload and reload everything on the bike at the checkpoints at both ends of the bridge. Between bombings it gets pretty boring here too.

Despite the heat the soldiers wear balaclavas – protection against the swarms of tiny voracious flies which bore visibly wide holes through the skin, and do it so subtly that they cannot be felt until a few minutes later.

After an hour or so up the other side of the canyon, I notice that the tent and spare tyre are no longer strapped to the rear rack. I retied them quickly at the bridge in order to escape the flies. I go back to the point where I know they were still attached but there is no sight of them. They could easily have rolled off down the steep canyon walls, but one truck has passed going down, and may well have picked them up as booty.

If the soldiers are being as thorough with the truck as they were with me, it may still be at the bridge. I head back down, but it's an hour before I arrive and the truck is long gone.

The soldiers now are sympathetic, console me with a drink of coke, and give me a bullet to remember them by.

I'm angry with myself for not securing the tent and spare tyre properly – the tyre was particularly precious because I don't know how long it will be before I can buy another, and both front and rear tyres are rapidly shredding themselves, pieces of rubber hang off in strips like they do on the tyres of buses and trucks. And I've spent two hours sweating in the hot desert canyon when I could have been climbing into cooler climes. I stop and collect water from the irrigation ditch that runs alongside the road, and curse aloud at my stupidity and haste.

A woman comes out of a nearby house that I hadn't noticed among the rocks and bushes. She hands me a bunch of small ripe bananas. Her clothes are rags, her house is no more than a few wooden stakes driven into the dust, and she stands here smiling and calm and giving away food to a stranger who is indulging in anger and self pity over a couple of lost possessions and who still has more than anybody else around will ever have.

The road leaves the valley of the Pampamarca and climbs up a narrow side canyon, following the course of a dry river bed composed of regular-sized six inch square rocks with a gap in between – a sort of natural cobblestone. It's a rough ride but it leads out of the desert heat, up to where the valley broadens, where trees shade groups of houses, and pigs and goats graze and snuffle through patches of green grass watered by streams fed by snow and ice far above.

I stop at the pass. A truck comes by and stops too. Everybody gets out for a piss.

'You must be the Englishman', says the driver. He passed Gérard earlier in the day, just leaving Ayacucho again.

Half way down the steep fifty kilometers to Andahuaylas the small remaining piece of the rear mudgard bequeathed me by Joseph in Belize, kept more for nostalgia than practicality, comes untaped and shoots around the wheel. In discarding it I notice that part of the lip of the rear tyre is outside the wheel rim. I pop it back in. The inner tube is visible in several places through rips in the side.

The few street lights are just coming on in the main street of Andahuaylas, but electricity is halted somewhere in its path to the hotel. The manager suspects the hold up is in the fuse box, hidden behind a tangle of wires high up on an outside wall. He whacks it with a piece of wood for a while and produces a colourful firework display, but the lights stay off.

I tour the town in search of bicycle tyres. Most of the shops are dimly lit by candles or oil lamps. A few have red flags hanging outside, indicating that meat is for sale, but most are plain adobe brick and must be entered in order to find out what might be for sale within.

My sudden appearance causes surprise in many shops. Not many gringos pass through here at present. In many I am offered a seat on sacks of grain or packing cases, plied with cups of coffee and questions about England.

When I ask about bicycle tyres in one shop, a woman cries, 'Oh, I saw you on television!' and rushes out to collect some friends. I assure them that it wasn't me, but that no doubt this famous personality will appear in a few days.

Loaded with coffee and goodwill but no tyres, I am intercepted by an official-looking man with a gun, who produces from his pocket a card identifying himself as a member of P.I.P.

'What is P.I.P.?' I ask him.

'P.I.P. stands for Peruvian Investigation Police', he tells me rather smugly, and asks me to accompany him to the police station for some investigation.

Where have I come from? Where am I going? What am I doing in Andahuaylas? Don't I know there's a state of emergency?

I say look, there are bicycles and tricycle barrows all over town so where are the bike shops, and he draws me a map on smartly headed P.I.P. notepaper marking the shops that might sell spares. These are general hardware stores. None have 27 inch tyres.

'Twenty seven inch tyres are no good', says the hardware store man. 'They are for racing bicycles. Nobody has racing bicycles here – they're no good. I've got twenty eight inch, twenty six inch, twenty inch. Any good?' I say no thanks they're no good.

My tyres are no good. The general opinion of the people who watch me work on the bike in the hotel courtyard is that the tyres will easily reach Cusco. I am not confident. The rear tyre in particular is ripped and torn and bald. I swap it over to the front where it will take less weight and where I can at least keep an eye on it.

'There are lots of tyres in Abancay. You'll be there in a few hours', they encourage as I leave.

Abancay is the next town – about a hundred miles away which will be at least two days over mountain roads.

Having spent two days in Andahuaylas recovering from a severe stomach disorder, I half expect that Gérard has passed me, but looking back down the switchbacks after several hours of climbing I see a small black dot of a figure on a bicycle. It is Gérard, swaying with a healthy regularity, pots and pans and an assortment of oddments dangling and clanging alongside.

He shows me where his frame has been welded together again. Our attention as we continue through the quiet mountainsides where noises are of the wind in the grass and the chink of a hand hoe biting dusty soil, is drawn to the racket of each others' bikes. The racket of our own we have become familiar with – each rattle and clank coming from particular objects in collision, each squeak and grind indicative of the idiosyncratic workings of a particular mechanical part. The whole represents normal functioning. Any new sound needs checking out. To our own ears the familiar sounds go unnoticed. To each other the noise is chaotic.

Gérard has a stack of Peruvian Touring Club maps which detail heights of passes, distances between the smallest of villages and locations of roadside eating houses. At the top of a pass we reach in the late afternoon he can accurately pinpoint us at 4080 metres above sea level, and work out that we've come up 2000 metres from Andahuaylas. He reaches into one of his panniers and pulls out an altimeter just to check. It reads 4230 metres.

Gérard predicts there's a village just around the next hill but the sun is going down and I get a puncture so we stop and camp on a piece of grass on a bend overlooking the valley. Rows of jagged mountains glow pink across the way.

I remember Leo telling me of how in Costa Rica Gérard had delved into his panniers and discovered a cast iron fire grate filched from a national park in the U.S. that he had inadvertently transported for a couple of thousand miles across the tropics, and I suggest to Gérard that he carries more than is necessary. He is of course aware of this. His bike and junk together weigh over sixty kilos but he heaves it around all day without getting excessively tired. His legs are like tree trunks.

Like me, he collects items along the way that are aesthetically pleasing and practically useless, and is given things that acquire sentimental value and are therefore kept. The compulsion to surround ourselves with bits and pieces that please us, that we define as home, that we come to depend on as a sanctuary of the familiar, a safe corner from which we can view the world, is only slightly diminished when we have to carry those bits and pieces around with us. The need is the same, though it comes in for some scrutiny.

Gérard, for example, regards my flute, coloured pencils, two hats and a heavy pair of boots as excessive baggage. I rally to their defence at once, and suggest to him that three cameras is excessively excessive. Not at all, he assures me. One is very old, one is new, and one doesn't work at all.

Rain spatters down on Gérard's tent in the night, though sleeping outside wrapped up in his two sleeping bags, ears plugged against any noise, he is blissfully unaware.

The morning is cold, wet and grey and everything is masked in thick mist when we set off. Gérard says that it's only twelve kilometers around the hillside to the next pass and just down the other side is a restaurant.

The wind at the pass blows the thick mist into curls and wisps and phantoms. His altimeter reads 4180 metres. The damp seeps through my waterproof trousers. Gérard is wearing shorts. He hasn't worn a pair of trousers since the U.S., though he has a professional pair of elasticated pads to keep his knees warm – very smart in comparison with the scarves and oddments of cloth I wrap around mine.

Sheltered a little way below is a smoky one-roomed adobe hut – the restaurant where we stop and eat a second leisurely breakfast of soup and rice and eggs.

We pore over Gérard's Touring Club maps. Food is fuel and he burns it up at a terrific rate. He checks out the next eating house.

'Hmm . . . forty nine kilometres down to the river – that's a drop of 2300 metres, then seventeen kilometres up to Abancay at 2378 metres. Think I'll have some more to eat.' He asks almost apologetically for some more.

When we break through the base of the cloud, much of the road to Abancay can be seen. It winds down to the bridge over the rushing Apurimac river, and joins the main Lima-Cusco road that has come over the mountains from the coast.

Gérard's French made Motobécane bicycle has three front sprockets and five rear ones, but even on the steep rocky seventeen kilometre ascent from the river up to Abancay he doesn't use the lowest gear combination.

'It's too low', he explains, 'you'd never get anywhere', and he pumps his legs up and down, scattering stones and raising dust as his bike is propelled up the track.

It is clear how Gérard has the reputation among the other French cyclists of being fast. It's not so much a question of speed, he just doesn't bother to slow down when he goes uphill.

Bicycles abound in Abancay, but none of the bike shops have 27 inch tyres. None of the newsstands sell the monthly magazine '*Caretas*', so Gérard cannot read about himself.

There are plenty of tyres and magazines in Cusco , we are told.

We take a room in a hotel. I eat something that cannot have been quite dead, and spend the night being woken by my stomach swollen to the size of a balloon, and rushing to the toilet. By morning I am exhausted and have a fever but the volcanic activity at least has ceased.

The management show concern for my health and want to take me to the hospital. Gérard says it is because I keep filling their toilets. He offers to remain with me until I am better. I tell him I'm going to be fine and to get going. I know he is keen to continue, not least to clock up the 25000 kilometers from Alaska which his gauge shows is imminent. It is good to travel together, for companionship, but only when convenient and spontaneous, for then the pleasure overrides the disadvantages.

We have both noticed how people react differently towards us when we are together – less inclined to approach us, to speak to us because it is obvious that we are a group, self-contained. Alone we are perhaps less threatening, people assume that we are lonely and more readily overcome the habit of reserve.

Alone too, it is easier to leave behind the European conditioning that we drag around with us, those bits and pieces of custom and tradition that we surround ourselves with, the ideological corner from which we view the world, the standard to measure things by that forms an unconscious barrier which separates us from what is around us, and prevents us from seeing things as they are in their own context.

Gérard heads off in the afternoon, leaving me a supply of dysentery pills.

I eat one for breakfast the following morning, along with a chunk of cake thrust into my arms by a market stall holder. They provide energy for the long climb out of the valley, up above the snow line and down again into the land of people and grazing llamas, parched fields of dust, down for a day and a half to the river at the bottom of a red and yellow canyon.

Huts of the civil guard and two cafes cluster at the end of the bridge. I stop to shelter from the sun.

'*El ciclista Ingles*', whisper the children who gather around
to watch me drink a lemonade, and then several uniformed men
come over from the huts of the civil guard. Everybody else gathers
around too.

'Are you the English cyclist?' asks the chief. It seems like a formal
occasion. I stand up.

'I am', I reply.

He ceremoniously hands me a scrap of paper, folded in two
with '*El ciclista Ingles*' written on and bearing an official civil guard
stamp. It's a note from Gérard, written in English, wishing me well
and informing me that it is just forty eight and a half kilometers to
the next pass and that there are a couple of restaurants on the way.

A translation is demanded. What do cycling gringos have to
communicate? I disappoint everybody by saying it's just a note from
my friend.

I disappoint the woman who runs the cafe too, with my meagre
appetite.

'Your friend ate two plates of rice and six eggs', she says.

I stop at one of the small isolated houses high up in the mountains,
to ask for some water. Two men and two women sit under the porch,
drinking from a bottle. One of the women takes me inside the house
and thrusts a plate of beans and corn into my hands.

'Eat, eat!'

We sit outside. The men slap me on the back, talk among
themselves in Quechua, and drink. Today is *Fiesta de la Paz*. They
will not be working in the fields today. They are already drunk and
it's only early morning.

One of the men wires up an ancient gramophone to a car battery,
and soon there is music from a record so old and scratched that only
a distorted rhythm can be heard. This is enough.

The older of the two women thrusts a crying baby into my arms
and all four of them set to with some dancing, stamping the ground
with their bare feet, raising clouds of dust.

The three young children grin at the antics of their parents, the
baby stops crying and even raises a smile. I tap a foot, but this is no
party for hangers on.

'I don't know this dance', I complain, but this doesn't matter,
and the old woman drags me to my feet, crushes my hand in her

powerful grip and twirls me around into a series of arm locks. I get the general idea, which is to prance around uninhibitedly and let it all hang out, so I wave my arms and stomp my feet and raise dust in the bright sunshine. Soon it's time to swap hats, fling each other about, whoop and shout, while the baby cries again, and pigs and dogs cringe fearfully behind crumbling mud walls.

The break in the music while the record is set to play again is time to swig from the bottle – distilled maize liquor that numbs the insides and spreads a warm glow right down to the toes.

After half an hour I am exhausted, but there is no let up in the pace and I have to go on because the women won't let me go and pass me to each other; unflagging in their energy they go on dancing and swigging from the bottle.

There is a problem with the car battery so we sit in the shade, me panting, the others drinking. And suddenly the woman who first handed me the baby starts wailing to her husband, to me.

She cannot look after the baby, look, she has enough children already, she cannot feed it, she cannot raise it, and she wants me to take it to England. I say I can't but she won't take no for an answer and goes on wailing, gives me the baby, shouts to her husband who tries to console her. Tears stream down her face.

I haven't drunk alcohol for six months so I'm already drunk which I think is probably a good thing otherwise this would all be too much to take, and I feel mean because I can't think of any reasonable excuse why I shouldn't take the baby so I point out the physical impossibility of packing it onto the bicycle. Her husband, who's been listening intently, and wondering too why I won't take it, sees the logic in this particular argument, and persuades the woman that perhaps they'd best keep it.

And suddenly it's all over, the woman dries her tears on her skirts and we're dancing again and there's no more mention of the baby.

I teeter off up the hill a little way before I remember the water bottle I stopped off to fill, and go back to collect it, and dance some more. The dancing comes easier after a few drinks.

A short way up the road, the front tube explodes with a loud bang. I put in a spare, and a little further up this too explodes. Strange, two in a row, but I'm too drunk to worry about it and simply put in the last spare, and concentrate on the final stretch of the steep climb out of the valley, over slopes of loose shiny slate.

Over the pass lies a broad plain dotted with fields and houses. A little way along the third tube explodes. I've no more spares so I'll have to mend the punctured ones, and my head is a little clearer now so I can investigate why they have all exploded. The outer tyre, split and torn, has one particularly long rip where the inflated inner tube pokes out, and hangs over the rim so that it rubs on the brake block with every turn of the wheel. With the front brake removed, and just enough air in the tube to ride over the bumps, but not so much that it pokes out and catches on stones, and by sitting back to keep my weight over the rear wheel, it should be O.K. And it's not far to Cusco now where there are sure to be plenty of 27 inch tyres.

The fields are unusually empty – it's a day off from back-breaking labour to be festive, to get drunk. People are gathered in houses, leaning against boulders, staggering and swaying along the road. Some lie collapsed by the roadside or are being dragged along by friends. People grin and shout drunken remarks as I ride slowly by, sitting upright, grinning foolishly, drunkenly back.

In tiny settlements and out in fields, bands of trumpets and horns, pipes and drums can be heard, playing out of time and tune, wafting on the breeze, and the plain is bathed in the mellowness of drunken melodies and gentle late afternoon sunshine.

Then suddenly, soberingly, the dirt road ends, laid over, replaced by smooth black asphalt with, incredibly, white lines down the middle, no dust, no grit, no rocks, no holes, no rivers to cross, no subsidences to negotiate. Smooth, purposeful, affluent asphalt.

I take a room in a shabby pension in Anta and sleep. The town celebrates, drinking and dancing.

During the night I am woken by a rapping at the door, and the bare light bulb is switched on from outside. No doubt it is the local P.I.P. man. The flimsy door is secured with a bolt to prevent it swinging back and forth, so he can't come in, and following the Peruvian custom of sleeping soundly when shouted at or shaken violently, I feign sleep and hope he will go away.

The ploy fails. I hear footsteps running towards the door, and then with a cracking and splintering of wood a policeman bursts into the room, and hurtles across to the far wall.

He dusts himself down, unabashed at such a dramatic entry.

'Good evening sir,' he says politely, 'how are you?'

'I'm very well thank you. Why have you broken down my door like this?'

'It's quite routine, sir,' he replies chummily, 'I need to ask a few questions.'

He asks the inevitable questions, a little drunkenly perhaps, inspects my passport, finds it worthy of further scrutiny, and leaves saying I can collect it at the police station in the morning. He leans the door up against the wall on the way out.

Agricultural development schemes abound in the Cusco valley. Tractors can be seen working alongside the bullock teams, and the lines of men and women with hand hoes.

Minibuses and private cars, clean and shiny and full of people dressed in smart city clothes, whizz along the road that is carefully manicured to give a favourable impression to tourists. Clean green signs with reflective lettering indicate distances, and by the new concrete checkpoint with glass in the windows on the rise overlooking Cusco, visitors are welcomed in four different languages.

The narrow streets of the city toot and beep with the sound of cars and jeeps, buses and coaches, bumping and clattering over the cobblestones.

Cusco has been both an Inca and Spanish capital and many buildings are an architectural fusion of styles – ground floors built of massive stone blocks, mortarless and solid, and above, further storeys of Spanish design, with flamboyant balconies and red-tiled roofs and all around are the fortress-like churches of the Conquistadores, standing next to modern concrete office blocks, supermarkets, banks and hotels, museums and bars, and everywhere neon signs advertising hamburgers, money changing, artisan markets, Kodak film, Indian costumes, folk music, fried chicken and pizza.

I sit on a bench in the central plaza. Many other foreigners are here, clean, dressed in smart clothes, big cameras swinging around their necks. It is uncomfortable to watch how they stand and stare, and point their cameras at the Indians.

I feel dirty and dusty. The bike has a uniform covering of dust. I feel out of place because suddenly I am treated as a tourist and people crowd around wanting to sell me tourist artefacts and souvenirs, polish my shoes, take me to a nice hotel, ask for money, and I'm no longer treated as an individual but as part of an industry that depends upon my being a representative of an alien culture, a source of dollars, an eater of hamburgers, an object on the other side of a carefully maintained cultural and ideological divide that I cannot cross because it exists primarily and firmly in people's imaginations.

And who am I to object when it provides a living for thousands of Peruvians who might otherwise be breaking their backs tilling dust, and amusement for thousands of tourists who otherwise might not even guess that there was anything outside their own culture?

10. Inca ruins and lemon pie

I tour the town from bike shop to bike shop, and eventually return to the first one I went to which has a monopoly on all the 27 inch tyres in Cusco. I buy them both.

I take the rear wheel to a welders' shop to use a bench vice to remove the freewheel in order to replace the broken spokes. The thing is on pretty hard – cranking over mountain roads effectively tightens it up – and the first thing to give is my freewheel tool, neatly shearing off the flanges that slot into the spaces of the freewheel.

The spokes have snapped in the middle, so by making a loop at the broken end that is attached to the hub, new spokes inserted through the spoke holes in the rim can be passed through the loop, and twisted together with a pair of pliers. It looks untidy but it sustains sufficient tension to hold the wheel in place.

The streets of Cusco are full of the smells of the food that is for sale on every corner. Spicy *empanadas*, doughnuts, potato and corn cakes, ice cream. Pie barrows parked in the road display an appetising selection of cakes and pies, that taste all the better for being eaten out of a piece of newspaper, sitting in the gutter. Sitting eating in the gutter is a common and acceptable practice in Peru.

I bump into Gérard, emerging from the American Express office with a stack of mail under his arm. We sit eating lemon pie in the gutter and he tells me of his visit to the Inca ruins of Machu Picchu. He's had news of Leo and Rudi and thinks they will arrive in Cusco any day now. He plans to head south again tomorrow towards lake Titicaca and Bolivia. He would have left today, but the family he is staying with won't let him leave. He is looking plumper than usual. He says they feed him so much he actually turns food down.

Machu Picchu was a fortress city of the Incas, situated in the mountains north west of Cusco along the Urubamba valley. No road goes there, but daily trains take visitors to the base of the mountain on which the city is built, and drop backpackers off on the way at the start of the 'Inca Trail' – a route across the mountains that follows Inca highways.

I hire a rucksack and a foam sleeping mat from a We-Hire-Camping-Gear shop, buy a couple of metres of polythene sheeting to use as a tent, deposit my junk in the hotel's 'we look after your things while you walk the Inca Trail' room, and catch the train down the Urubamba valley.

Many stops along the way are just a few houses. People get on and work their way from one end to the other, selling vegetables, corn cakes, pieces of roast pork and coffee.

The Indian woman opposite me argues with the conductor about paying for her child.

'He's older than three, he has to have a ticket', says the conductor.

'He's not and I won't buy one', she replies, 'I have no money'.

'You pay or he gets off', states the conductor. He speaks in Spanish and she replies in Quechua. Then he speaks in Quechua and she replies in Spanish, and eventually simply ignores him and stares out of the window.

The conductor steals her bowler hat and refuses to return it. The woman pays for a ticket, grumbling.

The train halts by a 'km 88' sign that is the start of the Inca Trail. A man with a National Park of Machu Picchu hat stands in a hut at the end of a bridge suspended over the river. He takes an entrance fee from the dozen of us who have clambered off, and we file past across the bridge and head off up the track into the mountains.

The sketch maps provided by the Cusco Tourist Office are open to considerable individual interpretation, and we all wander off up different valleys and canyons, following the path we judge to be the correct one, wandering back down again when we come to dead ends, puffing and panting under the weight of our packs loaded with three days' supply of food. Further up there is only one path, and by evening most of us are somewhere along it.

A young Dutch guy called Rob who speaks six different languages and is dressed like a Scoutmaster with a walking stick and plus-fours is up early in the morning, jollying everybody along, and trying unsuccessfully to organise the separate groups into a team. Nobody is much interested in anything but enjoying the scenery.

In places the track is made of the original stones laid by the Incas in the form of wide gentle steps or steep blocks. It descends into valleys hot and steaming with luxuriant vegetation, dark and damp under a canopy of trees hung with vines and creepers, flashing with darting humming birds and bright flowers, echoing with the calls of birds and animals unseen. It rises out of forests up mountainsides carpeted with flowers and thorny bushes and waving grass full of buzzing insects and butterflies, and higher into thinner colder air, over passes surrounded by ridges that drop away into the blue haze of deep valleys. Snow and ice glistens on distant peaks.

The trail is littered with overgrown Inca ruins, with names like Sayaqmarca, Llulluchapampa, Warmiwanusq'a, exuding old age in mossy silence. Rob has a booklet on archaeology and tries to marshal us into groups and tell us about them in six different languages, but nobody is much interested in archaeology when there are ruins to be enjoyed.

The ruins of Phuyupatamarca perch just below the craggy ridge of an eleven thousand foot pass, overlooking the valley of the Urubamba river that rushes unseen and unheard six thousand feet below. It's a good campsite. There is only a little land above – bare rock – but an Inca water system provides a steady trickle of clear water that runs through a series of stone gutters and pools.

The Scoutmaster is the last to arrive in the evening, with two Swiss girls who have taken pity and allowed him to be their guide and leader.

We huddle around a smoking fire, taking turns to encourage flames with vigorous fanning, telling gringo tales. The Swiss girls complain that the Scoutmaster continually got lost, wandered off up side tracks and fell behind. Everybody laughs and teases him. He warns us about hypothermia, dehydration and altitude sickness, and scolds me for having no tent.

It is an effort when walking to remember to concentrate on carefully placing the feet rather than gazing at the views. I join some green lizards and two Belgians – hairy giants – sunning themselves at midday on a flat rock overlooking the wide curve of the valley, watching butterflies wing out into space.

The lizards scamper off when the Scoutmaster comes blundering by. He doesn't notice us until we speak to him. He is out of breath and sweating, clearly muddle-headed and suffering from the

altitude, and he speaks to us alternately in six different languages.
We make him sit down and rest, drink some water and put on his
sun hat. He's lost the Swiss girls again and is worried that they might
have taken a wrong turning without him. We tell him it's O.K., they
passed by an hour or so ago, and continue together down a steeply
zigzagging path to the ruins of Winay Winay – bleached and
crumbling stone walls that peep out from a tangled mass of roots
and stems and flowers. The Swiss girls are here, relieved to see Rob
and scold him for becoming lost again.

The path rises again, sloping around the cliff of an enormous
basin, damp with plants that the sun cannot reach, that cling
precariously to rocky ledges. The path is no more than a ledge,
often covered with rocks from recent rockfalls, and in places fallen
completely away itself, leaving gaps that are bridged by wooden
poles covered in earth scooped out of the hillside above, providing
a platform that bounces with every step, and vibrates with an
ominously hollow thud. Between the spaces the Urubamba river
can be seen, a silver thread three thousand feet below.

The trail emerges from this precarious traverse at the ruins of
Inti Punke – Gate of the Sun – on a ridge overlooking Machu Picchu
a thousand feet below, itself on a spur several thousand feet above
the Urubamba river which describes a tortuous U-turn around it.

We set up our camps on the flat tops of the staggered walls of
Inti Punke, admiring the views all around, and eat our stews by
candlelight in cosy expectation.

Black storm clouds are advancing, engulfing peaks and ridges
to the north. I place my sleeping bag inside the polythene sack
in anticipation of a good dousing. The Scoutmaster kindly lends
me his umbrella which I secure to the frame of the rucksack
over the place where my head will lie. In comparison with the
fine selection of storm proof tents around it, this construction
is cause for some amusement, but there is something pleasing
about its Inca-like simplicity; when the storm has passed
the umbrella can simply be put down for a fine view of
the stars.

Thick mist envelopes everything in the morning and we stumble
down unwittingly upon Machu Picchu, swathed in bands of cloud.
We wander around through a maze of walls and corridors, along
passageways of stone blocks that open into wide terraces that loom

out of cloud and suddenly disappear. Track of time and direction is lost in the labyrinth of mist and stone.

When the cloud lifts the impregnable position of the site can be seen – the ground plunges away on three sides – nothing can approach without being seen, and this Inca city, once self supported with water and crops grown on the terraces that still remain on the adjoining peak, was never conquered.

The sense of wonderment at wandering around the ruins though is less impregnable, and quickly conquered when the train arrives. Walking through the mountains for three days, removed from evidence of modern man, it was easy for us to stumble out of the jungle imagining that we had been transported back to the time of the Incas, but the arrival at midday of hundreds of day trippers and the mechanical clicking of a hundred cameras, the boisterous insights into how cute those Incas were shatters the illusion. The Inca Trailers, identified by their lack of zoom lenses, their muddy boots and slept-in appearance, and their slight but well concealed resentment at this intrusion of the twentieth century that has revealed real life Machu Picchu to be a well organised tourist phenomenon accessible to all, are left rightly and inevitably disillusioned, with no alternative but to leave with the little pieces of magic that linger intact.

Leo has arrived in Cusco while I've been ruining. He came along the coast road with Rudi and tells me stories of the desert, of sharing his sleeping bag with a scorpion. He is still troubled by hepatitis and trucked here from Abancay. Jean-Louis and Max are also in town, and Rudi and Don are somewhere on the way from Abancay.

Although I have been a week in Cusco I have made no effort to visit any historic colonial houses, cathedrals or museums, but I can show Leo some modern landmarks – the cheap vegetable markets, the best pie barrows and the bicycle shops. Leo longs to be fit again. He says it is incredibly uncomfortable, not to mention frustrating, to travel in the back of a truck through such spectacular mountains.

South as far as Urcos the road is asphalt, beyond it is dirt, and the wind whips up sand and dust into great clouds that reduce visibility to a few feet.

Beyond Sicuani the surface of the road has been fashioned by wind into ridges, like a wash board, over which it is impossible to ride at much more than walking pace. Forward momentum is translated into a vertical bouncing. The paths worn alongside the road by feet and bicycles are smoother, and lead up the gently rising wide slope to the fifteen thousand foot pass that marks the northern limit of the Altiplano.

The Altiplano is a plateau five hundred miles long, averaging thirteen thousand feet in height and surrounded by the twenty thousand feet peaks of the Andes which divide here into two ranges, leaving a natural basin which holds Lake Titicaca, a hundred miles long and a thousand feet deep, and the smaller Lake Poopo, both remnants of a former massive lake. The rivers that flow down the mountains into Lake Titicaca never reach the sea, but drain to the lowest part of the Altiplano and evaporate in the vast salt-pans of the south.

The northern part of the Altiplano in Peru is widely used as pasture for mixed herds of animals that can survive on the tough Puna grass, and some land is cultivated, particularly around the lake where water can be guaranteed.

The southern Altiplano is largely desert, but in the north there is just enough rainfall to support crops of corn or potatoes, though it tends to come over a period of a few months in the form of violent storms which are as likely to wash away the dusty soil as provide life-giving moisture.

The plain stretches out as far as the eye can see, under a sky of electric blue. Columns of dust a hundred feet high twist an erratic path. Some of these whirlwinds carry no dust and are invisible. One takes me by surprise. Wind howls across the road a few yards in front while everywhere else it is still. Then from behind I am engulfed in a whistling rushing of wind which pushes me forward so forcefully and unexpectedly that I fall to the ground, and lie there holding my breath with my eyes closed as pebbles and stones are whipped violently about. In a few seconds it moves away and everything is calm.

A black dot appears on the plain ahead, moving along the smooth worn path that winds through the low bushes and clumps of grass. It is a man on a bicycle with a coffin strapped somehow across the rear rack. He's a wide load so I move off the path to let him by.

'Good day, sir. Thank you', he says politely as he passes.

Another dot appears, and turns out to be a young Japanese on a bicycle. He bought the bike a couple of weeks ago in Lima intending to make a tour of Peru, but now wishes he hadn't. He took the bus south from Lima because the desert was too hot, and a truck over the mountains to Puno because the hills were too steep. The Altiplano is not too hot and it's pretty flat, but it's far too high and he can't breathe.

'I like to travel by bicycle,' he assures me, 'but it's too hard, the people are dirty and poor, and the children throw stones.'

He's not having a good day. Earlier he rode his bike into a ditch and bent the front forks back so that he cannot pedal and turn corners at the same time.

He has a large camera and tripod with him, which he sets up on the plain, and takes a photo of us. He says he doesn't get the opportunity to use it very much because people object to having their photograph taken – it is considered rude and people take offence. I have given up trying, and stick to taking boring shots of mountains and bicycles.

The streets and railway tracks in Juliaca are lined with market stalls and people sitting on the ground surrounded by a pile of goods. Trains coming in and out of the big railway sidings interrupt proceedings from time to time, blasting their horns and inching forward as the line is cleared.

Many market stalls are simply tricycle barrows – the town is full of bikes and trikes and the streets jangle with bells and horns.

There are tricycle barrow kitchens with huge pots of food steaming over kerosene burners, or over wood and charcoal fires built into the frames. There are tricycle transport and removal barrows which move slowly along the streets, piled high with furniture, beds, building materials, the thick tyres squashed under the weight. The operator, leg muscles bulging and covered in sweat, completely hidden behind a mobile mountain, relies on people to get out of his way.

Most common is the tricycle barrow taxi, with its licence number displayed proudly at the front. These things tear along in convoys of chaos and speed, loaded down with up to six people sitting on the flat bed, clinging to the sides, as the vehicle is negotiated with varying degrees of skill through the crowded streets, usually in competition with another. Cumbersome

to manoeuvre and slow to stop, a collision or two is not
uncommon.

I take my rear wheel that has broken a couple more spokes since
Cusco, to one of the bike shops.

'I have some broken spokes and I want to remove the freewheel
so as to replace them', I say to the old man in the gloom of a shop
whose walls are covered with shelves of spare parts! Bicycle frames
hang from the ceiling like rusty Christmas decorations. He peers
down his nose, squints through a pair of spectacles held together
with elastoplast.

'You've broken some spokes', he confirms, pointing at the gaps.
'You'll need to take the freewheel off to replace them.'

'Yes, it's stuck on hard. I broke my tool trying to remove it. Do
you have one?' I ask.

'No problem. I'll get it off for you.'

We move outside to the backyard, to a wooden trestle-table
with a bench vice screwed on. He unscrews the quick release
wing nuts with a whistle. Quick release nuts are rare in
Peru.

'It's a fine machine you have here', he surmises. 'You have come
to Peru to race?'

'No, on holiday.'

'Where are you from?'

'From England.'

'Ah, England', he nods his head. 'In Peru we have many English
bicycles – good ones – Raleigh, Triumph, and Chinese ones too, but
the best ones are Peruvian – Lions.'

He slips the tool into the slots in the freewheel and places it in
the vice.

'It's stuck on pretty hard', I warn him, 'It has come over the
mountains from Lima.'

'By which route?'

I name some towns along the way and he whistles.

'*Puta mierda, gringo!* No wonder you break some spokes.'

He tries to turn the wheel. It doesn't budge. He tries again,
straining, and with a crack it turns.

'Done it!' he cries. I look the other way because it sounded like
the crack of a freewheel removing tool.

He pulls the wheel from the vice to inspect his work.

'Ah, the tool broke', he says, disappointed, but far from being upset at the destruction of his tool. He appears concerned not to have assisted me.

'Don't worry', he says 'We can go to my cousin Vicente who is also a bicycle mechanic. He will get it off.'

I say it's not that important, I can mend the spokes with wire like the others, but he waives this aside saying it's no trouble at all, and we walk a few blocks to his cousin's shop – a lock-up wooden shed filled with spares and broken bicycles and assorted bits and pieces that flow out into the street where they merge with the items flowing into the street from the wooden sheds either side.

Vicente is sitting outside on a crate, hammering at a rusty piece of metal. The two cousins embrace. The wheel is examined and Vicente hunts around on the ground and comes up with a tool that fits. The man from the used nuts, bolts, nails and assorted tools shed next door comes over to where we are standing inspecting the freewheel. Vicente notices it has six sprockets and points this out to the man next door.

'It's a Japanese freewheel and we're going to take it off for the gringo', he explains.

The family from the wooden shed at the other side come over now. They sell used glass bottles and jars, safety pins and assorted items fashioned from old tin gasolene cans. Vicente is getting quite excited.

'He's come from England on a Japanese bicycle with six sprockets on the freewheel and we're going to take it off for him', he shouts, pointing at me. He finds a spanner that fits over the freewheel tool. I try to take over the operation. There is no way the freewheel is going to come off with a spanner, and Vicente may feel bad about it. But he insists that he does it himself. We all stand back, watching expectantly as he tries to lever it off. He strains and puffs and his face goes red.

'Come along Vicente, put some effort into it', encourage the neighbours. Vicente strains till the veins bulge from his neck. Other passers-by gather around.

'Come on Vicente you old woman!' shouts the nuts and bolts man, and everybody joins in with a jibe of their own.

Suddenly the spanner slips. Vicente staggers back unbalanced, drops the wheel and jumps up and down holding his thumb. Howls of laughter are all the sympathy he gets.

'He's broken his thumb!' cries the nuts and bolts man, and everybody laughs louder.

The freewheel remains firmly on. The spokes are replaced with pieces of wire. The alternative to these Heath Robinson repairs is to buy a new wheel and freewheel, but there are no freewheels for sale in Peru that would give the low gearing necessary for comfortable riding over steep mountains. It is not important. So long as the wheels turn it doesn't matter what they look like. A bike held together with wire and string meets little resistance in a country where everything else just about holds together.

Smooth asphalt cuts a black line across the dusty brown plain towards Puno. The bike feels as if it is skimming across the ground, and I know that it is not just the physical contrast with the jarring ride over washboard dirt roads, but the excitement I feel at the prospect of seeing Lake Titicaca, that far off place with the exotic name that helped start me off on this trip.

In moments of despondency and aimlessness I have attributed it with all kinds of imaginary qualities to provide myself with a sense of direction and purpose.

The phrase 'Hey man, go to that lake in Peru' has become something of a joke that I say to myself whenever I find myself going somewhere I never intended, when I realise that my plans have been forgotten, abandoned.

Yet here it is, against all expectation, Lake Titicaca on the horizon, just the same as it ever was – a stretch of water just a short bicycle ride away.

Puno is the largest town on the lake. Down by the docks the water is polluted from the industrial waste and sewage that is either pumped into it direct or makes its way by force of gravity down from the streets every time it rains. But many people are casting lines from the quay and regularly pulling out fish.

Several large ships lie in the port. These were built in British shipyards at the turn of the century and sailed to the coast of Peru where they were taken apart into small pieces and carried across the Andes to the Altiplano on the backs of mules and men, to be reassembled over twelve thousand feet above sea level. Today they transport trains and trucks across the lake to Bolivia.

Small launches run ferry services for the inhabitants of the islands, who come to town to sell fish or tourist artefacts, and purchase provisions. They run on the same principle as the buses and trucks – if there is anyone still to get on they are not yet full.

On one thirty foot vessel I count at least a hundred people huddled together in the back, and more inside the small cabin, the roof of which is piled high with brightly coloured bundles.

'Let's go!' call some of the passengers to the captain, who stands with one foot on the concrete dock, ushering aboard more people. A large woman stumbles aboard, and hands reach out to steady her as the boat rocks heavily from side to side, low in the water. Startled cries and prayers can be heard as more people wriggle their way in among the sea of bodies and bundles.

'Let's go, I've got my children with me', goes up the cry towards the captain, who after a last scan along the quay for more prospective fares, to everybody's relief, climbs aboard too. The boat drifts slowly around bobbing up and down on the small waves before the outboard motor finally starts, and the overloaded craft chugs off across the lake.

I take a trip around the lake on a tourist launch, whose captain regards ten passengers as sufficient. We visit the floating islands built of totora reed that grow in the shallows, and bounce dutifully across admiring such an unstable habitat. The children take us by the hand and lead us around. Their faces are tanned and cracked by the wind and sun like faces of old men. They skip and run and laugh and show us their floating houses, the floating shop, the floating farmyard, the floating schoolhouse.

'What do you learn at school?' I ask my two escorts.

'Everything. Maths, science, geography. Where are you from, mister?'

'You guess', I say, thinking to test their geography. 'It's a country in Europe.'

'Germany.'

'No'.

'France?'

'No'.

'Italy?'

'No. It's an island.'

'Japan!'

'No. It's near to France.'

'Czechoslovakia!'

'No. It's England', I tell them, but they haven't heard of that one.

We buy our model boats and dolls and climb back into the boat lying against the floating quay. The water is clear and blue.

The captain is full of stories and history and he tells us how Manco Capac, founder of the Inca race, whose mother was the lake and whose father was the sun, was born – or rather arose – on the Island of the Sun, and of lake monsters that live in the thousand foot depths where it's always dark, guarding the gold sunk by a civilization on the run from the Spanish, that not even Jacques Cousteau and all his equipment could discover, and of the two Italian tourists who were swallowed up whole in 1978, and more legends about the lake which is now silver and blue and reflecting the sky like a mirror in the midday sun, and we're all infected with the enthusiasm with which the captain relates his tales, and he even sings a Titicaca song about how life used to be, with such heart-felt emotion that at the end he cries and we all applaud appreciatively, and he is plunged into melancholy reverie and doesn't say another word all the way back to Puno.

I send some postcards home before leaving Puno because I've forgotten to write for several months. Inflation is currently running at a hundred and fifty per cent, which although a modest rate by Latin American standards, is faster than the post office can print new stamps, and the hundred *soles* stamp is in fact the old forty *soles* stamp with 40 crossed out in official post office ink and 100 printed above – ingenuity typical of Latin American countries in dealing with inflation. Argentina for example has at a stroke wiped six noughts off its currency so as not to overload the computers of the national bank when converting the foreign debt from dollars to pesos – or so the story goes.

Stone houses nestle into the rocky outcrops along the lake shore, with stone walls enclosing small patches of ground, worked somehow into a soil that produces a few crops of vegetables and corn. The lake level fluctuates at this time of year. Many fields are underwater, and in the early mornings, frozen over, and young shoots stick up bright green above a layer of ice.

Away from the small cultivated lakeside plots the ground is dry, the red and brown dust constantly whipped up by the wind into columns and huge curtains, transported across the plain to wherever the wind goes – up into the hills, or out over the lake.

People by the road nod politely to me, wish me good day, wave back and grin if I wave to them, and some simply stare, or take no notice at all. Indians of the Altiplano are not an excitable people.

The sky is a bright clean electric blue, the road is straight, unobstructed. The way ahead seems very simple and clear.

A few piles of stones indicate a hazard ahead. Normally such warnings are only put up where the road suddenly disappears at a subsidence, or where a broken down vehicle is blocking the road around a sharp bend. Here there are no vehicles in sight, no buildings nearby, just a small bundle on the empty road.

The bundle is a corpse, covered in a dusty brown poncho all except for a pair of crusty bare feet sticking out at the bottom, toes pointing up to the sky. A group of men from a nearby field are standing around the body, silently, their cracked and weathered faces looking down the road, across the plain, some leaning on hoes, some crying.

I feel I should perhaps cross myself, or make some other gesture of customary politeness to convey my sympathy, but I cannot think of anything that however well intentioned would not seem an intrusion on their grief. Sincerity before appearance seems more fitting here, even if it is nothing.

The sight of a colourful procession a little further on jolts me out of morbid contemplation. A group of men and women in gaily coloured clothes are twirling along down a dusty track on the outskirts of a tiny village, followed by a group of musicians, also jigging happily, blowing rusty tin horns and trumpets, banging away on ancient drums.

Behind comes the rest of the villagers – men dressed in their smartest clothes – dark jackets, some even with ties, the women too in obviously recently cleaned skirts and shawls of red and purple, ribbons around their bowler hats and everybody passing around plastic containers, swigging at chicha.

A wedding took place early this morning. I am hailed loudly, invited to join in the celebrations.

Friends and relatives are helping to build a house for the newly weds. Four adobe walls are already half way up. I ask how long it will take to complete.

'Oh, whenever, later on, perhaps tomorrow. When it is finished we stop', explains one man, his suit already covered in dust.

A core of people work steadily op the construction, a few get to grips with the garden, turning over the dusty soil with hand hoes, but drinking and dancing take precedence over work.

Despite their harsh life, the Indian campesinos have the ability to abandon themselves to celebration. Or perhaps because of the hardship they are ready to welcome any opportunity to lay down the burden, to stand aside for just a little while.

I leave the main asphalted highway to go on the dirt tracks and footpaths that follow the lake shore towards Yunguyo which borders with Bolivia on a mountainous peninsula. The border on the peninsula is ill defined, many of the marker stones having been put to more practical purposes by the campesinos to build their houses with. They come and go as they please, by boat or on land. The customs and immigration post is itself situated on one of several alternative tracks. I miss the right one, but a man on a bicycle riding by points it out.

'Why don't you travel by truck?' he asks.

'I don't like them', I reply. He guffaws loudly.

There is nobody about at the border post when I get there, not even a soldier. I sit on the step in the shade, and presently a customs man appears.

'What do you want?' he asks.

'I want to leave Peru.'

We enter the hut, furnished with a chair and table, and he hunts around and comes up with the appropriate stamp which he whacks onto an empty space in my passport.

'Pleasant journey', he says, and disappears around the outside of the building for a piss. I ride over the chain and into Bolivia.

11. Tear-gassed in La Paz

The hum of a giant insect that blunders against my sleeping bag with a loud thwack wakes me at dawn. At the other end of the wide bay, the early morning sun reflects from the whitewashed walls of the town of Copacabana which lies in the shelter of a high spur of rock jutting out into the lake.

Eucalyptus trees line the pebble beach, tall and straight before the dry rocky mountainside that rises behind. Ducks chatter in the reedy shadow, and wild guinea pigs hop in and out of stony hillocks, squeaking sociably to one another.

The lake is clear and blue and gently waving. The sky too is clear and blue and still. An occasional cloud floats across, white and fluffy and slowly shrinking.

There is enough kindling within reach to boil a pot of water. A handful of twigs is plenty to brew a cup of tea. The smoke smells of Eucalyptus.

An old wooden rowboat drifts slowly away from the shore with two figures in it. An old man stands shading his eyes from the bright early morning sunshine under a wide brimmed hat, and a young boy, seated and hatless, pays out a long net from the back of the boat.

Several seagulls wheel overhead, squawking, diving now and then for fish. A pair of brown ducks paddle slowly past, bobbing up and down in the shallows, not fishing.

A young girl in a white smock, bowler hat and bare feet scrunches across the pebble beach leading a cow, straining on the rope attached to its neck, smacking its side to persuade it to drink. I doze back to sleep.

A mechanical whining hum wakes me from renewed slumber, and a small fast moving dot appears on the horizon. It's the Titicaca hydrofoil, announcing the arrival of the twentieth century, emissary and slave of speed and efficiency. It skis purposefully to the small harbour of Copacabana, vestigial stronghold of the Bolivian navy.

Celebrants of an all night fiesta are returning from the hilltop overlooking Copacabana where they have spent the night. Two groups of about thirty people gather in a field at the bottom of the hill. Some arrive unsteadily, supported by companions, and promptly keel over. Drunk and sober alike have a set of bamboo pipes – *zamponia* – of differing sizes. Each plays a different melody, and all combine to produce an intricate and harmonious wall of sound that ranges from the high pitched squeaking of the small pipes, to the deep booming of large bass pipes that is felt throughout the body more than heard by the ears. Those standing jig around in time with the music, or jump up and down to keep warm, and there is constant interchange of musicians between the two groups. Several individuals mill about on their own.

Time is beaten out for both groups on an enormous drum, held by two men and beaten by a third. People fall over, people stand up. The music is simple, the continuity haphazard and effortless, the sound is hypnotic.

The fiesta continues as the rest of the town wakes up. A brass band leads a procession through the streets. There's an old man bearing a tall pole with a framework of wood at the top to which are fastened fireworks which he periodically lights. Some fizz and whirr and engulf him in clouds of smoke. Others propel themselves free of their fastenings and shoot off into the air or smack into walls. The crowd of small children is delighted, and runs screaming from their path. One or two drop off by the old man's feet where they buzz and pop in the dust, making him skip around comically.

A few sticks of dynamite are exploded up on the hill by way of celebration, booming out shockwaves that rock the walls of buildings. Letting off dynamite is acceptable behaviour in Bolivia.

It is a hundred miles to the capital La Paz. I buy some bananas for the journey.

'What do you think of our country, gringo?' the old white-haired woman in the store asks me.

'I haven't seen much of it, but it seems nice.'

'Ha!' she exclaims, 'The country is all right, yes, but the government is full of shit. It's full of schemes and theories, and it's the same in Peru. The President of Bolivia and the President of Peru are bedfellows. Like this . . .' she winks conspiratorially, and lays the index finger of each hand beside each other to indicate what she means.

'Baulinde Terry, he is the old man, and Siles Zuazo, he is the old woman. Their policies are bad and they're both full of shit.'

Political opinions in Bolivia, of those who bother to hold any, are rarely middle of the road.

With the wind behind me on the asphalt road that runs along the Altiplano to La Paz it is easy to cruise along in top gear. When the wind changes by a hundred and eighty degrees it is as much as I can do to move at all in first gear.

It is early evening when I reach El Alto, the town of half a million inhabitants that perches on the lip of the canyon above the capital, and is really a continuation of the shanty towns surrounding the city.

La Paz itself lies two thousand feet down in the canyon that cuts away from the eastern edge of the Altiplano. A concrete motorway winds the twelve kilometers down, but I lose it in the darkness, and find descent instead through the shanty town full of smoky fires, barking dogs, and houses made of tin and polythene and cardboard that cling to the canyon walls, one on top of another for mile after mile, along perilously steep tracks of rough cobblestones and mud, slippery under the inch of hailstones that has just been deposited by a big storm which rolled down off the plain.

The city centre is bright with electric lights of buildings and street lamps, and the headlights of trucks and buses that nudge a passage through the crowded streets in the evening rush hour. The pavements are lit by the glow of gas lamps around the street traders whose wares cover the ground, around the food sellers with their big pots of soup and stew, where people sit and crouch eating from bowls and plates, and stand wrapped up in ponchos and blankets, bowler hats and balaclavas and wildly coloured woollen hats, around charcoal braziers of grilled corn, kebabs, fish, and frying pans of hot fat sizzling with hamburgers, bananas, pigs' trotters, in an overwhelming welter of noise and smells.

I'm exhausted and take refuge in the first hotel I find. I'm ravenously hungry too, and eat a meal in a basement restaurant by a busy roundabout just down the road.

A group of people charge into the room as I leave, falling over one another into a heap at the bottom of the stairs. Nobody pays particular attention to them, and thinking that this is part of the bustle and confusion that apparently constitutes normal evening activity in La Paz, I pay no heed to what they are saying.

I emerge into a street battle. A group of people up the hill are shouting at a group of police in riot gear lower down across the roundabout. The protesters have erected barricades of burning tyres, and dig up cobblestones to hurl as missiles at the police. The police crouch behind shields, clearly reluctant to advance on the crowd, but prevented from retreating by officers sheltering behind armoured cars.

The police call through loudhailers, 'Disperse, go home!' and a barrage of rocks and cobblestones comes hurtling and bouncing down across the roundabout, crashing into the line of shields. The police return fire with tear gas, which in the variable wind scatters both police and protesters spluttering and choking away from the spreading cloud.

My hotel is up the road that is now full of tear gas so I take a detour through some of the steep narrow side alleys. The alleyways are full of other people also seeking alternative routes. Everybody is coughing and spitting and rubbing their eyes.

I come out of the maze of alleys into a large square in the midst of a chanting crowd. I can see the sign of my hotel lower down the hill, but the way is blocked by police with shields and batons, jeeps and armoured cars.

The protesters seem amiable enough, high-spirited, enthusiastic, and their most popular chant seems reasonable, 'No to the govern-ment of starvation'.

A few tear gas canisters are fired up the street towards us, but the wind blows the gas back down again, making the people caught in between – street traders and food sellers – crouch gasping in doorways, mothers covering screaming babies with shawls and blankets.

Two police motorcyclists are dispatched to take a closer look at the crowd. They are driven back with a hail of rocks and stones. A lone policeman on the beat, caught up by chance among the crowd, talking to some civilian friends in a darkened doorway thinks it is time to join his comrades, and drawing his pistol makes a dash down the hill. He is seen on his way with jeers and whistles, considered perhaps too vulnerable for a good sporting stoning.

This old part of town is a labyrinth of steep narrow winding streets and alleyways. The leaders of the group of protesters have walkie-talkies and are planning where to disperse and regroup. Instructions are passed around as the police advance – a line of riot shields and riot sticks, then those on foot with machine guns and lastly the jeeps and armoured cars. A furious barrage of rocks and cobblestones greets them, but they keep coming, and when close enough, launch off tear gas. Everybody is choking and spluttering again, and scatters in different directions.

I've had enough running round the city being tear-gassed when all I want to do is to go to bed. Only those running away are the object of pursuit. Many bystanders are flattened into doorways or crouch on the ground protecting their children. I stand at the side of the street, trying to appear uninvolved, and the ranks of police barge past.

The interest payments alone on Bolivia's foreign debt are greater than its gross national product, and the recent austerity measures implemented by the government, under the auspices of the I.M.F. as conditions of interest payment rescheduling, were the cause of the demonstration. It is not a situation confined to Bolivia. The whole of Latin America pays more money to Western banks and creditor organisations than it receives in loans.

The economy of Bolivia is largely rural. Three-quarters of the population are subsistence farmers – campesinos – eking out a living on the Altiplano, or in the valleys of the eastern Andes. Inflation is currently running at two hundred per cent, and periodic massive devaluations of the Bolivian peso do not engender faith in the currency. People wake up to find their money worth half of what it was the day before, and those with savings, and businesses that require foreign capital for investment or for the purchase of imported goods, take to the streets in search of dollars that are not always available from the national bank.

In the small business centre of the city, in the street where the banks have their high rise office blocks, the pavement is a mass of money changers buying and selling dollars. Although illegal, trading goes on openly under the noses of the police.

The official exchange rate is two hundred pesos to the dollar. On the black, or parallel market as it is more respectably known, dollars are exchanged for eight hundred pesos.

Newspapers express public outrage at this illegal trade, and demand that the government take steps to stabilise the financial economy to undermine the need for its existence. The government claims it is taking steps, and makes token arrests of money changers every couple of weeks.

It is unnecessary to enter shops in La Paz. Everything can be bought in the street. Almost every road and alley in the old part of town is lined with traders. A piece of pavement on which to sit and spread out a few goods is all that is required. People sit all day by piles of vegetables and household goods.

I bump into Leo under the shade of polythene sheeting at one of the fruit juice stalls near the central market. A line of tables buckle under the weight of piles of fruit – oranges, mandarines, bananas, peaches, papayas and melons.

Leo arrived a few days ago with Michel, another French cyclist. They came together from Cusco, though nearly got split up at the border where Michel was threatened with imprisonment. Back in Lima he thought twenty dollars an exorbitant amount to pay to extend his visa, and simply changed 30 days to 80 with a pencil. As extensions are normally granted in multiples of thirty days, this was easily spotted by the immigration man at the border. A long argument followed, with Michel eventually convincing him of the legitimacy of this deceit by an impoverished gringo, so poor he was touring the world on a bicycle.

Leo and Michel plan to continue south over the Altiplano and cross the Atacama desert of northern Chile. Gérard went that way two weeks ago.

On the morning of their departure I pop round to their hotel to take some photos of them leaving. They're not there.

'They've gone out for the day', the hotel desk man explains.

Leo comes to my hotel in the evening. He has lost Michel. They both went out to buy a few goodies for the road and to drink a last couple of fruit juices because south of La Paz it looks like being desert for a thousand miles or so, but Michel never came back. All his things are still in the hotel room. Leo is worried that he might have had an accident. He has toured the hospitals and clinics, inquired at the French Alliance and Embassy, but Michel is nowhere to be found.

Leo comes around the following morning.

'I've found Michel', he says cheerfully. 'He's in jail.' He was caught changing dollars on the street. Leo is on his way back to the jail with Michel's sleeping bag and some bread because police hospitality does not extend to food and blankets.

The jail is a solid windowless concrete building in the courtyard of a military police post. It consists of two cells – one for men and the other for women. The men's cell is about twenty feet square and has forty people inside. The women's cell is slightly smaller and equally crowded. Light and ventilation come through the door of steel bars.

It is visiting time. Twenty people crowd around the doors waiting their chance to shout to friends and relatives, passing food through the bars. We stand in the crowd, shouting Michel's name. He appears, grinning, the lone head of red gringo hair. There is only one toilet, Michel says – a hole in the ground in the darkest corner. There is a high turnover of people because this is just a holding cell. At night they all sleep huddled on the floor, new arrivals nearest the toilet, though Michel says that as a foreigner he is allowed a more prestigious position near the door. At night before going to sleep they take turns to sing a song or relate an amusing tale. Michel only knows two songs so he hopes to be out soon. He is teaching the others to speak French.

'It's terrible', the woman standing next to me says. 'My son has been here for a week for demonstrating. They won't tell me when he can come out. They don't feed him. It's terrible. Do they have places like this in your country?' she asks.

'Yes, more or less', I reply.

Leo has brought along a few newspaper cuttings that Michel has collected along the way, and takes them to the jail office to plead the case of an impoverished gringo touring the world on his bicycle, so poor he has to change his dollars on the street. He gets no indication as to when Michel may be released. We both feel obliged to celebrate our freedom by drinking a few more fruit juices.

The central plaza is full of ice cream vendors, photographers, and people sitting on benches in the bright sunshine feeding pigeons from little bags of grain. The roof of the cathedral is falling in and scaffolding surrounds the walls of the presidential palace.

In the shopping precinct that leads off the plaza, closed to traffic, a crowd has gathered around a musician. He is skinny, dressed in rags, and plays a *charango* – a small ten stringed instrument that looks a cross between a banjo and a mandolin, the sound box is an armadillo shell – and a set of pan pipes secured around his neck with a piece of wire. He taps out a beat with his bare feet on the pavement and sings in a soft voice.

The audience has completely blocked off the street. Four burly policemen barge their way through to the centre, and tell everybody to disperse and the musician to move along because it is an offence to cause an obstruction in a public place. No one takes them seriously and the musician is urged to play some more songs. The police become angry and surround the young lad, telling him to stop playing and go away. He is frightened and makes to pack up and leave. The crowd becomes angry now, everybody shouts at the policemen, tells them not to pick on the lad, he's hungry, he's only trying to make a living, the people want him so leave him alone. The musician is clearly embarrassed by all this but the strength of public opinion is with him, the policemen withdraw, jeered and whistled at, to the cries of 'Play in the streets', 'Play in the markets', 'Play in the bread shops', 'Play where you want'.

For several days the city is engulfed by huge storms that roll down off the Altiplano, battering the city with rain and hail and shaking the ground with thunder. People take refuge under cover of doorways, tin roofs, polythene awnings, under arches, in cardboard boxes, as running water floods through houses, shops and restaurants, respecting only gravity. The streets become rivers full of floating rubbish and bobbing turds.

Michel is released after four days of confinement, with seven of the fifteen dollars he was caught attempting to change on the street returned to him. He is quite keen to be on the road again, and leaves the following morning with Leo after they've drunk a few fruit juices and changed some dollars.

Rudi and Don recently passed through La Paz on their way south, and Gérard wrote from somewhere in Chile. I've been content for the past few weeks to be undecided about where to go. South seems to be the way, if only out of inertia and habit. It has been a pleasant enough direction for over a year, and a southbound course stretches sufficiently far into the distance and into the future to seem more of a heading than a destination. The endlessness and continuity is the attraction, however short-lived or momentary it may turn out to be.

Diplomatic relations between Argentina and Britain remain severed following the Falklands war. I fill in forms at the Argentine Embassy to find out I am eligible to apply for a visa.

'This could take some time', warns the embassy man. 'It could be ninety days, or as long as three months.'

In just a few days I learn that my request for a visa application has been refused.

I hunt around for a tent but can find nothing in La Paz that remotely resembles camping equipment. The demand is not great here. There are plenty of plastic containers though, and in preparation for the dry southern Altiplano and the Atacama desert beyond I buy a large five litre water container to supplement the four pint bottles I already have. It is difficult with the other recent acquisitions – including a *charango* – to fit everything onto the bike.

At one of the welding shacks that line the major highway out of the city, I show a welder a sketch of a rack that would fit above the front wheel onto the existing rack that carries the two front panniers. He squints at it for a few seconds and hands it back to me, and with bits of metal that are lying around, constructs a contraption in a few minutes that fits perfectly.

'It should be strong enough', he says, and gets me to hold the bike while he stands on it to demonstrate its indestructibility. No graceful lines here, or lightweight alloys – it must weigh a kilo or two by itself – but it has a functional beauty all of its own.

The city is almost at a standstill because of the wave of strikes following the most recent austerity measures. Even the more pro–government newspapers are calling the President little more than a lackey of the I.M.F.

I leave the city on the paved road – one of three in the country – that runs up to the Altiplano and south to Oruro. Owners of private vehicles in Bolivia tend to use them only in the cities as most intercity routes are fit only for the sturdiest of buses and trucks, and even these soon shake free anything not securely bolted down. The bus and truck drivers are on strike today so the road is almost deserted.

12. Blinded by the salt

With no obstruction in their path, the storms and thunder clouds that lumber across the Altiplano can clearly be seen revolving clockwise, trailing a black curtain of rain and hail that leaves behind a carpet of white. Some have towering columns of dust at their edges. All have their own localised wind systems, and with timing it is possible to take advantage of the downdraughts, to be pushed along from behind or pulled along from in front.

I try to avoid them. Slow and monstrous though they are, some manage to sneak up behind and catch me unawares, engulfing me in blackness and booming thunder and dancing lightning. There is nowhere to shelter from the stinging hail that the wind near the centre of the storm whips into a fury of horizontally swirling pellets. The dusty ground hisses and gurgles.

A few herds of goats and llamas graze the tough grass, watched over by women and children who sit on the plain in clothes dyed bright colours that stand out for miles. The young children are skilled with slings, and loose off well aimed stones to direct straying animals back to the herd or away from the road.

Distances are deceptive in the clear air. The dark blobs on the horizon turn out to be trees twenty five miles away at the village of Sica Sica. The Altiplano is virtually treeless though here there are the remains of stumps that must once have been enormous trees.

Sica Sica is typical of Altiplano villages – adobe houses, dusty streets, one shop, dark and cool, that has only potatoes, flour and coca leaves for sale.

I am accompanied into the city of Oruro by a meteorologist – the only meteorologist in Oruro, he tells me proudly – returning on his bicycle from the weather station. He writes the weather reports and forecasts in the daily paper.

I mention how cold it was last night.

'Minus ten degrees centigrade', he tells me. 'Fifteen millimetres of rain have fallen in the past four days', he adds.

He asks me where I am going and I tell him I'm heading for Chile via Uyuni.

'Ah, Uyuni', he muses. 'It hasn't rained in Uyuni for two and a half years. It is the coldest town in Bolivia because it is by the great salt pan of Uyuni where the ground reflects all the heat back into the sky. During the day it can be twenty five degrees, but at night it can drop to minus twenty five. The inhabitants of Uyuni are the healthiest in all Bolivia because the wind blows off the salt pan where no germs can live. Many people die of old age. Some live to be sixty or more. In Bolivia this is old. Most people are dead at forty five, less in mining areas like this where miners die of lung diseases. Around Oruro they mine copper, zinc, tin and lead. There used to be silver but now it is all gone. The silver mined at Potosi is brought here for processing, but nothing is happening at the moment. The miners are on strike.'

In 1952, following the refusal of the army to recognize the democratically elected party of Revolutionary Nationalists, the miners of Oruro led a civilian uprising. Armed with sticks of dynamite they marched on La Paz and defeated the military in armed conflict. Being in the forefront of demands for political reform, the miners have always suffered at the hands of the army during reprisals in subsequent military regimes. But they remain militant. The miners' cooperative recently intercepted a consignment of new buses imported from Argentina on its way to La Paz. Oruro is a depressed region in greater need than the capital, they argue, and the fleet of buses is at present under guard in the mining complex, while representatives of the government and miners meet to discuss a solution.

Despite the recent storms the ground south of Oruro appears parched. A few sparse bushes grow out of the sand and dust, and a few crumbling remains of adobe walls mark where houses stood in former times before the current drought. Several tiny mineworks dot the far hillsides, mostly abandoned. Sometimes a single figure appears as if from nowhere, crosses the road and strides out across the hot plain.

It is very hot. I sit and rest and eat a mandarine. An old man comes wobbling down the road.

'Good morning', he says, raising his hat before passing by. A few seconds later there is the unmistakable sound of a bicycle and rider tumbling into the dirt. The old man dusts himself down.

'Whoops, a little crash', he says, grinning foolishly.

He comes and sits down and we eat mandarines. He used to live around here with his family, he tells me, many years ago, but it hasn't rained for years, the well dried up and there was no grazing for the animals. His family live in the city now, and he works in a small mine up in the mountains.

A truck overtakes me a few hundred yards up the road, the back loaded up with thirty or forty people and a pile of bundles. It stops up ahead and the driver leans out to speak to me. I can't understand what he is saying because of the noise of the engine and his unintelligible accent. I assume he is offering me a lift so I simply say no thanks and wave him on. Ten minutes later I look back and see one of the rear panniers is missing. It must have come loose when I laid the bike over to rest. The truck driver was probably telling me about the bag I'd left behind.

The heat must be addling my brain. Fancy not noticing. I race back to where it must have come off, but all that is there is a pile of mandarine peelings, already crisp and curling in the sun.

The pannier contained important items – sleeping bag, camera, some warm clothes, a few tools and spare parts. The truck driver must have picked it up. He's probably chuckling to himself now at the booty, wondering at the throwaway attitude of gringos.

Dammit you're an idiot! I feel like crying.

Two trails of dust appear on the horizon behind. It's two jeeps, speeding this way. I stand up as the first approaches, wave my arms to flag him down. He swerves around me. I've got to hitch a ride to catch the truck. The second jeep approaches and I stand in the middle of the road waving my arms. It swerves to go around me, beeping its horn, but I move over to block its path. It skids to a halt in a shower of gravel and a cloud of dust.

The jeep has 'Department of Transport' on the sides. There are three men inside. I explain my situation and they readily agree to give me a lift. They are on their way to repair a bridge on the road over the mountains to Potosi. Sacks of cement lie in the back.

'We're not supposed to stop to give lifts', explains the driver. 'There are bandits on the road.'

'Describe the truck', says the round-faced man squashed up against the door. The cab was red and there were thirty or forty people in the back, is all I can remember.

The round-faced man is surprised that I should come all the way from England to pushbike across the Altiplano. The driver reminds him that Englishmen do strange things, that England is the home of Margaret Thatcher, the famous Iron Lady, and that if I don't get my bag back she will probably send a fleet across the Atlantic to make war on Bolivia. They all crack a few jokes about the Falklands war and the fact that the brutal imperialist Britannic aggressors were led by a woman.

Outside Poopo there is a transit checkpoint hut where the driver presents his documents. He comes running back out.

'A red truck passed five minutes ago', he says, climbing behind the wheel and spinning off down the road. All three of them become excited now like schoolchildren, shouting and laughing as we give chase, tearing around bends, skidding all over the place, the driver beeping the horn to let everybody know that he is a maniac.

A blue truck comes towards us.

'Is that it?' the driver asks, slamming on the brakes and swerving to avoid a head on collision. Size determine right of way.

A trail of dust ahead indicates another vehicle, and closer to, I recognize it as the red truck.

The jeep driver toots his horn and tries to pass amid the cloud of dust, but the truck keeps to the middle of the road. It is normal for overtaking manoeuvres to take five minutes on narrow dirt roads, the lead vehicle waits for a suitably wide stretch to pull over.

The jeep driver is impatient, abandons convention, and turns the wheel so that we plunge down the small embankment. Thirty or forty pairs of curious and amused eyes watch as we bounce over the rocky plain and fly back up in front of the truck. We slow to a halt blocking the road, rather too suddenly for politeness. The truck grinds to a stop behind and everything is enveloped in a cloud of dust.

'Well, what are you going to do now?' the driver asks me.

'They'll cut your throat,' encourages the round-faced man.

I go to the side of the truck cab and the driver pokes his head out of the window.

'Hello gringo', he says, and adds a few words I cannot understand.

'Hello, do you have my bag?' I ask, feeling pretty stupid. He pops his head back inside, and after some discussion the other cab door opens and a young lad jumps down and hands me the pannier.

The driver speaks another stream of unintelligible words.

'Thank you', I say when he's finished. The jeep moves to the side to let him pass. Thirty or forty people grin and wave from the back.

The Department of Transport men get out now and slap me on the back.

'You're all right now then gringo!'

They appear as pleased as I am that the bag has been retrieved, and offer me a lift further down the road. I say no thanks, I'm all right now.

At Challapata the road turns eastwards to the mountains and Potosi. I stop in the shade of a withered tree in the dusty plaza where Indian women are selling glasses of peach water, and ask where the road to Uyuni is. I am met with blank stares. Perhaps they don't speak Spanish. I ask again.

'There is no road', answers one woman. 'There is a railway.' I'm sure there is a road as drivers have told me of its terrible condition. My maps mark it too, though this is no guarantee of its existence. The new 'Anniversary Edition' Ministry of Roads map I bought in La Paz marks it as a thin yellow line, and Bartholomew's 'South America' confidently marks it in the thick red normally reserved for major roads.

I buy a round slab of goat's cheese kept cool in a bucket of water from another woman. She dries it on her dusty apron. I ask her where the road leaves town for Uyuni, because I've been all around and I cannot find it. She leaves her bucket of cheeses and leads me through the few dusty streets to the edge of the village.

'There it is', she says, pointing to a barely discernible set of tyre tracks across the sand.

'It goes to Uyuni?' I ask.

'That's it. Don't look for it at your feet, look for it up ahead.'

'How many hours by truck is it to Uyuni?' I ask.

'Ten hours. You can make it in eleven, perhaps twelve.'

It's the drop handlebars and derailleur gears that suggest

to people that I race from place to place at incredible
speed.

I trundle off down the track at walking pace until the sand
becomes too deep. Then I walk. A few miles on there are many
parallel tracks, and a rusty bulldozer, abandoned, sits amid piles
of sand and dust.

A few bright green bushes dot the yellow plain. Now and then
I startle a flock of sand coloured doves, so well camouflaged that I
don't see them until they fly off from under my feet. There are dumpy
thick-billed birds that sit with their heads held back and their beaks
pointing at the sky. The sky is bright blue, everywhere.

Lightning flashes over the mountaintops away to the east at
night, but overhead the sky is clear, bright with stars and the
frequent trails of shooting stars. The nights are very pretty but are
becoming uncomfortably cold. I choose the shelter of boulders and
dips to help reduce the wind chill, but the filling of my sleeping bag
is old and bunched up, leaving cold spots, and though I sleep fully
dressed with hat, scarf, gloves and boots, I shiver in the hours before
dawn, and have to wriggle numbness from my fingers and toes.

The water bottles freeze solid during the night so I fill the pot with
water before I go to sleep, and set it up by the little alcohol burner
that is really no more than a tin can with a hole in the top, so that
in the hypothermic lethargy of early morning I need only venture out
an arm with a match to await a brew.

Sunrise is always breathtaking. By the time I've drunk a pot of
tea the first light puffs of wind are rustling the dust, a few birds fly
low over the ground with a whoosh that lingers in the silence and
the whole plain sparkles in the sharp clear air. It's a fine time to
practise playing the *charango*.

The road is still soft sand, impossible to ride. Groups of llamas
emerge from behind sand dunes, and disappear down gullies in
search of clumps of puna grass.

There's a dot on the horizon – a man walking towards me. After
half an hour he seems no nearer. The sight of another human being
is an irresistible focus of attention. By the time we are near I have
examined minutely his way of walking, his dress, the slant of his
hat angled against the sun, the way that his arms swing, how he
adjusts the strap of a bag slung over his shoulder, the way he looks
up from the ground, towards me, and back.

When we meet, we grin and shake hands, and it seems as if we already know each other. We make a few signs because he speaks no Spanish and I speak no Aymara, and I gather that it's not far to the little village of Sevaruyo and that he's heading for Challapata.

Sevaruyo is twenty to thirty thick-walled adobe buildings, a railway hut and a water tower. The railway line is the main street. A windowless house by a standpipe turns out to be a shop – the town centre. Several people come out of the doorway, as I fill up with water at the tap. Their clothes are covered in dust.

'Gringo!' calls out a thin wrinkled old man. 'Where are you going?'

'Uyuni.'

'Oooh, long way.'

'How far?' I ask. Several different answers are given, distances measured in truck hours.

I pull out the new map of Bolivia and everybody crowds around, admiring the colours, peering and squinting and pointing to the names of places they recognize.

They recommend I take the railway to Uyuni because it is flatter and firmer than the road and easier to follow.

I ask if any other cyclists have passed by. Yes, two came through quite recently, they decide.

'When was that?' I ask.

'Monday', says a young girl, 'Tuesday', says the old man, 'Wednesday', says a woman, all at once. It's only Thursday today, I think. It is difficult to keep track of time.

In the shop there is rice flour, bananas, coca leaves, some ancient tins of sardines and some stale bread rolls. I buy some bananas and pack them into the shopping bag on the top front rack where I keep all my food. The wrinkled old man, a bundle of amiable curiosity, pokes his face inside it.

'Mmmm . . .' he says, 'bread, goat's cheese, lemons, garlic, bananas, mandarines. You're well prepared.' He looks round at the circle of grinning faces.

'He's well prepared!' he announces. Everybody laughs and one of the women slaps his back and tells him not to be such a nosy old man.

It is possible to ride for much of the way alongside the railway, though in places sand has engulfed all but the rails.

The track is raised on an embankment with just a foot either side on which to ride. It requires concentration as the front wheel has a tendency to ski and swerve in the soft sand.

The landscape changes constantly: here gullies and ravines to be crossed on steel girder bridges; there groups of gentle rounded hills. The clumps of grass have disappeared and the ground takes on a metallic sheen. Larger mountains dot the plain – long flat-topped mesas purple and red, ice-capped mountains and conical volcanoes standing alone, rising way above the sea of sand.

The railway is not marked on the Ministry of Roads anniversary map, which doesn't matter because I know that it leads to Uyuni. The map is based on a satellite photograph, coloured in and overlaid with roads and towns. The larger volcanoes appear on it like craters in photos of the moon, and I try to work out my position on the map from the landscape, and imagine the towns and villages beyond. It makes the place seem less barren, less desolate.

While I'm busy imagining my security the bike veers from the track and heads down the embankment, here twenty feet high and too steep to stop. I hang on tight, slipping and sliding, and hit a boulder at the bottom. The bike stops dead and rolls onto its side with a dull thud. I describe a somersault over the boulder and land with a thwack in the soft sand. Quite an exciting diversion. I'm quite pleased, but on trying to move off I find that the front wheel is buckled, and catches on the brake blocks. I remove the front brake, but the wheel is so buckled that it cannot turn between the front forks. It takes some severe adjustment of the tension of the spokes and a couple of carefully aimed kicks to unmangle the thing sufficiently that it turns freely, if eccentrically between the forks. The brake must stay off but that's not important here.

It takes a long time now to cross the bridges over ravines as the front wheel slips from the rails, clumps down and wedges itself between the sleepers. The sleepers are cracked and worn.

I've just crossed a long bridge when a train comes along – a short line of rusty containers with a couple of passenger coaches tacked on the end, pulled by an ancient engine, all moving at such a leisurely pace that the driver has time to toot his whistle, ask after my health and offer a lift before passing by.

The railway tracks near the tiny settlement of Chita are buried in sand so I try taking the road. The road is two deep sandy ruts and I continue to walk. No vehicles pass.

There is an unusual, almost luminous quality to the light up ahead, and over a slight rise the dry salt lake – the Salar de Uyuni – stretches out brilliant white along the horizon.

These beds of salt are estimated to be twenty five metres deep in places, and extend for hundreds of miles throughout the high basins of the Andes along the borders of Bolivia, Chile and Argentina. In places they are overlaid with shallow salt lakes, which vary in position and depth from year to year according to rainfall in the mountains. Rivers are seasonal. When they do flow, they flow onto the salt pans and evaporate. This is the lowest part of the Altiplano. It is over twelve thousand feet high.

The sand here, still far from the salt pan, is covered with a crust of white. Only algae can grow, brightly coloured, clinging to boulders, feeding on rock and sunlight.

The ground holds no heat, so at night the temperature plummets, and the silence is broken by the occasional sharp cracks of distant boulders shattering with frost.

The air is so thin and so clear that all the dawn traces of red and orange have disappeared long before the sun bursts above the horizon, already white and bright.

The road and railway run parallel now, perfectly straight and flat over a white plain that glares blindingly with reflected sunlight. There is no distinction between land and sky, for the horizon is a shimmering mirage of silver grey. The bases of distant mountains and volcanoes are lost in the mirage, and their peaks seem to be floating in the sky with no visible support.

The glare gives me a headache, makes me squint behind sunglasses. The salt air makes my nose run, and the hot dry wind sucks out moisture at a faster rate than my stomach can absorb it, leaving me thirsty no matter how much I drink. A gallon of water goes in no time, and does nothing to quench my thirst. The sight of the buildings of Uyuni floating above the mirage of the horizon is welcome.

Uyuni is larger than might be expected for a town stuck out in the middle of the southern Altiplano where nothing can grow and drinking water must be piped in. It owes its size to its importance as a railway junction. The line from La Paz in the north divides here, one track winds through the mountains that enclose the Altiplano to the south, to Argentina, the other crosses a hundred miles of salt pan west to Chile.

Uyuni seems to grow out of the dust. Within a few blocks of single storey whitewashed adobe buildings is the centre – a concrete customs building, a bank, hotel, cinema, market and shops, and the railway station and sidings. The wind whips down the mainstreet that is free of traffic, blowing dust over the street traders who sit by their wares on the ground, wrapped in blankets and shawls and wearing wide-brimmed hats.

The municipal building is one of the few with two storeys. The national flag and banners hang from the upper windows, and a small crowd has gathered below, amid a flutter of leaflets dropped from above where the local government workers have barricaded themselves in. It is their fifth day on hunger strike in protest against the recent public service cutbacks, deemed necessary as part of the economic recovery process for scrimping together enough money to make the next interest payment on the foreign debt.

My hotel room is a concrete fridge with a bed that sags under the weight of ten blankets, and a chamber pot half full of frozen urine.

'I recommend that you take the train to Chile,' says the hotel manager. 'Once a month a truck goes out to the army post but it takes a different track each time. There is no road.'

'When does the train leave?' I ask.

'Not for three days.'

I say it will only take me two days to ride. I can follow the railway line.

'There's nothing out there but salt', he says. 'A little while back two soldiers got lost out there. Their compasses were no good because of the magnetic fields around the volcanoes which have a lot of iron and many other minerals in them. By the time they were found two days later, their corpses were all dried up – shrivelled like prunes.'

A little more adjustment to the spokes of the front wheel rounds it up so that when the spring of the brake is bent out, and the blocks set as wide apart as they will go, the rim is just gripped when the brake lever is fully on. When I've checked bits and pieces, tightened the nuts and bolts that have worked loose, and oiled the chain, I spray the whole bike with WD40. Every piece of metal in Uyuni is covered in rust.

The roads out of town don't so much end as peter out into sand and salt. I follow the railway west onto the flat white expanse that disappears into a horizon that is already just a glassy mirage, though the sun is barely up and directly behind.

A little way from town there is a side track, packed end to end with old steam engines and boxcars long abandoned, stripped of anything that might be of use, just skeletons of rust which crumble to the touch.

The hills near Uyuni float above the ground, and the conical peaks of distant volcanoes that rise twenty thousand feet into the air are simply hanging in the sky.

The ground in places has a hard thin crust which gives way to soft white powder. Elsewhere the salt has formed huge hexagons with lips at their edges, that pattern the plain as if covered with giant white lily pads. Mostly the ground is smooth and unbroken and dazzlingly white. The salt-laden air smells like the sea. It makes my eyes water and my nose run like a tap.

The railway crosses a stream – the Salt River – flowing slowly, thick and sticky with dissolved salt.

The white plain goes on and on immeasurably. How far ahead is that volcano? It looks so close but it gets no nearer.

The effects of sensory deprivation become apparent after a few hours. The brain is accustomed to receiving a constant barrage of ever-changing stimuli from the world around it. The lack of input from the white plain gives it nothing to think about, nothing to process. But habit dies hard and it must do something, so it seizes upon the tiniest of things, anything, and applies its full whack of attention to it. The smallest event becomes fascinating, full of details and aspects normally unnoticed because swamped by a multitude of other distracting signals.

The metallic creak of the steel railway lines expanding in the heat booms out like a gong across the plain, full of chords and harmonics that echo around my head long after the sound must have dissipated.

A stone rolling down the small embankment becomes a landslide, a rockfall. I watch it tumble as if in slow motion, knocking and clonking against other stones that produce their own individual sounds.

The wind gives life to a dead llama – a pile of bleached bones and wafting hair – playing tunes through its fleece, rattling and whistling around its bones, it sounds like an orchestra.

The things that originate in my own head are also subject to this magnification and elaboration. I follow a train of thoughts with such complete absorption that I forget about where I am. I am wherever I think about, people become alive in front of my eyes, speak without me being aware of putting words in their mouths. I have conversations with friends, their voices and images so real that sometimes I answer aloud and look around to see where they've gone, and suddenly find myself back on the salt pan, and I sit down to recover from the illusion by drinking some water, or checking something on the bike, even though I know nothing needs checking, or take something out of the panniers and set it down on the plain just to look at something familiar, because even my hands don't normally look like this I'm sure – all craggy and vibrant, in so many hues of pink, pulsing with warm blood I can feel coursing through veins and arteries – gripping everyday objects that are themselves almost unrecognisable, and I wonder what I am doing, carting such intricate contraptions around through scenery that looks like the moon.

But those volcanoes really are too much, floating and glowing so high in a bright blue sky, frozen tops shining like beacons over a landscape devoid of all life that is simply, awesomely beautiful. Overwhelmingly beautiful and devastatingly empty. I feel I have entered a realm of magic, and at times become so enchanted that I stop and take off my clothes, and stroll around completely overawed.

It comes and goes in waves. During periods of relative sanity I tell myself to put my shorts on, and get on the bike dammit, and not to worry about it – enchantment is a perfectly natural condition.

A line of hills and lava flows lie across the plain and come down to meet the track up ahead. There are sand dunes here too, red and brown and yellow, and among them a cluster of huts.

No people are about. A rusty metal pump stands in the centre of the huts. I pump it for water but it doesn't work. A small girl comes out of one of the huts.

'It doesn't work', she says.

'Is there no water?' I ask. She lifts a piece of rusty tin nearby that covers a well. Several other men and women come out of the huts and stand around looking at me. We smile and say hello.

'Where are you going?' inquires one man.

'To Chile', I reply, pointing west along the railway track.

'Ah Chile', he says, nodding. 'On the bicycle?'

'Yes. On the bicycle.'

This conversation over, there doesn't seem to be anything more to say so we stand around just grinning at each other. How can they possibly live out here?

'We stay here when there is work on the railway', the man says, as if reading my mind, or an expression that has flicked across my face.

'May I take some water from your well?' I ask.

'Of course. Take all you want.'

There is an old rusty bucket with a rope attached, lying next to the well. There are holes in the bottom. The bottom of the well cannot be seen. I guess it's forty feet before the bucket comes to rest.

'The well is deep', I say.

'It hasn't rained for many years', says the man.

By the time I've hauled up the bucket all the water has drained out of the holes in the bottom. I turn the bucket over in exaggerated examination.

'There are holes in the bucket', I conclude. Everybody is grinning. The man sends a young boy off to one of the huts, He returns with a bright red plastic bucket and hands it to me ceremoniously.

'Thank you', I say, bowing slightly, happy to be a part of this play. I examine it closely, tap the solid bottom.

'It's a good bucket. There are no holes.' Everybody is still grinning.

'It's the visitors' bucket!' explains the man. Everybody laughs.

I pull up a full bucket. The water tastes of salt but it's drinkable.

'Why do you cross the Salar like this?' the man asks as I mount the bike to leave.

'I go to Chile. The Salar is here so I cross it.' It sounds banal but he nods understandingly.

'Why do you go to Chile?' he asks. I reply using the Spanish verb *'conocer'* – to see, to know, to acquaint oneself with.

'Good', he says.

We all shake hands and then I go and we disappear into each other's mirage.

A set of tyre tracks cross the railway, and then run roughly parallel alongside. I follow these to make a change. They run more or less in a straight line, but angle away slightly from the railway track until both the low embankment and the crooked telegraph poles are out of sight.

'To acquaint oneself with.' Yes, that is as accurate a description of travelling for its own sake as my knowledge of Spanish will translate. And yet here it is not quite apt. Here something is different. Here I am aware of a need to get from one place to another. Normally I am not conscious of this because normally there is no need. I no longer travel for the purpose of getting to a particular place. It is enough just to be on the road. Living and sleeping and eating by the roadside now feels like being home. And it's not just my home. Just as after so long sitting on a saddle, the bike has come to feel like an extension of me, so by the same principle, the road has come to be an extension of the bike with which it is in constant contact. All one. And the road stretches out for as far as the eye can see and beyond, across the country, across the continent, from the past to the future, the world is linked by its network, the bloodstream of a huge living organism. As long as I am in contact with it I am in contact with all of humanity and it doesn't matter how far I travel in a day, or really even where, because there is nowhere to go but the road. It's the road to nowhere, one place is as good as another, every bit is different, every bit is unique, every bit is a part of the same thing. I have no need to get anywhere because I am always here.

But this place is off limits, here it feels different because I have never seen such extreme conditions of desolation. Nothing lives here because nothing can, and though it is a place of eerie unearthly beauty, of enchantment, a place to indulge in hallucination, to experience seeing what one is because there is nothing else to see, and to eavesdrop on the gods and demons that live in the imagination because there is nothing else to hear, it is a place primarily to be passed through on the way to somewhere else. The inhospitality is not hostile but it is utterly indifferent. It is no good just being here, it is not home, and certainly no place to sit around in idle speculation, concocting cosy and rhetorical definitions of one's place in the universe. But it is still very simple: here I am and there I must go.

As if to mock such easy simplicity, the tyre tracks stop. They simply end. Ahead is a perfectly white unmarked plain. It shines.

The sun is overhead. This doesn't mean that it is noon because it appears to be overhead all day long except at sunrise and sunset, and gives no clue as to the direction it might be taking across the sky, or which way might be west. This doesn't matter though because a volcano of distinctive shape and colour that has been hanging up in the sky ahead like a triangular heavenly body serves as a signpost, and as dusk approaches, as the mirages retreat to no more than a line on the horizon and distant mountains once more become visible, and the peaks of volcanoes come down at last to rest for the night on the earth after another day floating in the sky, the line of telegraph posts and the railway track come into view and I feel in touch with humanity again.

In touch with humanity but cold. Seriously cold. The water bottles freeze before the sun dips, cold and still white, below the horizon. The plain continues to glow faintly under the bombardment of starlight from out of a crystal clear night sky.

I wake with a pain in the tip of my nose where it pokes out of the sleeping bag into the chill wind. No cosy minus ten degrees this. Exposed skin can freeze at minus twenty three degrees centigrade, the Oruro meteorologist told me. I bring my nose inside awhile to warm up. Why don't I have a tent? The condensation on the inside of my sleeping bag turns to ice which crackles and flakes and tinkles over my face when I move.

It's my own fault that I feel so cold. I made a bad mistake of half leaving the sleeping bag to take a piss, when I should have used an empty water bottle inside. I never warmed up again. Idiot! I can't get back to sleep because it's so cold. My feet are numb, my teeth are chattering and I shiver uncontrollably. After a while I stop shivering. The Oruro meteorologist would no doubt explain what a bad sign this is. 'Come on sun' is my only thought. It loiters up over the horizon after an age, and I lie thawing out in a suddenly bright world, stagger around physically uncoordinated, mentally dulled, confidently doing stupid things like sticking the flesh of my hand to the cold metal bike frame by picking it up without any gloves on.

By mid-morning it is hot and I'm in cap and shorts, though lumps of ice are knocking and sloshing coolly in the five litre water bottle.

I stop to take a photo of a group of squat domes near the railway camp of Julaca, painted in army camouflage patterns of grey and green, which seems ludicrous on a white plain. A soldier appears beside one, waving his arms at me. I wave back. He comes running over.

'This way, this way', he says excitedly, pointing at the domes. I point towards the buildings of Julaca further along the track.

'No this way. I go this way.'

'No please, this way. To check your documents.'

A dozen soldiers are posted here. In Julaca itself are a couple of hundred people – railway workers and their families, many of whom live in disused railway carriages.

Water is piped in from Uyuni. Six foot icicles still hang from the large pump that waters the trains.

Beyond Julaca lava flows reach down from the slopes of volcanoes in big folded sheets and knobbly mounds of black rock. There are small cones of grey and black volcanic ash a few hundred feet high.

Mineral deposits colour the sides of volcanoes, in patches and stripes, and bands of red, yellow, orange and brown. The air is acrid with the smell of sulphur.

Volcano Ollague stands ahead, a dark brown cone streaked with ice, intermittently puffing out smoke and steam that drifts away, twenty thousand feet high.

There is less salt here, and deep sand. The lower slopes of mountains and volcanoes join to enclose the salt pan. It also marks the boundary between Bolivia and Chile.

The few buildings of the border post of Ollague are visible a few miles ahead. A small rusty sign that reads 'Policia' with an arrow pointing towards a hut set back off the railway track suggests that passers-by should pop in.

'Hello', I say to the policeman sitting behind a desk inside the hut, making him jump out of his chair in surprise.

'Good afternoon', he says composing himself, straightening his tunic. 'Where are you going?'

'To Chile.'

'And from where have you come?'

'From Uyuni.'

He steps outside, regards the bicycle, looks up and down the railway line and comes back inside.

'Passport', he says, and opens a large book to write down the details.

'You have no exit stamp', he observes.

'I'll get one in Ollague', I assure him.

'You cannot leave the country without an exit stamp.'

'I don't intend to. I'll get it in Ollague.'

'You cannot go to Ollague without an exit stamp. This is a military zone. Ollague is in Chile.'

This last piece of information throws a new light on things. I dig out the Ministry of Transport road service anniversary edition map of Bolivia.

'Look', I say, pointing, 'Ollague is at least ten kilometres inside Bolivia.'

He shows me his large scale military map of the region stuck on the wall that shows Ollague as being in Chile. We compare them awhile.

In its enthusiasm to produce a memorable and pleasing edition, the national road service has put patriotic optimism before cartographic accuracy. I'm pretty pissed off about it.

'Well I'm going to Chile anyway', I say to the policeman. He checks the Interpol poster on the wall next to the military map, with photos of international terrorists and other wanted persons and lists underneath of their pseudonyms, and finding that I'm not on it, and perhaps suspecting that I'm a bit crazy to ride out here anyway, he becomes more sympathetic.

'Do what you want', he says, 'There is nothing I can do about it, but now that your particulars are noted in the exit book as having passed, if you leave the country without an exit visa you will automatically be registered as an 'escapado' and if you try to re-enter the country you will be imprisoned.'

This seems a little harsh. It's probably untrue. If it is true it could be a problem. If I cannot get a visa for Argentina which seems likely,

I may want to return from Chile by way of Bolivia some time in the future. Perhaps by this very hut. For the sake of a couple of days it is not worth having it prey on my mind. If I leave now I can be back in Uyuni by tomorrow evening. And I must admit, having crossed the salt pan once, its vastness is not such a fearsome unknown thing, and the prospect of immersing myself in its strangeness again is attractive.

'Where are you going?' calls the policeman as I leave.

'To Chile', I reply, though I'm not, and he goes back into his hut to report the *escapado*, or *desperado*, or do whatever it is he does all day out here.

A set of tyre tracks lead away from the hut, and as the last few miles alongside the railway were deep sand I follow these. They wind around the low hills and convoluted lava formations away from the railway, and then swoop down onto the plain. For several hours huge boulders dot the land, white of course, eroded into strange smooth shapes. I camp in the shelter of one twenty foot monolith. The wind plays tunes through its holes. Shelter from the wind and a water bottle in which to piss is comfort here indeed.

My nose has been running constantly for two days and occasionally bleeding. My eyes have been streaming and sore but I have paid them little attention. When I open them in the morning they hurt, like when waking in the middle of the night to a bright light, and I have to close them again. But it doesn't get better. After ten minutes, blinking and squinting, the stinging pain is no less. I pull my black woolly hat down over my face, and looking through this I can keep my eyes open for several seconds at a time before the pain makes me close them. It's enough to pack up the bike by.

I guess this is the result of the constant bright glare, like snow blindness that sometimes affects climbers and skiers. The nerve endings in the eyes get burnt out and need a few days of darkness to recover.

I ride as best I can, opening my eyes every few seconds. The white tyre tracks over the white plain are not easily distinguishable at the best of times and prove almost impossible to follow with just occasional glimpses. I keep hitting bumps, losing my balance, and falling off. I walk.

The tyre tracks I assume will lead to the army camp I passed through yesterday. With the distance I covered coming back yesterday I figure I'm midway between there and the border, about twenty miles. I think it's going to be a long day.

My eyes are burning now even when they're closed. It feels like they're full of hot needles. The act of opening and closing them is so painful that I cry out loud every time I do so. Mostly I keep them closed and try to feel the way. Inevitably, I open my eyes to find the road gone. Perhaps it just ended. More likely I wandered off, but it's no longer there.

I stop, and with a few minutes rest between glimpses make a methodical 360 degree scan of the surroundings. No sign of a road, or the railway, just blinding whiteness, a blur.

It's O.K., keep calm.

Somewhere out there is a town, but the chance of finding such a small dot on a vast and otherwise deserted plain where I could walk for days in a straight line and not come across anything or anybody, are clearly slim. Especially as I can't see where I am going. I might pass within a mile and not know it was there even if I could see because it could be lost in a mirage.

Keep calm.

Obviously the thing to do is find the railway. I can hardly stumble across that without realising it, and it should be solid enough to follow without actually having to look at it.

So where is it?

The tyre tracks may have brought me a long way from it but I know that it runs somewhere south of here. I can take a course by the sun because it's just a few hours up. I know where the sun is because when I face it, even through closed eyes and a woolly hat it is particularly painful.

The ground becomes difficult. The crust gives way beneath my feet, beneath the bike wheels I sink into deep powder. I stop often to rest, to sip water, to occasionally take a peek for any sign of the railway in the dark blur that is all I can see of the world now. The vision worsens noticeably every time I open my eyes and the pain is intense. I guess they have only a limited number of glimpses left in them so I open them one at a time to make them last, covering the particular eye I am going to use with cupped hands and then opening just a crack between fingers to reduce the glare.

Following the course I thought to be south, judging by the sun, turns out to be unreliable. I find myself travelling up a slope towards the blur of a mountain that was earlier 180 degrees in the opposite direction. The railway certainly never passed so close to a mountain.

The sun is no good as a guide. I am wandering round in circles. What was all white is now all black, the wonder and magic has become a nightmare of pain and darkness of such complete contrast that I wonder if I am really in some outrageous dream from which I must soon awake, though I know really it's no dream, and that considering that it might be is a distraction from having to acknowledge the seriousness of the situation, to keep at bay a mounting feeling of hopelessness. I can't pretend any longer, and lean on the bike, take stock of the situation.

I'm hot, I'm exhausted, I'm thirsty. I have enough water for a day. I'm lost in the middle of a vast salt pan in the middle of a desert and I'm going blind. There is a pause now in the flow of thoughts. There is a logical progression which I am blocking out, some thought that I have been holding back all morning is gaining momentum and I don't want to know what it is. But here it comes now, irrepressible, thundering into my brain like an express train it smashes through every defence and it says 'There is no way out, you're going to die.'

My heart pounds and adrenalin rushes around my body, demanding that I do something, which makes everything worse because there is nothing I can think of to do. I am overcome with panic and fear, and have to lie down and take deep breaths to stop myself from fainting.

The voice is shouting from outside now, 'You're going to die.'

'It doesn't help to panic', I tell myself logically, reasonably, feebly, but it has no effect on the shouting going on outside my head, or the turmoil that has consumed the inside as well now, born of fear that knows no reason.

I escape into irrationality. I wish time would go backward, I promise to give everything I have to the soldier who appears with a truck, I'll believe forever in the first god who appears to return my sight. I'll make any deal for my salvation.

Pretending does no good so I rant and rave and submit to fear, what the hell does it matter? I curse myself, I curse my eyes, I shout 'I will not die,' at the top of my voice at the sun and the salt and the plain I cannot see, at the blackness that is pressing in and mostly at myself for getting into this situation.

It does no good either, only now I am hoarse.

Perhaps the railway is just over there and I've missed it. I work round in a circle but there's only a blur, no indication of the existence of man. Anything would be welcome.

I will die out here and no one will ever find me. No one will even know that I'm dead.

And here is pride with a parting shot. 'I'm off', it says. 'You're a complete asshole. To wander out here because you had to, or because you didn't know what it would be like, O.K. But to come out here into such desolation of your own volition, for your own amusement and then to die, is the height of folly. You deserve all you get.'

I try crying to relieve my despair, but it stings so bad I pretty soon stop. Good grief how ridiculous! What can you do when you can't even curl up in a ball and cry your eyes out? I have to laugh - heartily, cruelly.

I'm running out of emotions. None of them help. Everything is draining away.

Things are becoming calm. There is nothing left to get excited about. The complete absence of life makes death not such a big step. And anyway, wouldn't I gladly discard this exhausted carcass of a body?

I really am an idiot though. Not to come out here, but to waste my life fearing death when I don't even know what it is. Except that it happens to everything.

I can think clearly now. There is no clutter. I am still free to act as I see fit, and I will not die a nervous wreck.

I could wait until sunset and take advantage of the couple of hours when I could be sure of direction. Likewise at sunrise, but that might take several days to reach the railway and I have enough water for one, maybe two.

There is a light breeze, and though wind is variable on this part of the Altiplano, in one day it tends to blow in the same direction. Early this morning it was coming from the west and I've noticed no lull that usually proceeds a change. That's it then. All I can do.

I concentrate on walking in a straight line, keeping the breeze on the right hand side of my face, filling my lungs with air, resting, waiting, sometimes taking a peep even though it makes me shout and I can't see anything anyway, it doesn't matter because everything is now so clear and calm. Life is good one step at a time, from heartbeat to heartbeat. Even if you're going round in circles in the dark. No regrets. No fears.

I'm so pleased with this peace of mind after the emotional outpouring earlier that I even entertain thoughts of actually getting out of here, though I'm careful not to betray any outward expression of hope lest the desolation neutralise such presumption with some new twist of fate. I might break a leg. No, don't even think about it! Concentrate on the breeze, on walking in a straight line, stick to reality, a breath, a step, a second, a lifetime.

There's something new in the dark blur outside. It's a big black blob. 'It's a house! It's a train!' babbles a voice which I ignore. It turns out to be a large pile of railway sleepers stacked up beside the railway track. I lie down in its shade and fall asleep. I'm so tired, I just want to go on sleeping, but I make myself clamber up the embankment. Which way now? I turn my back on the wind because I haven't got the strength to walk against it.

Back between the lines, back in the mainstream, I can indulge again in hopes and fears and speculation. Here comes pride, well what a surprise! Back from exile with all its entourage of knowledge and vanity, its preoccupations and delusions, and I have to laugh out loud at the things it comes out with. Yes, everybody climbs back on board and recounts their own particular version of events, and vents their disgruntlement at being temporarily banished, they conjecture and propose and interpret and disagree, but I pay them no mind because I'm happy just to put one foot in front of the other and feel the bike bump over the sleepers down the middle of the track.

Clink, clink. Metal struck on metal. Voices of men working on the line up ahead. There are other sounds as well, I guess it's Julaca.

'Hey amigo, where are you going with your hat over your face?'

'I'm going to the village to rest in the shade. I can't see.'

'Ah, you are blind. It is the salt', the voice says matter of factly, apparently unsurprised and unmoved by my appearance and condition.

'Is it far to the village?' I ask.

'No it's right here.'

A little further along I hear children's voices and the heavy footsteps of somebody running towards me.

'Where are you going?' a soldier's voice, I guess by the tone.

'Is there somewhere I can rest in the shade. I've come across the Salar and I can't see.'

'Oh man', says the soldier, 'this way', and he helps me down the embankment. I feel suddenly weak and can hardly stand up.

Another soldier comes over, wants to see my passport, wants to know what I'm doing in a military zone. I pull out my passport, clumsily disgorging other things from the pannier – clothes, the saucepan, other objects that roll and clank away in the wind. Children who have gathered chase them across the dirt, bring them back, laughing.

'Here you are mister.' They thrust things into my hands and I try to put them back but more things just tumble out. They see that I cannot manage and take over.

'He's a poor blind gringo', they say, stuffing things back on the bike wherever they can. 'In here. No, in here', they shout. It's a good game.

Meanwhile the second soldier is flipping through the pages of my passport. I imagine him looking at the photograph, trying to compare it with what he can see of my face that isn't covered by my hat - a nose that pours snot over cracked lips and a dirty unshaven chin.

'There is a goods train going to Uyuni later tonight', the first soldier tells me, and he leads me over to sit against a wall, fetches a glass of water and tells the children to leave me alone, though I'm hardly aware of what is going on because I'm so overcome with weariness and gratitude, and tears of relief flood down my face.

The soldier helps me into an empty box car of the goods train and the driver helps me out when we arrive at Uyuni in the middle of the night. He leads me to the station building where I find a space on the floor amid the sleeping bodies waiting for the passenger train that leaves early in the morning.

I wait until everybody has gathered their belongings and boarded the train so as not to tread on anyone, and shuffle out of the station building over towards the sound of a primus stove and the quiet chatter of people taking breakfast. The conversation stops as I draw near.

'Good morning gringito. Coffee?' asks a woman's voice.

'Yes please', I say sitting down on the ground, wishing a general good morning in the direction I imagine other people are sitting.

'What's the matter with your face?' asks a man. 'Why don't you sit on a stool?'

'I've come across the Salar and I can't see.'

There follows talk of the effects of the bright glare and tales are told of people who have become lost on the salt pan and gone crazy. The woman thrusts bread rolls into my hands.

'Take, take', she says.

I ask if there is a doctor in town, and one of the men jumps up and leads me by the arm down the street, giving a running commentary of what is going on.

'We're going to the clinic', he says. 'There is the doctor now, standing outside.' I thank him but he's already gone. I explain my problem to the doctor and he takes me inside the clinic, looks at my eyes, washes them out and squirts various solutions into them, tut-tutting professionally all the while. He sticks on a couple of patches secured with a bandage, and with the help of a nurse leads me to a bed.

'Stay here awhile', he says, then adds, 'Have you had breakfast?' I say yes thank you but the nurse comes back in a few minutes with a cup of tea and a saucer of biscuits.

She comes back later with some lunch, and seeing the biscuits scattered over the floor, stays and spoon feeds me a bowl of soup and a plate of rice and meat.

The doctor comes by from time to time to look at my eyes, humming and hawing reassuringly, he squirts more solutions in them and covers them over again.

It's early evening when he removes the patches for the last time, and says I'll be all right now if I stay out of bright lights and don't go wandering out across the Salar again.

The clinic is just a few rooms. I poke my head into each one on the way out, thanking everybody I see, which is just three nurses, for all their kind attention, and apologising for having wasted their time and not knowing really how to express the gratitude I feel. They wave aside my thanks. 'It's nothing, it's our job', and wish me well and show me where they've parked the bike.

Outside it is a real treat just to look at things, shapes, colours. I go to the hotel and find the manager standing outside. He's surprised to see me and enjoys hearing my tale.

'I told you so', he says. 'You'd better stay here and wait for the train now', he advises again, and I agree it's a good idea.

It's three days until the next train leaves and I soon get to know all the wide dusty windswept streets with no traffic, and stock up with a few things, like alcohol for the stove.

'It's not for cooking, it's for drinking', the old white haired lady tells me as she syphons a bottleful out of a big drum, but it burns better than meths. In the afternoons I sit in the shade and eat ice cream. The schoolchildren get to know that I can help them with their English homework.

The local government workers are still on hunger strike. On the tenth day one of them is lowered down from the first floor window on a stretcher, to the applause of a crowd of onlookers, and driven away in a Ministry of Health jeep. It's the only vehicle I ever see move in Uyuni.

13. Out of sight, out of mind, almost out of tea

The train to the border stops at the watering points, at Julaca where the locals sell hot food through the windows. It stops in the middle of nowhere, and sometimes goes backwards inexplicably for a short distance. It stops at the police hut at the border where everybody is obliged to weigh their baggage. The train is full of people – mostly Chileans returning from La Paz. The baggage consists largely of boxes of biscuits.

'Things are so cheap in Bolivia at the moment that it is worth the train fare to load up with biscuits to take back to Chile to sell', one Chilean tells me.

The baggage scales are not designed for weighing bicycles, which need to be supported by hand. I manage to reduce the weight and thereby the fare, but it still weighs forty kilos.

I leave the train and the baggage weighing queue and ride the five miles along the track to Ollague. The international border is marked with a piece of rusty tin set on a pole lying at an angle by the track, with Bolivia scratched on one side and Chile on the other.

Ollague is a tiny border town sitting among railway yards. The arrival of the passenger train is a major event and all of Ollague's tiny population comes out to watch, as passengers line up on the flat sand outside the concrete customs building amid a colourful spread of belongings – mostly boxes of biscuits – waiting to be cleared by the customs and immigration officers who travel up to the border from Antofagasta twice a week to meet the train. Volcano Ollague towers icily above, massive, impassive, puffing out white clouds into the sky.

Not being with the train, and in possession of a bicycle, I am required to fill out a vehicle entry form and sign the vehicle registration book – a large and ancient leather bound volume bearing no more than a dozen entries in its recently recorded history. Half of these are cyclists who have come through in the last month. Rudi passed by three weeks ago, Leo and Michel last week, and Don just a few days ago. Gérard is on his own on a previous page.

The train toots off out of sight leaving Ollague to its quiet isolation. The next town is marked on my map as being over a hundred miles away, but there is somewhere to get water before then I am told by the people in the little cafe. They wonder at the recent abundance of cyclists – 'Is there a race on?'.

The sandy track out of Ollague winds around the base of the volcano, through hills of folded lava, rounded cones of black ash and over dunes of white sand.

Occasional signs warn of the dangers of straying. 'Mines', one reads simply beneath a skull and crossbones. 'Don't leave the international highway. Guard your life', advises another, rather grandly. 'Minefields marked by yellow rocks', another sign reads helpfully, though the ground is littered with bright yellow sulphur bearing rocks anyway so it is difficult to distinguish those placed as warnings from those occurring naturally.

The sky is a hard clear blue. There are no clouds or birds, or plants or animals, no sound except for the distant whistle of wind playing around a volcano and the soft scrunch of bicycle tyres through sand, no movement except that of the ground itself, shimmering in rising waves of hot air.

It is impossible to gauge scale or distance. The road disappears up over a ridge of black rock that descends the side of volcano Ollague. It seems just a few miles away, but when darkness falls it's no nearer. Fine black ash and sand cover the steep slopes on either side and there is little choice but to sleep on the road itself. I build a couple of piles of the bright yellow rocks in the customary precautionary manner, but nothing passes in the night. It's a quiet little international highway.

There is something pleasing in the energy-saving aspect of waking on the road itself. From the pass, the slopes of smooth black sand strewn with bright yellow boulders fall away down to the flat white salt basins. All around are volcanoes, dark brown and red, and streaked with ice, some puffing smoke, all dotted with side cones and steam vents surrounded by the spew of sulphur and ash. The air is bitter with invisible gases.

The road traces a line across another salt pan – the Salar de Ascotan – and up into the volcanoes on the far side. The water in the lake in the middle of the salt pan is bright red and surrounded by a patchwork of other vivid colours – red, orange and green – tints produced by salt water algae. The bright white salt of the surrounding plain is criss-crossed with coloured lines, wavy and straight, that mark the courses of salt streams that drain into the basin, water from hot springs that bubble and steam and deposit minerals in all the colours of the rainbow.

What strange planet is this that rumbles and gurgles and smokes, and glows with coloured patterns in a wasteland of black and white?

And what's this now? Tall thin shapes moving slowly on long legs, dark against the mirage behind. Flamingos. Bright pink flamingos are wading leisurely through the shallows. This is too much. I have to stop and find a place to sit between the coloured lines on the hot ground in the freezing air, brew a pot of tea and voice my surprise at the unexpected pleasure of resting in the company of fellow lifeforms. It's Earth after all and it's good to be here even if what I am seeing is so unlikely that I fear it will disappear if I blink my eyes, even if the wind is so cold that the little alcohol burner, which is really no more than a small tin can with a hole in the top, can do no more than take the chill off the pot.

A collection of railway huts, deserted except for two big dogs, sit at the edge of the salt basin where the road and railway run briefly alongside before taking their own course again up through more mountains and volcanoes.

There's a standpipe outside one of the huts. I fill up with water with one hand while fending off the advances of the dogs with a chain in the other.

These mountains are enormous. The road rises between two volcanoes to a pass that divides the salt pans and plateaux of the High Andes from the Atacama desert. Beyond, chains of mountain ridges and volcanoes creep like giant fingers west towards the Pacific Ocean two hundred miles away, sandy plains and mountains that extend both north and south for a thousand miles. It is said to be the driest place on earth.

The pass is fifteen thousand feet high and it bristles with minefields. I lob a few rocks around that I might make some noisy impression on surroundings of such immense and imperturbable grandeur, but they thud dully and my passage goes unnoticed. No matter. It is in the contrast of an insignificant tiny sac of blood and bones with a vast and splendid desolation that the beauty lies. The enormity of the whole is hidden from eyes that look at it as separate.

I've gone over the top so from here it ought to be mostly downhill. The volcanoes are adorned here with different coloured mineral deposits – purple, orange and yellow, in streaks and patches of startling intensity around small side vents.

Over the hard sandy ridges in the middle of the road the bike bounces up and down. At the sides in deep soft sand it slides to a halt. The smoothest and fastest ride is to be had where sand fills the grooves between ridges but not so deeply that the wheels sink in and slide. By concentrating on gauging this fine line it is possible where the road descends steeply, to cover a mile or two at speed, though eventually concentration lapses and the bike veers and skis off the road, or a stretch of deep sand is too long to plough through, and I fall off in a heap. But it's only soft sand so I speed down anyway.

There is evidence of bicycles and riders before me doing exactly the same thing. Wheel tracks follow the line between ridge and sand, and then there are skid marks and the impression of a crumpled body. Sometimes I see these and laugh so much that I fall off too.

There are footprints too in the stretches of deep sand where a bike has been pushed. Sometimes the footprints leave the road and walk around a little way, or wander over to a rock and stop, and these traces provide me with company and the feeling that I am travelling with friends. The distancing effects of time and space are elastic. The arbitrarily finite measurements with which we calibrate infinity seem inapplicable here and impossible to sustain without a huge amount of faith, because everything appears so vast and endless. The picture dissolves because it is unnecessary. Or rather, it retreats from the outside world back into the imagination.

The echoes of Leo and Michel are here, and Rudi, and Don who I've never met, and I wonder how they're doing and if they find the desert as enchanting as I do. They are alongside, in their own time, and we chat, and make up little stories. Strange how it goes – never short of company, riding alone through the desert.

The weird unearthly landscape of high volcanoes and salt gives way to more conventional desert as the valley opens out to join a wide gently sloping plain. The mountains here are of gentler, more credible appearance, smoother, rounder, in softer pastel shades of brown and buff and pink and grey.

Small side tracks come out of nowhere, forming crossroads, and more misleading Y junctions, and disappear back into nowhere. They leave me wondering if I'm following the right track because my head is addled with the heat and altitude, and I can't remember exactly how many days ago I left Ollague, though it can surely be only one or two.

Still no sign of life. No vehicles. Not much of anything really, to speak of, but I say a few words aloud anyway, for the novelty of hearing a voice, to maintain a little order and control on a world that is acquiring an unfamiliar presence and immediacy. This is how we control the world, render it familiar. 'Sand', 'Sky', 'Future', I try them out, repeat them.

A roadsign up ahead intrudes upon my thoughts. A short pole with a metal plate wired on. It reads 'Zona Archeologica' and an arrow points along a sandy track to some buildings in the distance. Perhaps there is water there, and people too. I ting a few stones at the metal sign to reassure myself that it's really there. Yes, let's try and be sensible or we'll get lost or go crazy. It's a real pole all right.

The buildings of the archaeological site are mobile cabins plonked down in a group. A little way off is a deep ravine. A track leads steeply down to the bottom. There are watered flower beds around the cabins, where the fragrance and bright colours, and the buzzing of insects and the greenness is overwhelming. I sit awhile, listening and smelling. Juicy moist flowers, succulent water plump geraniums, poppies, carnations. I follow a hose to an outside tap and fill my bottles. Where are the archaeologists? Down the ravine probably, but I haven't spare energy to investigate.

It is hard to break away from the spell of the greenery, the insects, the casually coiled self-assurance of an idle water hose, and to re-enter the heat and the glare and the endless sand. But the bike feels reassuringly heavy with a gallon and a half of water, and it can't be too far now to a town. And there's food enough for another couple of days. Rice flour mostly – not particularly exciting fare, but nutritious enough, and compact. You can pack a lot into a pannier, it goes a long way, and with a little water and a little fuel it is quick to cook into a gruel. Additional vitamins and variety are provided by garlic and lemons, also compact, slow to dehydrate. Rice flour with lemon and salt for breakfast, rice flour with garlic and salt for supper. Washed down with a cup of tea that also serves to clean the pot, every meal is a feast. Be nice to have some more tea though. I'm down to recycling the last tea bag – carefully sucking out residual moisture after each brew and replacing it in its own polythene bag. It has seen better days, and though it no longer imparts much taste or colour, its ritual addition to the pot is comforting and provides some entertainment. Sometimes I catch myself lifting up the pot lid and chuckling at its limp form, bubbling pathetically, redundant. Desert theatre is essential and austere.

The headwind is strong and laden with abrasive sand that gets up the nose, into the ears, down the throat, but despite the irritation and battling the wind, the bumps, the getting off to walk through deep sand and the falling off, trains of thoughts flow by uninterrupted. Long forgotten memories of events long past come back complete, though I'm not aware of delving down to uncover them. Well well! Yes what a surprise, I remember that, ha ha ha! Half remembered snatches of pieces of classical music are reproduced from start to finish, played by a full orchestra. These are games, distractions. Other memories, forgotten not through irrelevance but through design, because unpleasant, come bubbling harmlessly to the fore. Painful embarrassing memories, taboo subjects, hang ups, blocked out as protection from that part of ourselves which does not conform to our cosy self image, as a defence against a world which betrays our trust, mocks the vanity of our intellect, wounds our pride, breaks our hearts.

It's time to stop. The first stars are faintly twinkling, the wind has dropped and the air is cool again. I roll out my sleeping bag, and stomp around a little on the ground beneath my feet, to assure myself of the solidity that was there all the time.

The first few hours of the day is the time to make progress, when the air is still cool and the wind blows gently from the east. By mid-morning it comes from the opposite direction and blows hard for the rest of the day, and then there is no point in struggling to move at much more than walking pace because after half an hour heat exhaustion will occur. By midday the air throbs and everything is moving in wavy lines of heat.

The road meets the railway line again, and where they cross sits a station building, waving and shimmering under a bombardment of sunshine, wind, and blown sand, appearing and disappearing at first, then closer up, remaining in view, just trembling slightly. I'm trembling slightly too. The walls are rough like sandpaper. There is no one here. I ride on.

It rides on. The body is a machine that knows what to do. It eats and it drinks and it lies down at night to rest. The brain too ticks and whirs mechanically and figures out what adjustments to make to the bicycle, and finds its own amusement, and they both seem to be doing O.K. so I might just abandon them for a while and leave them to their heat and dust and effort and intrigue, and soar off somewhere a bit cooler where there's no responsibility and where everything doesn't hum and breathe and occasionally vanish, and vibrate in sympathy with everything else. No, stay around for a little while just to make sure they're O.K., because if there is any responsibility it is to be in control of yourself and your thoughts and your actions, even though all your life you've been taught to relinquish it, because to everybody else when you are in control you are out of control, and there's nothing more frightening than freedom. But there is nobody around now to offend so it doesn't matter any more, and you might be needed after all because look, down there in the desert on that road that is two wheel ruts across the sand, there is a cycling machine that thinks it should move from the left hand rut to the right hand rut because it's always smoother and easier on the other side of the road. But it can't move over no matter how hard it tries, it just keeps right on going, and listen to it talking to itself – 'Move over you asshole' – what a scream, how ridiculous, but quietly now, don't let it know we're up here watching, let's see what else it gets up to, yes more clicking and whirring of its brain now – it knows the heat is affecting it and that's why it's having difficulty riding over the ridge of sand between the two tyre tracks that are really the same, but it has a point to prove so it's going to cross over anyway even if it has to walk dammit, but when it stops and puts its foot down, it doesn't support its weight and it topples right over.

But it's O.K. We're coming back down now.

There are no clouds still, but way in the distance just above the horizon is a layer of hazy white, not moving or getting nearer – just hanging there like it might be smoke. Perhaps it is a town. It's about time I reached a town because I'd really like to see someone, and maybe sit in the shade and cool off. It is much lower down here, the water bottles didn't freeze last night and the wind burns as if blown from a hair dryer. The desert is all becoming the same – the sky, the sun, the sand, the road – merging in the heat, just different shapes, different sizes, different arrangements of atoms, the same atoms, people, rocks, sky, all the same stuff, forming, dissolving, reforming – which is all very well, just so long as there is a town there, because all I want to do is sit in some shade and maybe talk to someone.

The road winds down the sides of a gorge and follows the course of a dry river bed. There is a tiny village where the gorge opens out and a stream appears from among boulders and is diverted through some fields pale green with young shoots.

Cactus and eucalyptus trees all covered in dust line the few sandy streets. There are several small houses, a chapel and a store. I call in at the store.

Tinned food, sweets and bottles of drink line a few wooden shelves. There are bars of soap and candles in display counters. Sacks of flour and rice sit on the floor.

'Hello', I call out, and a young man appears from out back.

'Good morning, how are you?' he says, coming over, shaking my hand warmly. His wife enters the store with two young children and we all shake hands too.

'Where do you come from?' the man asks.

'From England.'

'And how have you come?'

'On bicycle.'

'Good God you must be tired! Come and sit down.'

We sit outside in the shade of the porch and he tells me about an Americano who passed through a few days ago – 'Señor Don' – and he too was on a bicycle, but he was a little sick and maybe a little crazy from the desert.

His wife comes out with cups of coffee on a tray, and soft bread rolls and a pot of marmalade.

'Eat,' she says, and we all tuck in, and the man tells me that the village is called Chiu Chiu. 'It is the same site as the village of an ancient pre-Inca civilization, one of many dotted around – perhaps you've seen the camps of archaeologists who uncover them? Though there is not much to find anymore. The river Loa springs from the ground which is why the village can exist here.'

I nod and grunt appreciatively at the bread and marmalade that tastes so good after however many days it is of boiled rice flour and sand, and I ask where exactly Chiu Chiu is because it is not marked on my map and I've been meandering along tiny tracks down from the mountains of Bolivia so for all I know it could be anywhere, and not that it matters because I'm just pleased to be here, but it would be nice to get a little perspective because things have all become a little vague and indefinite recently. He draws a map in the sand on the floor of the porch and says it is only thirty kilometers to Calama which is a big city, so you're all right now, you can't possibly get lost, and from Calama the paved road starts and it goes to Antofagasta and all the way south to Santiago, and if you want you can stay here with us until you want to leave.

'Have you seen our museum yet?' he asks before I leave, though first I have to convince him that I'm really feeling O.K., 'It's full of things dug out of the desert from long ago.'

I pop in on the way out of town. Just a small museum – one room with three glass cases of pieces of pottery and coins, a skeleton and an enormous fossilised shoe. There are two girls here labelling exhibits and they stop work to show me around. They don't get many visitors they say, but a few days ago a giant gringo came by on a bicycle, and they show me where he slept on the floor, and giggle at the memory.

The white hazy band that has been visible in the sky for the past couple of days is man-made and comes from the chimneys of the huge copper works of Chuquicamata. The mine started production over a century ago under the direction of British engineers who also built the railway. The rich copper deposits were a surprise bonus for Chile, still pleased with the nitrate deposits newly seized from Bolivia. As the largest opencast copper mine in the world, Chuquicamata produces a proportionally enormous cloud of pollution.

Other things are in the air. Nearing Calama, paper bags and plastic squeezy bottles and bits of cloth come bowling down the road in the wind, and the towering whirlwinds of swirling dust that periodically totter and teeter in tall drunken columns across the plain now carry cardboard boxes and sheets of newspaper and other rubbish high over the desert. I try to prepare myself for the city and envisage what it will be like from what it discards, but fail and get completely zapped out.

Calama is a modern city, with tall concrete buildings and hard paved roads, sidewalks lined with shops displaying modern consumer goods – fashionable clothes, computers, refrigerators - and streets so full of shiny cars and smartly dressed people rushing around purposefully in every direction that I have to get out of the road and walk along the pavement for fear of being run down in the abstraction of colour and activity, or riding through a plate glass window. Even the litter bins that line the streets are clean and bright, and full of things people make a living selling in Bolivia, and everything bought in the shops comes with a receipt and is wrapped up in paper bags and tied up with clean white string that must later be untied and unwrapped and consigned to the litter bins that fill up so quickly it must cost a fortune just paying someone to take them out of town and empty them into the desert. It's not surprising things seem so expensive.

It's a smooth black asphalt road now, with a little traffic that whizzes by at eighty miles an hour, mostly modern long distance coaches bound for Santiago one thousand miles to the south via the cities of the coast, and big trucks hauling stuff up to Calama and the mines from Antofagasta.

Short posts with green signs give the distance to Santiago every five kilometers, and I play with the numbers and try to convert kilometers to miles and when I cannot manage the simplest of sums I know it is time to stop and lean the bike against a pole and sit in the three inch strip of shade for a while because with fast moving heavy vehicles that come suddenly out of nowhere it's important to remain in a fit state not to wander from side to side according to addlement and whim, as seems to have become a habit.

The town of Carmen Alto is a petrol station and cafe. I stop and buy a cup of tea and sit outside in the shade of a wall and eat bread and fresh fruit from Calama.

A coach pulls in for fuel and the passengers file off to stretch their legs and drink from the water hose. Some come and join me in the shade and talk, and by their freshness make me aware of being dirty and covered in dust.

The asphalt soaks up the sun, and flows in viscous waves into the sand either side that itself is too hot to sit on without first scooping away the top layer, a black strip that disappears into the distance, ever downwards to the coast, then through an avenue of giant billboards a kilometer apart that welcome visitors to Antofagasta from the national airline, Coca Cola, Toyota trucks and the tourist board with the assurance 'Antofagasta – you will always be our North', then steeply down through a high-walled canyon that opens suddenly to reveal the whole city – the shanties that back up against the cliffs, the residential suburbs and tall white high rise blocks of the city centre and cranes of the harbour – and all the way down to the Pacific Ocean beyond, blue and white and heaving and sighing, where seagulls wheel and squawk and brown pelicans surf glide the air currents in front of the waves.

The cental plaza in the middle of the maze of concrete and glass seems like a botanical garden, full of flowering trees and date palms with their trunks painted white, and glossy-leaved shrubs, all echoing to the twitters and hums of birds and insects, and stone benches set along the pathways patrolled by ice cream vendors, and a decorative pond where a fountain spurts clear water arrogantly up into the dry desert air.

There are reminders of home – pillar boxes in the same mould as those of the British Royal Mail, but blue, and on one side of the clocktower engraved with the sayings of national heroes of favourable historic events, a plaque and a Union Jack commemorate the British colonists of Antofagasta 1810–1910.

Something in the mentality of the people too is reminiscent of home – perhaps because of the culture brought over with the thousands of European settlers during Chile's more recent past – there is something familiar in the way in which people act and move and walk and talk, in the pedestrian shopping precincts dotted with payphones and newspaper stands, cold drink and doughnut stalls, lined with delicatessens and bakers and greetings card shops, and full of people – families pushing prams out for a stroll, groups of youths standing around, parading their fashion and modernity, smoking cigarettes and drinking beer from bottles – it calls out like a funfair.

'This way sir', says the teller behind the counter at the national bank, and leads me into the manager's office where the manager beams at me from behind his desk. 'How many dollars do you want to change?' he asks, pulling his own wallet from his inside jacket pocket.

I dump my junk in a pension called London where the two proprietresses sit in armchairs in the high-ceilinged lounge, embroidering and drinking tea like in an English guest house.

Outside in the streets everybody has time to stop and talk, and invite me back for tea. 'What do you hear of Chile in England?' people want to know, because they are proud of their country and concerned for its image in the world, and when I say that mostly people in England hear only of ongoing political oppression and the latest atrocity against human rights by the Pinochet regime there is usually an embarrassed silence because discussion of politics is difficult without first being sure of who you are talking to, feeling out the ground and speaking of the schools and hospitals that have been built in the last ten years, and the benefits of piped drinking water to every town, because everybody is scared and it is easier and safer not to think about politics at all in a country where trade unions and political parties are illegal and every day somebody goes missing. The students, however, are keen to talk politics, preferably in English, even though they may be too young to remember what happened in 1973, when President Allende was bombed out of office in the presidential palace by the air force, they are in the forefront of popular demand for a return to democracy and they know what it is to be scared because they are forever being beaten and tear-gassed by the army and riot police. But, they all agree, the whole country agrees, they say, everybody wants a return to democracy, it is only on the means of achieving this goal that people disagree – 'You saw how much notice was taken of your non violent protest – absolutely none – the only thing that is noticed is the bombing of police stations and the blowing up of power lines', 'Yes, but the barracks have their own power supply and the only people harmed in the end are ourselves when they come back with bigger sticks and hatred and beat us in the dark.' 'Yes, and at least there is a system at all here – look at Bolivia, you've been there gringo, you've seen – they've got ten different political parties and they've all got 'Revolutionary' somewhere in their title, they vote for who they like and they're all living in poverty and dying of malnutrition', and so it goes, everybody has a point to make, everyone is right, on into the evening when the neon lights flicker on and the music and shrieking from bars and discos rolls out into the night, into the streets, into the desert, into the floodlit stage of the central plaza where the vultures that sit by day on the ledges and gargoyles of the cathedral, glide down in lazy circles to roost in the trees, and crash land on branches barely able to support their weight, dislodging in the process half a dozen of their dozing fellows who amid much squawking and flapping of giant wings, climb back into the sky, and circle down for another landing.

4. A desert full of flowers

The road climbs back into the mountains between the grey and brown cliffs of a deep canyon, and out onto a wide sandy plain dotted with clusters of pink and orange hills.

A few clouds blow in from the west, but having crossed the cold sea current that runs up the coast of South America from the Antarctic, they shrink rapidly on contact with the hot desert, and long before they are overhead, evaporate into nothing.

The road maps from the tourist office at Antofagasta show the next water to be obtainable two hundred and sixty kilometers away at a petrol station. Bartholomew, optimistic as ever, shows a town – Rosario – a hundred kilometers on. But scarcity of water is no longer such an important factor because this is the Pan-American highway, and though it may be an hour between vehicles, there is no way you could die of thirst. Drivers toot and wave and stop to offer lifts.

There's a wayside shrine at the top of a pass, housed in a wooden shed and enclosed by a wire fence that is covered in orange licence plates left by passing vehicles. They flap and clang in the wind like prayer flags.

A couple of geraniums in flower pots sit in the shade of a small Eucalyptus tree, watered by travellers. There are also the tracks of bicycle tyres, sandalled footprints, and some curling carrot peelings just a few hours old.

Giant green roadsigns every fifty kilometers or so give distances to towns, always phenomenally large numbers – 649 kms, 921 kms, 1227 kms – as if there is nothing in between, and always to different towns from the sign before which makes it hard to work out where you are. They are best ignored. But of course they cannot be ignored because in landscape so barren they blast their way into the most absorbing of daydreams.

Another slowly growing dot on the horizon turns out to be Posada Rosario – a cafe with a huge truck park out front. Under the porch are two gringos and a bicycle. One is Rudi, the Swiss cyclist I met briefly in Lima. The other I don't recognise, but he's tall and says 'You must be Cris' in an American accent, and I know he must be Don.

Rudi got here an hour ago and has been mending a puncture. Don's bicycle is inside. He is ill. He arrived here three days ago and felt too weak to continue, indeed was forbidden to leave by the family of the cafe who insisted he stay until his health improved. He says they've been cooking him food that he has been unable to eat, fussing over him, washing his clothes – though not his T-shirt it seems – and all he is able to do is sit on the bench all day looking out at the desert. Michel and Leo joined him on his bench this morning for breakfast, and all these bicyclists whizzing by down south convince him that he is fit enough to travel again, even though he looks pretty weak and sickly still. He sets about loading up his junk.

Don is hugged and kissed farewell by the family of the cafe, and they stand on the porch waving as we leave. We must appear an untidy bunch of bicyclists – in matching dust coloured shorts, and T-shirts full of holes – but that is unavoidable. Lack of attention to appearance is essential here. Preoccupation with cleanliness when there is no water for washing, or with brushing off the layer of dust and sand that covers everything when as soon as it is gone another layer will be deposited, is a neurotic waste of energy. Energy is better spent just getting through the desert.

'Give me plenty of room,' says Don, weaving all over the road, 'I'm a bad driver,' and we all try to avoid colliding, as we pass and drop behind at our own pace, on an empty road that is suddenly crowded.

Don's bike is a Fuji like mine, though twice as big, and different pieces are held together with wire and string. I tell him about my freewheel, how it refuses to come off, and show him the spokes in the rear wheel joined midway between hub and rim with a twist of wire. Don is impressed. He has a couple of broken spokes himself, but belonging to the non interventionist school of maintenance he is not overly concerned.

When Don reached Antofagasta after the ride down from Bolivia, he was so impressed with all the things on offer that he had to buy something. He bought a dynamo and lights, and when it gets dark he is keen to try them out, and also to take advantage of the cool of night because he is finding it tough going during the heat of the day after not eating for three days.

Rudi and I stop by a smooth mound of sand that shines silver in the moonlight. Rudi left Switzerland eighteen months ago for Canada, intending to stay for a few months and find some work. Then he bought a bicycle and rode west, got into the swing of things and just kept going. Now he's heading for Buenos Aires in Argentina, and maybe Africa. He attempted to cross the border further north along one of the dirt tracks that lead out of Calama up into the high desert, but found the pass across the mountains still blocked by snow and ice, and the border police unwilling to let him pass for his own safety, even though he wrote a note taking full responsibility for his actions. So he returned to Calama – 'A ten day round trip in the heat and cold on a bumpy track.' He's weary of the desert. 'It's all the same. It only changes at dawn and dusk.' He will try to cross into Argentina again a little further south.

We catch up with Don the following morning ten miles up the road, eating from a big black saucepan.

'Hi Don, how are you feeling this morning?'

'Pretty good, pretty good', says Don, looking pretty sick still. I join him in his ditch. The air is still cool. Nothing is shimmering yet. It's a pleasant time of day.

'What have you got for breakfast, Don?'

'Oats.'

How enjoyable it is to make conversation, to speak to someone other than myself in the morning, of things close to my heart.

'Ah, oats. I like oats. Do you have them on their own?'

'No. With water and sugar. I used to eat them raw and I was going to go home. Now I cook them and I want to travel for the rest of my life.'

By midday everything is shimmering again. The road is soft and gooey, too hot to touch. I let a little air from the tyres that have become rock hard.

Agua Verde is two truckstop cafes and a petrol station. It's late afternoon and I've come a hundred miles since this morning. A hundred miles on smooth asphalt seems about right. No sooner than the bike is leant against the cafe wall a woman comes out and hands me a can of cold Pepsi Cola.

'Your two French friends were here this morning', she says. 'Are you on your own?'

'No, there are two more of my friends somewhere behind.'

Inside the cafe is a seismologist from Santiago. He calls me over to his table and orders me up a meal. He studied geology at Imperial College in London and he tells me about the history of mining industries in the Atacama, and the role played by British companies.

'All the mines are state-owned now – Britain only prospects, and holds shares in the railway that doesn't run', he says, and tells me about the deposits of minerals that he is investigating around the nearby volcanoes.

The woman of the cafe refuses to accept money from the seismologist for the supper I have eaten.

'He's my guest', she says.

Cheated out of paying for my meal, he offers to rent me a room for the night.

'They're only two hundred pesos, with clean sheets and warm blankets', he says.

I say it's free outside, with clean air and a million stars, and have to add that it's really what I prefer because he is genuinely offended that I refuse his offer.

The dawn is damp with thick fog so I doze awhile waiting for it to clear. Then there is a small earthquake, an agreeable rippling and a low rumbling growl that continues for half a minute. Too wide awake to doze, I enter the cafe for a cup of tea.

'There's just been an earthquake', I say to the woman who is bustling around in the kitchen.

'Yes, it often happens. The earth moves a lot up here. Now what do you want for breakfast?'

It's hot and dry in no time at all, but thick banks of fog remain and lie in solid walls across the road, and fill gullies as if with foam. Inside one bank of fog is a pearly rainbow, a complete circle of faintly sparkling colour.

Two figures on bicycles are rolling down the switchbacks of a long hill ahead of me. Did Don and Rudi pass by in the fog? I catch them as they are eating lunch. It's Leo and Michel. They tell me how they ran out of water crossing the salt around Uyuni, how the soldier threatened to shoot them where they crossed the border into Chile for having no exit visa. Leo recalls sharing his sleeping bag with another scorpion. I tell them how I went blind and we all have a good laugh.

Michel is sitting in a fold-up chair with his feet up on a rock, relaxing like he might be on the beach. A chair seems to be an important piece of desert equipment. Rudi has one too, and I was impressed with the way he never missed an opportunity to put it up, stretch his legs out and take a little nap.

We ride in a line against the strong wind, three abreast when it blows from the side, across wide plains of grey and orange sand where every few hours we pass a clump of yellow grass or a lone gnarled cactus, or we see a vulture high overhead to show that life goes on here, then up and up through gorges of yellow rock criss-crossed by black bands, to a high pass that looks over into a landscape of convoluted rocky mountains.

A billboard here marks the boundary between two of the twelve administrative departments that divide the country.

'*Bienvenidos a la Regeon de Atacama*' it reads in giant letters, '*Donde florece el Desierto*' – 'Where the desert flowers' – which makes us laugh because ahead is the same barren desolation as that from which we have come. The sign is colourful though.

We freewheel down the long descents and plod slowly up the hills. Bicycles are the ideal form of transport on good roads through mountainous desert – there is the constant breeze of your own momentum, and for half the time, propulsion comes courtesy of gravity. For twenty miles at a stretch you can simply sit back and watch as the desert unfolds in front and rolls right on by.

By evening we reach a high piece of flat ground where mist billows almost like cloud and the wind hums softly around smooth boulders.

The sky looks stormy and Leo and Michel bang away at pegs to hold up their tents. Leo says his tent is useless against the rain. Fine against the wind and sand and the grinding immensity of the desert, but rain goes straight through. In big blobs. He has a sheet of polythene for in-tent rainstorms. He says if it rains on him here in the Atacama desert he's going home.

There's a man thoughtfully examining the bicycle when I come out of the vegetable store in the coastal town of Chanaral.

'Nice bike', he says, peering to see what make it is.

'Ah, Zefal!' he nods to himself, 'A good one.'

I point out that he's reading the pump and that the make of the bicycle is Fuji.

'Ah, Fuji! A good one.'

He asks me where I come from and where I am going and then launches off into a monologue about what a fascinating life I must lead and how interested other people must be in what I am doing, and all the time nervously jerking his body around in awkward movements and making twitching gestures with his hands as he describes the life of the great outdoors, the fresh air and healthy living, in a never-ending stream of statements that he appears to want me to agree with, and I begin to wonder if he knows that I am here or if perhaps I have become an object for him to speak at, and I look around, but no I'm really here and there is nobody else about so it must be me he is talking to, and perhaps this is how everybody appears to talk when you've just come out of the desert, but no, the man in the vegetable shop was perfectly understandable, so it must be him, so what the hell is it he wants? I'm about to interrupt, because if this is going to go on much longer we'd better go and sit down somewhere in the shade, but he's working up to something and finally it's out.

'I work for Radio Chanaral, can you give an interview?'

'Yes, sure', I say, relieved that he has shut up, and realising almost immediately that I meant to say no, not really, because if that was an example of radio communication we may as well all just go into the desert, stick our heads in the sand and listen to the sound of blood pounding in our ears.

'Wait here, I'll be back in five minutes', he says, and hurries off down the street.

After ten minutes he has not returned, and released from the obligation of thoughtless acceptance, I leave town, more hastily than is perhaps proper from a desert oasis.

Up ahead is a bright purple band. It is made of flowers. Tiny flowers. Not tough thick stemmed desert-hard cactus but delicate, small, fragrant flowers with big bright soft petals and thin green stalks that waver in the slightest breeze.

They grow out of the sand, out of the rock, out of the cracks in boulders, out from under the asphalt at the side of the road.

Further on there are more, different colours – red, yellow, pink, white – in clumps and patches, and finally in such profusion that they cover the whole desert, the plains and the mountain ridges in sheets of brilliant colour, so bright, so vivid, so delightfully unexpected.

There are tiny insects too, flies and bees and ants and spiders, scurrying around in their shade, and butterflies flitting from flower to flower, bumble bees blundering into things, small lizards and sparrows that eat the insects, and hawks and vultures overhead.

I am amazed by the flowers. I have to keep stopping to sit among them, and listen and smell.

'I am amazed by the flowers', I say to the girl at the next truckstop cafe.

'Oh yes, they come most years', she tells me. 'There are a few days of rain and they all spring up. They last for a few weeks drinking the mist. Some years there is no rain. Further north where they have rain perhaps only once in twenty years, they have flowers too. The seeds live in the sand.'

Some valleys have no flowers. Flowers are forgotten, there is only sand and bare rock and heat, and then over a rise is another world where the desert sings only of life because it is buried under a living carpet of glowing colour that hums with the clatter of a million tiny feet and the buzz of a million pairs of tiny wings and the murmur of a million things eating and drinking and fighting and making love.

There are those wasps that you always see battling with tarantulas on T.V. programmes, dragging around fat caterpillars and shovelling out holes in the sand with their back legs in which to bury them. And big beetles, comedians every one – an inch long with white stripes down their black backs – they rush from flower to flower, nibbling at unopened buds, bumping into stones, and frequently into each other, for they are numerous. With a social life of a few weeks on a good year they can't afford to be prudish, and whenever they meet they try to mate, no matter what sex, any beetle will do, they clamber up onto each other's backs, sometimes forming long lines of nine or ten that weave a procreative conga among the flowers. Their hard carapaces hang down below their hind legs, and when they run along the road they drag along, click-click-click over the asphalt. On sensing danger they stand still, hoping perhaps not to be seen, a tactic they apply equally to a roving finger or the vibrations of an approaching vehicle. All the beetles clicking along the road stop together. Then a thirty ton truck thunders through and bowls them along around its wheels before flinging them aside to roll another hundred yards where they lie still. Then, click-click-click, up they get and beetle off.

In Copiapo the Sunday charity marathon is in full swing. Hundreds of runners are pounding around the closed off streets of the city centre.

A crowd has gathered in the central plaza. The attraction is Leo and Michel. They are trying to eat some lunch, unsuccessfully, because they are surrounded by people asking where they come from, where they are going, what are all these things they carry on their bicycles, and what is the purpose of it all. They look for somewhere quieter to eat their lunch. After they have gone, an old man, clutching a bottle and swaying slightly, becomes angry that they have left so soon. He turns to me and starts shouting.

'They come out of the desert and they stay for ten minutes and then – off they go. Why do they come, what is their mission?'

People nearby try to shut him up, and apologise to me for his behaviour, he's drunk, he doesn't know what he's saying, but he won't be shut up and I say to him, 'Mission? They have no mission, they are not missionaries. They are travellers, they travel, that is how they like to live. They don't spend their money on buying houses and cars and bottles of drink but they use it to travel, and when they leave after ten minutes it is not through rudeness or discourtesy but because that is their custom and there is no reason for you to take offence.'

'Pah! Rich gringos on holiday. You think you don't need anything or anybody. You're just antisocial', he concludes, and totters off.

It's a problem we all have, taking offence at things that are not intended to be offensive.

The snow-covered peaks of the High Andes are clearly visible away to the east, high above the plain of flowers and cacti. A dirt track leaves the road and winds across the plain to a flat topped hill that overlooks the valley way in the distance.

'Southern European Observatory. 35 kms' reads a small sign.

An enormous refrigerated truck grinds to a halt, reverses up and stops. The driver jumps down, opens up the back, pulls out a couple of ice creams.

'Hello, gringo. How's it going?' he says, handing me one. I point to the building on the hill and ask him if that is the observatory.

'Observatory "La Silla" it is called. North American and European scientists work there all the year round. The skies are very clear here, the clearest in the world', he says. We suck ice creams. 'The government and the gringos are going to build another one, bigger still, further south, high in the mountains. It has been delayed though because the site they have chosen is the exact location on which a group from the World Spiritual Society has been camping for the past year. They say the place is a focus for spiritual vibrations and the signals are so strong that something big is going to happen there soon. They refuse to leave. They say they don't want noisy construction crews and unbelieving scientists upsetting the vibrations. They're all crazy of course.'

'So will the observatory not be built?' I ask.

'The government says that it understands and is sympathetic to the Spirituals, but that if they don't move they will be removed. How come there are so many cyclists these days?' he asks. I say I don't know. We just seem to have accumulated.

'I hear about you all on the C.B. One of your friends, the Americano, was picked up a couple of days ago. He was sick. A truck took him back to Antofagasta. There's another cyclist a hundred kilometers behind you, and two more a hundred kilometers ahead. Why don't you travel in a group?' he asks.

'We do', I say. 'We just get a bit spaced out sometimes.'

He leaves me his home address in Santiago and work telephone number and says not to hesitate to call if I have any problems on the road. He rumbles off.

Mist and fog swirl in from the sea and engulf the desert. For several days the sun is obscured and it's impossible to tell the time. I'm damp and cold for two days, and then it rains at night, real heavy raindrops that spatter and plonk and give me a fever and everything becomes soft and grey and feverish, ghostly boulders and cacti, apparitions in the mist.

When the fog lifts it seems a different land. Villages and towns spring up in every valley, bushes and scrub and green plants crowd out the cacti, and further south there are fields of wheat and oats, green meadows where cows graze, apple orchards and market gardens, tractors and men on horseback.

Life is not so simple for the vagabond, he must pick his spot to sleep at night, for there are hedges and ditches and fences, roadsigns and farm tracks, and passers-by to be mindful of. In my dreams I hear the scrunch of feet on gravel, and think perhaps I should wake up, but it's too late because suddenly I get a face full of boot and gravel and a man stumbles over me, and his mate trips up right after him. Grunting with surprise we all sprawl on the ground apologising to each other.

Just as I top the pass that leads into the Santiago valley, there are clanking sounds as the chain goes floppy and plays tunes on the spokes. Sounds serious. I was hoping to make good time today because Santiago is one of South America's largest cities and I expect to spend some time lost on freeways and one-way systems.

The rear derailleur is not springing back to keep the chain taut. It is not simply stiff with dirt and dust because the whole roller cage swings freely back and forth. I unscrew the pivot bolt cylinder and find that the spring inside has snapped off where it should slot into the hole that anchors it. The steel is too tough to make the precise right angle bend at the end with a pair of pliers, which would temporarily suffice. So I put the chain in a middle gear, and tie the swinging roller cage back against the changer body with a piece of string. The chain is held taut now so I can safely pedal along. But I can't change gear, so it's a bit slow pulling away. The front chainwheels are also well worn, which doesn't help any because when too much pressure is put on the pedals, the chain just slips over the teeth.

I try not to stop. Everything else is trying hard not to stop either, and I draught along with the traffic into the bustle of the city centre without stopping even to get lost, into the bright lights and advertisements, cinemas and burger bars, neon-lit shopping precincts and supermarkets and pavements spilling people into the six-lane highways, and roadworks and construction sites and all the earth covered over in concrete and steel and high walls and barbed wire fences, and everywhere alarm systems and security guards and machine-gun toting policemen. Yes, everything is here and it gives me a good zapping and leaves me bewildered because I'm still out in the desert somewhere.

It seems for the moment that the expensive things and big buildings are more important than the people, who are here to fill in the gaps, to hand over money, to pass pieces of paper, and to dress themselves up smartly enough to be worthy to walk the streets, and pretending all the time that they really like it.

It takes a few days to acclimatise, to assume the habit of excluding everything which does not directly concern me, to acquire the city shell of affected detachment, to enjoy the cosy reassurance of an unlimited supply of consumables, of being surrounded by a million other like-motivated people. Soon I can stroll down the streets unaffected by the bombardment of advertisements and the beeping of car horns, the cries and shouts and revving of engines, down the hot dog and ice cream boulevard, between the rows of travel agencies and steak houses, jewellers and tailors, past the blind man shuffling barefooted along the gutter outside a shop selling pairs of two hundred dollar shoes. I don't bat an eye, it's O.K. this is the city so walk on by, past the girl with no legs begging for a peso, propped up against the plate glass window that separates her from a hundred thousand dollars worth of computers and kitchen appliances, it's O.K., walk on by, this is the city, any city, all cities, no need to think about it, switch off your brain, just look ahead, look up with a vision corrected gleam in your eye through the smog filled air at what remains of the sky that has not been obscured by the multi storied fortress of the national bank which cares about you, see the sunshine reflecting from the mirrored glass of the public welfare building, yes how well we are, how good we feel, see those rays of sunshine glinting on the gold dome of the cathedral, flashing out its message of concern for the poor and the oppressed, roll up roll up, gather round, this is the city, shrug off the embarrassing weight of individual responsibility, no need to run away and live in the forest or hide in a cave, this is the place to come if you can't cope, if you want to cop out, if you need to escape from yourself, from the world, come serve out your days in the security of collective resignation and unending confusion as only we civilized technology-liberated citizens know how.

But recognise your complicity in the running of the machine you love to hate, with your stash of gringo dollars and your two year holidays and your antisocial customs. You are the machine, you are the monster, so change your ways or shut up.

O.K., I'll change my ways. But I'll have to put it off until tomorrow because today I'm far too busy – I have to collect some money I've had transferred to Santiago from my bank in England. It's been waiting here for a couple of months.

'How would you like your money, sir?' the clerk asks me.

'Dollars please', I say because dollars can be exchanged on the street for ten per cent more than the bank rate.

'I'm sorry, you can have it either in the currency in which it has been sent, or in Chilean pesos', he replies.

'In what currency has it been sent?'

'In pounds sterling.'

'O.K. I'd like it in pounds sterling please.'

'I'm sorry sir, we don't have any pounds sterling. Choose again.'

Human contact smashes down the city walls. I ask a girl wheeling a bicycle down the street where I might find a bike shop. She takes me home for tea to meet her mother, whose parents were English and came to Chile to build the railways. We sit in the backyard in the shade of vines laden with grapes, speaking in English and drinking *maté*.

Nowhere can I find the spare parts that I want – a set of chain wheels that will fit my crank arms, a large freewheel, a replacement spring for the rear derailleur. The cycling club of Chile say they import their derailleurs from Italy and France, and when bits break they get new ones.

It seems ludicrous to trash the whole gear system for the sake of a broken spring, so I take it back to the repair shop I first visited, where I bought a few nuts and bolts and they tried unsuccessfully to remove the freewheel and succeeded only in cracking the ring that screws in to hold the outer and inner sections together. With their tools I manage to fashion a serviceable replacement.

Leo and Michel arrive in town after sojourning on beaches further north. We chuckle over an article in a newspaper from Coquimbo where they were interviewed – half of which is what they told the reporter and half is what he invented to make it all sound exciting and dangerous.

Leo collects some letters from the other French cyclists. Gérard is down south in Patagonia somewhere. Max and Jean-Louis wrote from Bolivia where they have hepatitis. But then Jean-Louis turns up in Santiago. He sold his bicycle in Calama for sixty dollars. It cost him sixty dollars when he bought it so he figures he's had a twenty thousand mile trip for nothing. He passed through Antofagasta two weeks ago, and who did he come across in the hospital? Don. Don was in a bed, confined to a ward, with instructions not to go wandering off for thirty days. He had hepatitis. Poor Don. We guess Americans turn white rather than yellow and have a little chuckle at his expense. Nobody knows where Rudi is.

Jean-Louis has no bicycle but he has a box full of bicycle bits that he collected at the post office, sent by companies in France who have supplied him with all manner of spare parts along the way. For free.

'Why don't you write to English companies for spare parts?' he asks.

Why not indeed? I have been meaning to change my saddle, which I have to pad out with items of clothing, for the last ten thousand miles. I write a letter to Brooks in England, asking them, even though they don't know who I am, if they would like to give me a saddle, and post it to me in Chile. It seems a bit of a long shot, especially as I don't know their address and enclose the letter in one to my parents asking them to track it down.

During an unofficial Day of Action, announced by students and supported by the labour organisations and the church, in protest at the recent killing of two students during a demonstration for the return to democracy at Concepcion University, Bruce, a young Australian staying at my hotel, returns in a state of shock with his arms and legs bruised and swollen. He was sitting in the shopping precinct he says, eating an ice cream in the sunshine, minding his own business, taking no particular notice of the police in riot gear that are a permanent feature of the city centre, when without warning and apparently for no reason, they started laying into passers-by. He couldn't believe it. He sat there just taking a beating till he realised that they weren't going to stop. He ran off, pursued, and only escaped by rolling under one of the metal shop fronts as it was hastily being pulled down, and together with the shopkeeper and his wife, held it down as it was pounded from outside.

In the afternoon a march blocks off one of the main streets. Thousands of shoppers and pedestrians swell the numbers, out of curiosity, and in passive solidarity. Coachloads of riot police arrive. The army turns up in jeeps and armoured cars. The demonstrators are calling for an end to the Pinochet dictatorship, for a return to democracy. The banners of banned political parties are waved. The crowd is told through loudhailers that it constitutes an illegal gathering. It must disperse. There is nowhere to disperse because police can be seen lurking down every sidestreet. A few people break away and are chased and beaten to the ground by the police. The crowd roars its anger at the lines of police who are dressed like alien beings, in helmets with dark visors, brandishing long lightweight alloy batons, behind a wall of perspex shields. Rocks are thrown at them, tear gas is fired and the crowd is split up into smaller groups, herded into sidestreets.

I'm in a crowd of people – demonstrators, students, churchmen, families out doing their afternoon shopping, mothers with small children in push chairs, everybody standing around rubbing their eyes, coughing, crying, wondering where to run to next. Riot police stand at one end of the street, silent. Then they charge and everybody stands still for a second, listening to an atrocious sound of thumping boots and heavy panting. Then we run, we hobble, we limp, we push our prams, we fall down and trip over one another, we pick each other up, we flee from the guardians of the Pinochet regime who are mindlessly clubbing away for law and order at running, screaming, defenceless people.

From the opposite end of the shopping precinct an armoured car appears and mounts the pavement. As it approaches it turns on a water cannon. It bowls along, tearing away pavement stalls, dodging drunkenly around public payphones, knocking down litter bins like a rampaging elephant, but we all keep running towards it, and past it, despite the jet of water which blasts people off their feet, rips off their clothes, pins them against walls, because it's better than a beating.

A curfew is announced over the radio and television. Power is cut off. Nobody is to be on the streets after eight at night. Even the normally crowded and noisy bars and brothels in the alleyways of the red light district around my hotel are silent, as if in mourning.

Four more people are shot dead in the night during disturbances in the suburbs. Two students, a clergyman and a seven year old girl. All, it is explained, were engaged in subversive activities. The following day's newspapers have empty spaces where reports and photographs have been censored. People crowd around the newsstands. This is the acceptable form of protest in Chile – gazing in silence at blank spaces.

But there's good news too in the more pro-government papers. Front page headlines – 'Bank of England to make substantial loans to support the flailing economy.' More good news: several ex-British air force fighter planes are to be sold to Chile, coincidentally, for exactly the same amount as the loan.

One morning, the central market building which is always full of people, suddenly filled with smoke. Everybody rushes outside. One of the shops that form the outside of the complex is on fire. It's a fried chicken and chips take away bar. Somebody finds a hose from the now abandoned market building, and squirts a tiny stream of water into the shop. It doesn't do any good. Electric cables fizz and hot fat sizzles, the shop becomes engulfed in flame and billowing black smoke. People are driven back by the heat. Incredibly, someone emerges from the blazing furnace. It's the manager, staggering out with the cash register in his arms.

The fire brigade arrives in six fire engines, two with turntable ladders, and an assortment of water tenders. A couple of ambulances arrive next, though no one appears to be injured except the manager, who has hurt his back carrying the cash register.

A coachload of police turn up to keep back the large crowd, the newspaper reporters and photographers, the T.V. film crews.

What a show it is too. The firemen who have scaled up onto the roof are playing to the crowd now – leaping about between jets of flame, heaving up sections of the tin roof with shiny axes to get at the fire below. The crowd whistles and cheers its approval at special acts of bravado. Ten minutes later there is just a blackened shell of a shop, a few curling whisps of smoke, and streams of water gurgling down the drains.

The crowd that goes to witness the opening of the new plaza outside the Moneda palace – the presidential residence –

is much smaller and less enthusiastic. General Pinochet puts in an appearance, peeping around his bodyguards to wave from behind the bullet proof glass of his armoured limousine. He likes to keep in touch with the people, he knows how they feel – impatient rabble – what's the matter with them, why can't they wait another ten years for an election?

15. Rolling south to the Useless Bay

After waiting for four weeks, the girl at the Argentine consulate in an undiplomatic display of honesty says that unless I have relatives in Argentina, a reply to my visa application that was sent to Buenos Aires is unlikely to come.

So it's southwards again, with another cheap Taiwanese tent because everybody says it rains a lot down south, but until it does, why put it up? Sure, it's a nice colour, but you only have to take it down again in the morning and it cuts you off from all the happenings of the night, and the smell of diesel in the truck parks of petrol stations and cafes keeps away the mosquitos which are about the most unpleasant things a bicycling gringo is likely to come across sleeping on the streets in Chile.

This is the most populous region of the country – the fertile valleys south of Santiago, watered by the clear rivers that run down from the Andes that rise in a snowy line of peaks to the east that glow pink every evening.

I'm spoilt for choice because there are so many cosy truck parks to sleep in, and while I stand around trying to decide which looks the most comfortable, even though I'm back in my travelling clothes that are covered in patches and holes, that I never seem to throw away because they're always good for just one more day, a family in a brand new Japanese van pulls up.

'Hi there, we live in Talca, why not come back to our house for something to eat and a wash?' and it doesn't matter if you're ragged and dirty because if you're a stranger in Chile you sleep in a bed between clean sheets, and nobody pays attention to your road habits, you're one of the family and everybody bubbles over with generosity, asking questions, showing you things. I'm completely overwhelmed, tired too because I've come over a hundred miles today and I'm sleeping on my feet, but that's O.K. too, it's understood, and in the morning there's a cup of tea in bed, and you can't leave until you've eaten a large breakfast and had a guided tour of the city, and 'Hey, is that your only shirt?' and I'm back on the road with hugs and kisses like I've known them all my life, a pack of sandwiches and a new shirt, and a momentary feeling that it's time I found my family and friends again and settled down to relearning the simple joys of conversation. But the motion soon takes over and it's only a thousand kilometers now to Puerto Mont at the end of the Pan American highway, and a little bit further south to the Straits of Magellan, where even if they are good for another day I'll ditch the more unacceptable rags of this vagabond existence, and though the wind is strong it's an easy hundred and fifty kilometers a day, through villages and towns and past fields of wheat and corn, grapes and oranges and melons, and all the way roadside fruit and vegetable stalls bowing under the weight of fresh produce, and sometimes almost like England really, with apple orchards and rolling meadows with buttercups and Friesian cows and weeping willows beside streams, and just the odd volcano or two towering high and white in the background.

And even when the wind is strong it is not a problem because the gaily coloured carts and wagons pulled along by stoic old horses that pay no heed to the articulated trucks that thunder by provide excellent windbreaks – they just keep plodding along, even when the occupants are so drunk on the wine they've taken to market that they slump down asleep in their seats and nod their heads rhythmically, just like the old horse that is following its own nose home – there's no need to stop, everything plods along contentedly in the folly of its own purpose and momentum and all I want to do is fill my lungs with air and head south sitting in the sunshine.

I only stop by in Linares to buy some bananas, but it's midday and the shops are closed so I buy an ice cream instead, sit down to eat it on a bench in the plaza next to some visitors from Santiago and talk about English popular music because the Beatles are singing 'Once there was a way to get back homeward', over the loudspeakers.

A man on a bicycle loaded down with portable radio equipment comes by. He works for the local radio station Radio Linares and asks if we mind being interviewed 'Live from the Plaza', and outlines the sort of questions he thinks will be of interest to local listeners – the impressions of Linares from the family from Santiago and my impressions generally as a foreigner about Chile. Once we are actually broadcasting he slips in a few questions of a political nature, like what do I think of the Falklands war, and topical themes like the disturbances in the capital, and I get a chance to let off some steam about not getting a visa to visit Argentina because of the infantile behaviour of the British and Argentine governments in severing diplomatic relations, and how war is between governments fought by brainwashed robots, not between people, who generally get along fine and can sort out their differences between themselves without paying other people to go around killing and shooting each other to pieces, and as to the disturbances well isn't a State of Emergency a contradiction in itself? What is more disturbing than things not being permitted to emerge?

He nods encouragingly and asks me if I can be more specific so I specify the suppression of free speech and the absence of any political freedom in Chile, and he's nodding frantically and grinning from ear to ear as he fiddles with dials, and now that I'm up on a soap box there seems no point in being diplomatic so I vent a little anger over the fact that Chileans are tear-gassed and pinned to walls by water cannon just because they go out shopping, and sling in a few personal opinions about Pinochet as well.

'Well, thanks very much, and now, back to the studio', he says, clicking off switches and slapping me on the back. A few people have gathered around the bench and he seems to be hustling me away, to follow him back to the radio station where the controller, a tiny man with long silver hair and a smart suit, suggests that I stay in town tonight, and I get to meet his family and cousins and friends who live in different parts of the city, and I never get to eat one banana.

Clonkety plop! That's an unusual sound. The freewheel has dismantled itself. Well, you son of a bitch, I've been trying to get you off for six months and there's a trail of broken tools and thumbs all the way to Peru and now off you plop cool as you please.

Closer inspection reveals that it is just the outer section that holds the cog wheels that has worked loose, because the ring that holds the two sections together is cracked and cannot be completely tightened. One of the tiny hairsprings that works the ratchet has disappeared.

The other is broken. I cut small strips from an elastic band and wedge them, folded over, behind the flanges of the ratchet where the springs should be. Seems to work O.K. In Temuco I buy a bag of ballbearings to replace those that got spewed down the road, and head up the dirt tracks into the Lake District where everybody has been telling me to go because it's so beautiful. It really is beautiful too – a land of clear lakes, mountains and volcanoes, mist and waterfalls, and along the muddy trails on the far side of the lakes through forests of monkey puzzle and araucaria trees full of birdsong and dripping leaves, woodsmoke and pine scent and greenery, and a night-time silence so deep that you can't help but relax right down to your bones.

And just when I think I'm completely relaxed I wake up with a start, growling like an animal at the dogs that have come scrunching over the pebble beach and are sniffing and barking and yelping round my head, looking for something, then disappearing, noses to the ground, sniffing into the trees, and ten seconds later a fox comes along, trotting silently over the pebbles, following the scent of the dogs with a grin on its face that says 'Come on, life's a gas.'

The village of Conaripe on the shores of Lake Calafquen was buried in lava and volcanic ash that swept down from the volcano Villarica which rises up behind. That was in 1967. Today the mainstreet is black sand, young forests cover the black slopes of the mountains, and the lakeside is packed out with Chilean holiday makers camping on the black volcanic shingle, playing beach games, fishing, relaxing, swimming in the lake and cooking over woodfires, the old ones sitting in deckchairs snoozing, the young ones smoking grass and discussing politics, and in the evening everybody is drinking the local wine that is cheaper than Coca Cola, singing and dancing and playing guitars, and I whack out the tunes I've learnt on the *charango* and howl at the moon with everybody else while volcano Villarica sends smoke signals to the stars.

The town of Entre Lagos on the shores of Lake Puyehue is celebrating its tenth anniversary. The grassy lakeside is full of tents and stalls, but people say, 'Come on gringo, welcome, there's plenty of room!' and I find a space to squeeze in my tent and join in with the festivities, singing and drinking and milling around between groups of people sitting around fires as the whole sky and lake glows a deep pink in the sunset.

At dusk the mayor makes a speech from the podium, surrounded by local dignitaries, but carefully worded and apolitical in nature because the new part of town that is celebrating its tenth anniversary was built with money made available by the short-lived socialist Allende government whose good works are no longer officially mentioned in an attempt to erase their memory from the minds of the people. A flotilla of rafts is launched from the shore, decorated with ribbons and flowers and candles. It is a solemn moment, people are crying, but then an impromptu battle commences between some of the rafts, two particularly unlakeworthy vessels are sunk, one is set ablaze, and the lake is full of the splashing of swimming bodies making for the shore or neighbouring rafts, and the solemn crowd is cheering and laughing now and some even leap right into the water fully clothed just for the hell of it.

A rock band from Santiago plays in the village hall in the evening. The whole town is there, shouting and whistling and stamping their feet, though nobody is dancing down at the front because there is a crowd of discouraging policemen who know that dancing to pop music is the sort of thing that students do to work themselves into a subversive frenzy. When the band stops, salsa records are played and everybody immediately takes to the floor in a swaying drunken melee whose movements are sufficiently patriotic for the policemen to go home, and though I can't dance salsa I've drunk enough wine for it not to be important, and there are some charming young ladies who have drunk enough wine for them not to feel embarrassed to teach the curiously jigging foreigner a few native steps.

It is light when I return to the tent. While I've been partying someone has been going through my tent. An unexposed black and white film, a pack of playing cards and a small piece of cheese are all that is missing. No doubt the thief was disappointed at such meagre booty. I have to smile at the thought of whoever it was opening so many pockets and panniers and finding only holey socks, greasy tools and worn out pieces of bicycle. Junk, junk, junk.

A roadsign reads 'Welcome to Puerto Mont', and down below a town stretches around a wide bay. Puerto Mont is the southern end of the Pan-American highway, but there are roads south of here: to

the island of Chiloe – the largest and most northerly island of the
archipelago that stretches a thousand miles south to Cape Horn –
and a road recently opened that follows the inlets and estuaries of
the mainland as far as Cochrane where it crosses the Andes into
Argentina, for beyond, the spine of the Andes is buried in glaciers
and ice unmelted since the last ice age.

It is the beginning of December. The schools have broken up
for the long summer holidays and the kids are celebrating, rushing
through the streets of the town centre, whooping and shouting and
throwing each other into the fountains.

A van with a bear in a cage and a vulture clinging to a bar above
the cab tours the streets announcing the arrival of a circus.

A group of men and women are sitting outside a cafe drinking
wine, in one of the crooked cobbled lanes lined with dilapidated
wooden houses near the harbour in the old part of town that rings
with the sound of seagulls and cries from the fishmarket.

'Hey gringo, where are you going?' calls out one of the
women.

'I'm looking for a place to stay.'

'Stay here, we've a room upstairs. Sit and drink some wine.'

I sit and drink some wine, and start to doze off.

'Come, you must be tired', says the wife of the red-faced man who
is in the middle of telling me a lengthy joke. 'Leave him alone. You
drink too much', she says, slapping him roughly on the shoulder.
They don't get along very well.

One of the double doors that opens onto the wooden staircase
that leads to the rooms above the cafe is nailed shut with planks, so
I start to remove the panniers from the bike, which only takes ten
seconds, but before I have finished a small boy has appeared with
a crowbar and jemmied off the planks.

I book a passage on a ferry that ships trucks from Puerto Mont
through the islands of the archipelago to Puerto Natales and Punta
Arenas that lie on the pampas of Patagonia south of the ice bound
mountains.

On the land across the creek where the fishing boats lie out of
the wind, the red-faced man who is always drunk, and his wife
are patching up an old wooden bungalow where he is going to
live after they get divorced, because they don't get on. I keep the
two children amused on the muddy beach in the windy summer

sunshine while they have arguments and storm off in opposite directions.

The ferry takes four days to motor through the channels and straits to Puerto Natales, through a wild land of steep forested mountains and fiords, where a few tiny fishing settlements of Araucano Indians shelter in coves and inlets from the raging winds of the roaring forties, and south into the furious fifties where the sea swells and the boat rolls and everybody is sick, where only sea birds live among the towering black cliffs, huge waterfalls, rainbows and ice, emerging at last from the cloud and mist into a wide gulf where the white roofs of Puerto Natales, squat and windswept, gleam in the sunshine.

North for a while now, along the dirt track that leads to the Paine Towers national park. It's good to be on dry land again, even if the wind blows a gale day and night. Windspeeds of fifty miles an hour are common here, an everyday occurrence. Anything not rooted to the ground is swept away across the grassy plains. Stones and grit are whipped along like dust. Every bush and wind-stunted tree grows at an angle of forty five degrees. Even the condors fly sideways. In a cross wind I ride leaning right over into the wind, and frequently thud to the ground in a sudden lull, or get turned around and blown a hundred yards across the pampas before I have reached the brake.

There are fiercer gusts of wind that knock me off the bike. They are fearsome things, usually accompanied by towering swirling columns of dust, or long curtains a hundred feet high and half a mile long that roar across the plain with the sound of a train, and all I can do is lie flat in the road and hold my breath.

Rheas appear from time to time, and bound along on long legs, heads swaying on long necks, pursued by a crowd of darting chicks. Thousands of geese nest in the open grassland, taking off and landing like a snowstorm.

The day is full of new things, but a feeling of emptiness is creeping over me. I half expected that it might. It happens sometimes, usually the first day on the road after spending time with other people. Loneliness. I know that it will only last for a day or two and be gone – it always does, but right now that is no help – it never is. Overpowering loneliness and a sense of pointlessness in what I am doing, how I am living. The whole trip seems stupid and I'm a fool to continue, to even be here at all. I shelter the tent behind a group of short stumpy trees, but the wind still rips the guy ropes from the fly sheet, and pulls up the pegs, and shrugs off the rocks that weigh down the sides. And I can't get a fire to stay alight. Stupid lonely trip.

And then I wake up in the morning and everything is fine and bright, like after a long illness when you still feel weak, but cleansed, and you know everything's going to be all right, the storm has passed and everything is clear again.

I build a fire and brew a pot of tea, toss in some mint that is growing nearby, and just sit around in the sunshine drinking tea, humming a tune to the bees, singing a song to the brown and white skunk that snuffles right up to my feet, because the world is bursting with joy.

Loneliness is just a memory. Still alone, yes, but that is not a problem. Alone but not lonely. Loneliness is a state of mind that comes with forgetfulness, deliberate or otherwise, of the fact that we are never really alone, that we never can be alone. Forgetfulness of the fact that we are always connected, always in relationship, like atoms in a molecule, stars in a galaxy, invisibly, from a distance of a million miles perhaps, but part of the same thing, made of the same stuff. Alone, all-one. Loneliness is forgetfulness, loneliness is blindness, loneliness is delusion.

The granite towers of the Paine mountains rise ten thousand feet, in bands of yellow and grey and white above the pampas, above the six huge lakes, green and turquoise and milky with a suspension of minerals from the glaciers that feed them, above wind-torn deciduous forests draped in hanging creepers and twisting vines that echo with the knocking of woodpeckers, cawing choughs, and the honking of gawdy buff-neck ibises that seem to be made up from the spare parts of other birds.

The area is a national park. Two Australians, an American and a Dutch guy are the only other visitors in the whole park, and will be for some time because the one road in and out becomes flooded under two metres of water.

'It happens every year about this time', explains a park ranger. 'During the spring a lake forms within one of the glaciers, and when the ice wall that contains it finally melts, millions of gallons flood out in a few hours. All the lakes rise.'

The level of Lago del Toro where we are camped rises steadily as we watch. Access into and out of the park is by inflatable dingy, on the days when the wind is less strong.

It is an interesting place to be stranded: views to admire, wildlife to spot, trails to walk and always the prospect of being swept away among the pieces of bobbing ice when crossing the swollen rivers. Pale blue chunks of ice wash up on the lake shores, huge frozen statues shaped by the pounding waves whipped up by the gales that always blow.

We think for a moment that the local mushrooms we had for breakfast are colouring our vision when the dark greens of the forest turn to blue, but no, it's glacier Grey we can see through the trees, a bright blue beast three miles wide and ten miles long, scouring its way down from the frozen heights of Paine Chico to the shores of Lake Grey, here scrunched up, there smooth, and everywhere tremendous and varied sounds that belie its motionless passivity: the dripping of drops from the roofs of ice caves, the rushing gurgling of streams describing the shape of each crevasse, the squeaking and grating and creaking of each massive block of ice as it rubs its neighbour, the booming and slopping of each wave that runs under the overhanging shelf where the ice meets the lake in a sixty foot cliff, forcing its way up into cracks, and the whole symphony punctuated by the cracking and crunching of house-sized blocks of ice as they tumble from the wall, and thud into the water with a roar that shakes the ground and sends out huge waves that dislodge yet more.

The heights of the Paine Towers amass black storm clouds from an otherwise clear sky, which circle awhile, shedding bolts of lightning before being ripped away at regular intervals, tearing off as fluffy rings, a line of flying doughnuts, pink and orange in the sunset.

The road south of Puerto Natales is a thin strip of gravel that rises and falls over an undulating plain of waving grass. A sign here and there points down a side track to an unseen farm. The horizon is wide. Storm clouds drag across, trailing curtains of rain. I try to miss them, stay in the sunshine – it's a game.

Oh yes and it's Christmas Day, and there is nothing about but a sea of rolling green and a single stunted tree, gnarled and leaning, with dead twigs enough for a fire, and there's no one about except for one bus that rumbles past in a cloud of dust with toots and waves, and a horserider shepherding a flock of sheep and a swarm of flies along the road, and there's all the time in the world for a brew of tea and a bit of a lie down, to watch a silky grey pampas fox trotting along with its head above the grass, and the antics of the buff-neck ibis nesting in a rocky outcrop, honking and squawking above the sound of the wind which is now so familiar that it howls unnoticed.

Punta Arenas is a large port city of office blocks and shipping warehouses and the prosperous independent air of a region remote from the rest of the country. But it's all quiet during siesta time.

Down by the shingle beach seabirds wheel over the Straits of Magellan, over the hundreds of ships that are docked. Oil tankers and container ships lie offshore.

'Hotel, Dancing, Bar' reads a sign above a narrow doorway. I enter to take a room, though some surprise is shown that I want to sleep here, but an old woman shows me to a room at the end of a corridor upstairs. A few clothes lie strewn around, there's a book, a toothbrush and a face towel.

'There isn't somebody in this room already?' I ask.

'Oh no, there's nobody here', the old woman replies. 'This is the biggest and the best room in the house', she assures me, when in fact they are all exactly the same. She removes the few belongings.

It is of course primarily a brothel, but now that I am installed I can't be bothered to move to somewhere quieter, and I'm too tired to be troubled by the music and laughter from below that continues through the night, or the stumbling up and down stairs and regular squeaking of bedsprings.

It is just getting light when the girl whose room I've been given comes in after a long night's work to find her things gone and a stranger in her bed, but she shows no surprise and apologises for disturbing me.

I ask the man at the immigration office where I have to renew my visa for a further three months if he can renew my vehicle papers too.

'What kind of vehicle is it?' he asks.

'It's a bicycle.'

He roars with laughter, and assures me that the customs men on my arrival in the country must have been having a little joke at my expense, and that the visa extension certainly includes a bicycle. While in lighthearted mood, he hands me a stack of government printed postcards from a drawer in his desk, to send to my friends back home – picturesque views of Santiago, mountains and lakes, air force jets, with 'Land where hope reblossoms', 'Peace, Freedom, Prosperity' and other rousing phrases printed boldly on.

Back at the brothel I can't get back in to collect my things. It's all locked up, the electric doorbell is turned off, and I have to hammer on the door for some time, which annoys all the local dogs and amuses the people working in the office block across the road, before being admitted.

The ferry terminal for the service that runs between the mainland and the island of Tierra del Fuego is five miles outside Punta Arenas. It is a car park and a concrete ramp – a final modification to the American continent before it slopes at last into the sea.

Five cars, a bulldozer, fifty foot passengers and a herd of cows disembark when the ferry arrives. And a Swiss bicyclist. He's come by way of Ushuaia – the town at the southern end of the Argentine part of the island – the most southerly town in the world. He bumped into a couple of French cyclists camping on the beach there, having a bit of a rest because they'd come down from Alaska and there was nowhere else to go now.

The dark headlands of Tierra del Fuego can be seen ten miles across the water. I'm not going to get there tonight because the evening ferry has been cancelled.

The wind, as usual, is blowing a gale, and I'm tempted to head back up north right now and forget all about Tierra del Fuego – after all, I'm only going to say that I have been there, to follow in the wake of fellow cyclists who have gone before me. No, more than this – to exorcise the ghost of a goal that will haunt me if I do not go. I put the tent up in the car park.

A portly businessman from Punta Arenas comes by on a bicycle in a jogging suit. He says he is out to lose some weight, and tells me about his ancestors the Araucano Indians who lived around here, whose fires were seen by Magellan, who lived off fish and guanaco and who successfully repelled both Inca and Spanish aggressors, and even today a few still live as they did then – in poverty and squalor.

I notice his bicycle is a Fuji and I ask him if there is a Fuji dealer in town because if there is, there are a hundred bits and pieces I want to buy. He says no, a friend brought it down from California on the cruise liner that has just arrived in port, and he's only borrowing it for a couple of weeks while his friend takes a trip to the antarctic peninsula a thousand miles to the south, where twenty volunteer families are pioneering Chilean colonisation of that part of the continent which Chile claims to possess. The same bit that Argentina claims to possess.

The sun rises after just a few hours of darkness, not very far along the horizon from where it set. I board the ferry to Porvenir – the only town of any size on the Chilean side of Tierra del Fuego. It's the last day of the year, bright and sunny.

A family dressed like gypsies, drinking vodka in the grocery store at Porvenir tell me about various beautiful places on the island. Their enthusiasm is contagious, and I nearly stock up with food for a week's tour. But the wind is cold and it looks like it might rain, and it's probably all just pampas anyway. Sure, pampas are beautiful too, but I only really want a short ride around.

The gravel track winds south over gentle rolling hills of green grass, past small lakes dotted with geese and black-necked swans, then around the rocky deserted coastline of a wide bay.

I pile rocks up around the tent until it is half buried, to stop it from blowing away down the long empty shingle beach. The stones and pebbles hiss and crackle, pounded by grey waves of the sea that is whipped into foam by the wind. The sun stabs out brilliant yellow shafts between the black arms of magnificent thunderstorms, that glisten on the wet shingle and sparkle in the spray.

The bay is the end of my road south, and it is tempting to consider it an absurd destination for a year and a half's journeying. On my map it has a name: Bahia Inutil – Useless Bay. Certainly, no use appears to have been found for it. No row of electricity pylons stride reassuringly across the horizon. No distant hilltop is used to advertise religious wares, where for a small tax deductible holy offering we might renounce our individual spirituality, peep in at the one, true, securely imprisoned god, and stake our claim on a piece of the afterlife. No friendly gurgle of chemical waste pours from the gaping mouth of a cunningly concealed pipeline, nor the distant pall of airborn pollution to indicate that man's industrious quest for excellence continues. There are no monuments, no obvious attractions as a place of pilgrimage, except of course that it is a wilderness without obvious attractions. Its personal use for me, as a place to turn around at the end of a road is of no great significance. It is indeed a useless bay. And it is a fine place.

I find myself thinking of things that have come and gone along the way. Some things I remember like they happened a couple of days ago, and then realise that they must have happened months ago. I remember the first time that I woke up and could not remember where I was, or what I was doing there, and even more worryingly, what my name was. I panicked, got up pretty quick and looked outside the tent, and in a few seconds it all came flooding back: oh yes, here I am, out for a ride, of course I know my name.

The second time it happened I didn't panic because I knew what was happening. I couldn't remember where I was, but I didn't feel lost. Not like I feel lost sometimes when I know where I am, like we all get lost in the workings of our own little beliefs, lost within the labyrinths of our imaginations, in the safe little worlds where we can hide, preferably right in the centre where we are farthest away from the real world outside, whose order is orderless and beyond our control.

We cut ourselves off from the real world, until we are hidden even from ourselves, until we don't know who or what we are, except that we are buckling under the strain of pushing around a wheelbarrow full of philosophies and beliefs. We impose our will, our way, on everything and everybody, until our relationships are just one more possession, one more layer in a system of defence that has become so protective that we fear just about everything. Like the real world. Like ourselves. What is it that we fear about ourselves? That we might be individuals? That we might all be the same?

Shoals of tiny silvery fish, chased perhaps by bigger fish, leap above the surface of the waves, splatter back down like a shower of rain and re-emerge a few yards on. Seagulls watch their submarine progress, anticipate their aerial leaps and await their flight with open beaks.

I'm still busy remembering things. Some things I can't remember if they really happened or if I dreamed them.

I find myself consulting with the bicycle on a few points. I talk at length, not the usual grunt of encouragement, or expletive, or passing comment that I often make, directed indirectly at myself, but a real conversation. I pretend that the bike can hear me, I believe that it has a soul, because I feel the need to share the experience of the trip, how hard and how easy, and because it is harder to doubt the reality of a shared experience. We reminisce, recall particularly amusing events, dispel doubts about events that we can't quite remember, to make them seem more real. I talk with a machine while fish jump out of the sea into the mouths of seagulls.

How far do we go in the name of reality before stumbling into insanity? When does the fish cease, and become a bird? Is this the end of the road, or the beginning?

But to hell with all this speculation! Just for today I'm in Useless Bay and I have no use for answers. I have an overwhelming sense of wellbeing that I feel I must express, but all that comes out is laughter.

Fins break the waves out to sea, and a black and white porpoise shoots out of the water. It waddles along on its tail like they do in dolphinariums, eyes bright, mouth open, click-laughing. It's laughing at something different from me. We laugh together. There's a slightly fishy levity in the squawking of a seagull, and even the bike is chuckling now. Everything is having a good time. Everybody sees the grand joke. It's all O.K. down in Useless Bay.

6. Trouble at the border

I arrive back in Santiago in the middle of March. To get into the British Embassy where I am hoping to collect some mail, I have to explain my way through ranks of heavily armed police who are staking out the Vatican City Consulate in the same block, where a man who blew up a government minister has taken refuge. He's been there three months.

Among several letters are a number from the parcels post office, notifying me of parcels I should collect, several reminders to collect them, and one informing me that a parcel has been returned to sender after having been uncollected for three months.

This turns out to have been a saddle, from Brooks in England. I write thanking them for sending it, apologise for having such an unreliable timetable, and ask them if they could possibly send it back again.

The parcels from my parents are still here though – a set of chainwheels and a magnificent Sun Tour freewheel with thirty six teeth on the largest cog.

By the time the Brooks saddle has made its third transatlantic crossing I have only a few days to leave Chile before my visa extension expires.

The quickest land exit open to me is also the furthest geographically – the coast road north through the Atacama desert to Peru.

I take the bus to Arica and cycle the ten miles to the border. I clear immigration control, but there seems to be some hold up at customs. I am kept waiting around.

'I'm afraid this is very bad', a customs man eventually tells me. 'Your vehicle document is three months out of date. I'm sorry but

you cannot leave the country, and your vehicle must be impounded.'
He holds the offending document in the air.

'But I was told when I extended my visa at the immigration offices
in Punta Arenas that this covered the bicycle too', I explain.

'Oh, they're immigration. This is a customs matter. They don't
know anything', and he points to the expiry date clearly printed on
the vehicle registration document, which no amount of pleading of
ignorance, or of having been officially misled can alter.

An old man appears, dressed casually in a cardigan and slippers,
smoking a pipe. He is the chief customs officer here. He is kindly and
sympathetic, and he spends half an hour searching the thick customs
manual for redeeming clauses. There are none. He phones customs
administration in Arica to find out if they know of any. They don't.

'Our hands are tied', he says, shrugging apologetically.
'You have to go back to the customs offices in Arica.'

I pile in the back of a customs pick up truck and get driven back
to the huge customs complex in Arica. The bicycle is locked away in
a vehicle pound, behind bars. I am escorted inside, ushered from
office to office, official to official, always accompanied by a burly
guard, as if I am going to make a run for it. I explain my case to
a dozen different people. I argue, appeal for sympathy. I express
indignation. It begins to sound limp in the retelling. Customs is
customs, immigration is immigration, and Punta Arenas is three
thousand miles away. People are losing patience with me and the
position is finally made clear: pay the fine or go to jail.

Six people work in the office concerned with the payment of fines.
I find sympathy here. They all agree it is a ridiculous case.

'How much did the bike cost?' one man asks. He needs to know in
order to work out the fine, I tell him two hundred and fifty dollars.
The fine is worked out as increasing percentages of the vehicle's total
cost for every day of its infringement.

'Two hundred and fifty dollars is a lot to pay for a bicycle', he
says. Everybody agrees.

'Two hundred sounds more reasonable', someone suggests.

'Well, I brought a bike and it cost me a hundred dollars – a good
one too', somebody else chips in.

Various lesser figures are thrown around the room, and
eventually it is agreed that a half decent bike can be picked
up for fifty dollars. The fine is calculated accordingly. It amounts

to fifty six dollars, which is a sizeable portion of what I have
with me.

Transgression of the law forgiven in the internationally recognised
manner, the bicycle is unlocked and I am free to leave the country,
I even get a receipt.

Darkness falls as I am riding along the ten mile strip of no man's
land that separates the border controls of Chile and Peru. I sleep
here, behind a bank of sand, happy to imagine myself free of nations
and their regulations for a while.

The Peruvian border control is busy in the morning. Many
people visit Tacna for the day from Arica, and vice versa. At
precisely 8.00 a.m., fifty tourists in transit are left to their own
devices while Peruvian customs and immigration staff rush into the
yard, buttoning shirts, straightening ties, to salute the raising of the
national flag. Marching music blares from loudspeakers.

Tacna is the most southerly town in Peru. It is twenty miles north
of the border. I arrive in time for lunch, eat a raw octopus salad
and read a newspaper. 'Pinochet Asesino' proclaims the headline of
a report on yesterday's Day of Action in Chile, during which three
people were shot dead. One of them was a popular Peruvian singer
on holiday in Santiago. The other two were schoolchildren. All were
of course engaged in subversive activities at the time.

When it is cooler I ride the twenty miles back to the border. I
intend to re-enter Chile, and cross over the Andes by way of the
volcanoes and salt pans to Bolivia. Unforeseen circumstances prevail
however.

I leave Peru, cross the ten miles of no man's land, and get
stamped into Chile by immigration for another three months.
But there seems to be a hold up at customs. I am kept waiting
around.

'I'm afraid there is a problem', a customs man tells me. It
seems that any foreign vehicle which during its stay in the country
has contravened any regulation, is prohibited from re-entering the
country for a period of six months.

The old chief customs man with pipe and slippers, searches the
customs regulation manual for clauses exempting bicycles. There
are none. He is sorry, his hands are tied. I am free to enter Chile,
but not the bicycle.

I thank him for his help. It's not important. I can go over the mountains to Bolivia by way of Peru. Peru is fine.

It is dark again as I recross the ten mile strip of no man's land back towards Peru. During this afternoon's frantic paper shuffling, I was given back two important documents that I had to submit on leaving Chile yesterday. As far as I can tell, these are the only pieces of evidence preventing the bicycle from re-entering Chile. They certainly won't now find their way into the customs computerised information system, so perhaps there is a border a little further east of here where I can cross. I'm scheming and planning as I bed down for the second night in no man's land.

A jeep, crawling along the road, flashing torchlight onto the sand stops nearby. A man climbs out. It is the old chief customs man. He apologises for disturbing my sleep, but says that I am in possession of some documents that should be with customs, and that I must return them. I return them – another plan goes out the window. He warns me to be careful as this whole area is mined, then he wishes me goodnight and returns to the jeep, retracing the footprints of his slippered feet.

I doze off. I'm not out of sight like last night, and soon another vehicle screeches to a halt. It is the Peruvian international police. They direct their car headlights onto me.

'What are you doing?' one of the two policemen calls out.

'I'm sleeping.'

'You can't sleep here. This is a minefield.'

'It's fine. It's no problem.'

'It's prohibited to sleep here. This is Chilean territory.'

'They don't mind. The chief of Chilean customs has just wished me goodnight.'

This is obviously a tall story, and one of the policemen searches around for the tracks of my bicycle in the sand and follows them over.

'You can't sleep here. It is prohibited to sleep here,' he repeats stubbornly. The smell of alcohol wafts down. 'Which way are you going?'

'To Peru. I'll go in the morning.'

'No, you must leave now.'

'I have no lights. I won't be able to follow the road.'

'I'll get a truck', he says.

I am too tired to argue more, it is easier to comply.

Ten minutes later a van comes along. The policemen wave it down and tell the driver to take me to the Peruvian border. They follow behind in their car.

The driver of the van is a Peruvian. He is returning from Arica where he sells clothes. He says that his day permit was issued on the understanding that he brought some beer back for the customs men. He has a crate under the dashboard.

'They'll all be drunk tonight', he says, tipping his hand to his mouth as if swigging from a bottle.

As soon as I get out of the van at the Peruvian border control, the two policemen who picked me up come over and escort me to the immigration shed.

It is Saturday night. A radio is playing. Groups of customs men are standing around, drinking from bottles, accepting bottles from returning Peruvians, and looking like the archetypal unruly border officials – sweaty, fat, unshaven.

'We found him sleeping in the minefield', my two escorts announce, and they all crowd around.

The immigration officer behind the counter is not drunk or unruly.

'Where is your safe conduct pass?' he asks. I don't have one.

'You must have one to enter the country from Chile. You should have received one as you left Chile.'

'I have not actually entered Chile', I explain.

'But your passport is stamped into Peru this morning, and out this afternoon, To re-enter the country you must have your safe conduct pass.'

I point to the most recent entry stamp into Chile, which has been crossed out.

'Look, I did not officially enter Chile. I have nowhere to be safely conducted from so I have no safe conduct pass.'

'Why then did you leave Peru?'

I tell the story – a mistake. At the mention of the word 'fine' all the customs men who are crowded around suddenly come to life, all asking questions and shouting at the same time.

'A fine eh? How much was it?'

'You are a thief? You stole the bicycle?'

'Where is your bicycle licence?'

'Why did you stay only one day in Peru?'

'Why didn't you declare that you had an illegal vehicle when you entered the country this morning?'

'You will have to pay the fine here too.'

Bicycles entering Peru are not required to register as vehicles. I explain, logically it seems to me, that I was fined in Chile, through no fault of my own, for having infringed a minor regulation that does not even exist in Peru, so how can I possibly pay a fine for it?

Logic is unacceptable on a Saturday night. They want money. I'm tired and angry now, and determined not to pay anything. We argue. They take all the things out of my panniers for inspection. My passport is passed around. The receipt for fifty six dollars is drooled over. They are getting quite excited. One man waves the form in the air.

'You'll have to pay again to enter this country', he shouts. Everyone is shouting.

After a while the quiet immigration man takes me into an office. He phones the immigration chief in an adjoining building, explains the situation, and gets the reply that this morning's exit stamp is to be stamped over '*Anulado*' and I am to be allowed to leave. There is half an hour's worth of new forms to fill in to obtain the 'annulled' stamp. Easy in theory, difficult in practice, surrounded by a mob of drunken customs men. There is plenty of arguing and heckling among the customs and immigration men now, jabbing of fingers, wild gesticulations, but eventually I get the required stamp. This signals a lull in the debate. I stuff everything hastily back onto the bike and start wheeling it away.

A small, smartly dressed older customs man, with ribbons of rank on his shoulders bars my way.

'You cannot leave', he says, quietly, authoritatively, which is more threatening than the ravings of the drunken customs men.

He says that they are going to stamp my passport as having entered with a bicycle and that when I leave the country I will have to pay road tax. I can pay it now if I prefer.

I say that this regulation did not apply when I entered Peru this morning, or in the past.

'It is a new regulation,' he says, with a smarmy grin, 'it's just been introduced.'

He is a thoroughly nasty little man. There is a principle at stake here as well as my fast diminishing funds. I say I won't pay. We argue. He takes my passport.

The rest of the drunken mob crowd round and join in, shouting and shoving me. I try to remain calm but I'm too tired and angry to think straight, and soon we are all shouting loudly. There is some jostling, and a group of Chileans and Peruvians from a tourist coach form a circle around us.

Smarmy face stands there smug and grinning with his arms folded. It is a personal thing between us now. I have to hold my hands behind my back in an effort not to punch him right in his smarmy face. He knows it too, and just wants it to happen so that they can all lay into the uncooperative gringo and extract the money he refuses to pay.

It is getting close to a brawl when the quiet immigration man steps in. He speaks calmly, quietly, explaining rationally that I am free to go. Nobody listens. Everybody starts shouting again.

Smarmy face sees that I'm probably not going to hit him now, and takes my passport off to find the customs chief who may take a different view of things from the immigration chief. I sit down. He returns in a few minutes with my passport still in his hands. His chief is too busy to see him at the moment he says, and while he is disappointed and unsure of himself I gently take the passport out of his hands.

I wheel the bike slowly away. The atmosphere is still charged with animosity, the customs men are still heatedly debating the case, and I half expect to be set upon, or at least physically restrained from leaving.

There is just one soldier on duty at the final barrier. It is out of sight of the main customs area and I hope that he is unaware of what has been going on.

He examines my passport.

'Where are you going?'

'To Tacna.'

'You can't go tonight. You must stay in the compound. You can leave tomorrow.'

He leads me to the customs car park out back. It is brightly floodlit, but I sleep anyway because I am exhausted.

In the morning there is a thick mist. Everywhere is quiet, everyone I hope, is sleeping off last night's beer. I am just visible through the mist to the soldier at the final barrier, but he only looks around once in a while. I pack up my sleeping bag, and lie down flat pretending to sleep every time he looks my way. Then I dodge from car to car, and when he is looking the other way, sneak over the low car park wall and race off down the road towards Tacna. `

Moquegua lies in the valley of the river Osmore, a green strip in a landscape of desert gorges. Up in the mountains it is the end of the rainy season, and the road that leads over the high mountains and down to the Altiplano has recently reopened after being impassable for two months.

The mountains rise out of sight, into a haze. Several tiny villages cling to the mountainsides near the bottom of gorges, where streams run down from the high rains, but no one lives alongside the road.

Abandoned terraces cover vast areas of the steep slopes, long disused, rounded over, washed and blown away. Once they were part of a massive Inca desert cultivation system, irrigated by hundreds of miles of stone canals that can still be seen. Now only cacti grow among the rock and sand.

A truck coming down stops to change a wheel on the bend where I'm camped.

'It's raining up there', says the driver, pointing at the mass of black clouds that obscure the mountains not far above. 'The road is a bog.'

The back of the truck is full of people wrapped up in ponchos and blankets against the cold.

'What's it like up there?' I ask.

'It's snowing', replies a woman with her feet resting on a goat. 'You're not half way up yet.'

'Is it far to the next village?' I ask.

'There isn't one', she replies. 'How long will it take you to reach Puno?' she asks.

'A few days', I reply. People laugh with surprise.

As the truck is about to leave, a man throws me down a cooked maize cob, and the woman with the goat heaves it off a pile of canes and hands me one. In towns the canes are ground through a press to extract the juice. It's a popular drink. In the mountains you just chew it and spit out the bits, It's refreshing and sweet, with just a hint of goat.

The cloud base is a soft heavy ceiling, above which the world is transformed from dry desert sunshine to cold misty gloom, where rivulets of rainwater gouge channels through the sand, around bushes and clumps of grass.

Higher still the rain turns to snow, driven horizontally by the wind. It drifts against the bushes, against boulders that are covered with bright green velvety moss, hides the muddy ruts of the road, lightens the bleak dark mountains that drift in and out of view through breaks in the blizzard.

The map shows a number of 16,000 foot passes. I guess I'm in the middle of them because the road levels out, the air is very thin and it's very cold.

I haven't been warm all day, though I've got all my clothes on and I haven't stopped on the steep uphill climb all afternoon for fear of freezing up.

My head pounds with the sudden increase in altitude, my body is numb and feverish, like a foreign thing. I make it clear a patch of ground and put up the tent, shout out loud to remind it to hold onto everything three times as tightly as it thinks it needs, and hurry up and get inside out of the wind and snow.

The tent is torn down several times in the night. I scuttle around outside to restore it, but after the third time I'm more concerned just to keep warm, so pull the flailing pegs and poles inside, and let it collapse around me.

By morning the storm has passed. The sun peeps out between remaining clouds, dazzling the high plains dusted in white, the bright green clumps of tough grass, and a bundle of rags that shakes off a covering of snow.

The high plains between the passes are bleak and windswept. Two articulated lorries are stuck up to their axles in mud. They've been here two days. Half a dozen people stand around huddled up in blankets, conferring, digging up rocks and grass to put under the wheels, not moving.

A natural bridge crosses the river Hot Water, at a place where it steams and bubbles and spurts out jets from conical mounds of brightly coloured mineral deposits. Small frogs hop around, and lizards lie flat-bellied on hot rocks.

Apart from a few stone houses and llama corrals, the plain seems uninhabited, but where two dirt roads converge a hundred or so people are milling around. It is a market – a disorderly, rag-bag, everything spread out on the ground market, where people sit next to piles of popcorn, flour, bread, cans of cooking oil and kerosene and twenty different types of potato, or wander about, chatting, joking, greeting acquaintances, looking under the bonnets of battered trucks and fiddling with the engines so that they might make it back home again, or just sit on the ground on a blanket next to a smoky fire, eating lunch in the middle of nowhere, while the kids slap the horses and donkey, and throw stones at the dogs.

The road winds up to a final pass, and then descends through a steep gorge to the Altiplano, down to Puno on the shores of Lake Titicaca. The lake level is a couple of metres higher than when I was here before. The adobe dwellings nearest the lake are half submerged now. Families have moved in with neighbours occupying higher, less flooded ground, or with relatives in the shanties in the surrounding hills, or sleep on the streets until the water level drops again. The air here is full of flies and smells of sewage.

'Coming or going?' asks the customs man at the quiet lakeside border with Bolivia.

'Going.'

'What's this?' he asks, pointing at the big red letters '*Anulado*' in my passport.

'It's a long story.'

'Not important then', he concludes, whacking down an exit stamp.

17. Tigers in the night

Things appear quite relaxed in Bolivia. The man I find swinging in a hammock in the backyard of the customs building tells me they are closed.

'Go ahead into town and get your stamp there', he calls. 'But hey, do you want to change some dollars?'

It is a familiar road that I follow across the Altiplano to La Paz. Toll booths and barriers lie a short way down the motorway from El Alto on the canyon rim.

'It's prohibited for bicycles', shouts a toll booth man as I sneak under a barrier, 'Come back!'

The economy of Bolivia is still in dire straits. Inflation is running at over a thousand per cent. Exports are down. The price of tin on the world market has slumped. Tin is a major export earner.

The biggest export earner is cocaine. Profits are huge. Hundred per cent pure cocaine powder refined in Bolivia sells on the streets of La Paz for three dollars a gram. The same stuff, cut by perhaps fifty per cent, will sell on the streets of the U.S. and Europe for a hundred dollars a gram. The Bolivian economy, however, does not profit.

Bolivia is unable to make the interest payments on its foreign debt. The finance minister is touring the globe, securing more loans to pay the debt. Some come from other Latin American countries, despite crippling debts of their own. Terms are finally agreed with the I.M.F. for a postponement of interest payments. There is little real alternative. Bolivia is bankrupt.

There are now five hundred Bolivian pesos to the dollar. The black market on Calle Camacho changes dollars at two thousand pesos, and buzzes with rumours of new devaluations. Rumours of a coup abound too. Many people believe that a coup would be a good thing.

I meet Anna in a hardware store where she works for two days a week. She lives in one of the shanties on the west canyon wall near the suburb of Nuevo Potosi. Her mother died a month ago, leaving her alone to bring up her four year old sister. Her father died five years ago.

Anna's house is one room. Three walls are adobe and the other is wooden planks. The roof is sheets of tin, which lets in the rain. It is one of a thousand similar dwellings and lean-tos stacked one above the other. There is no electricity or running water, except the filthy streams which trickle down the gullies, in the maze of alleyways that have no names, that also serve as toilets. There is dysentery, hepatitis, gonorrhoea and T.B. Half a million people live in places like this.

My presence here is tolerated because I am with Anna. Nobody is fooled by the holes in my clothes or my boots that are falling apart. I am affluent, I am a tourist, I am a gringo playing at being poor for a while.

Anna thinks of taking her sister back to Sorata, the village in the mountains east of Lake Titicaca where she was born, where some of her family still live.

'While I have work we can stay in the city', she says. It has been her home for five years.

People in the shanty towns work at what they can in the city, as mechanics, labourers, shoe-shiners. They sell on the streets what they can buy wholesale, what they can get a commission for selling, or what they can steal. They are beggars and thieves, prostitutes and drug dealers, and it doesn't matter what they do so long as they do something, because their children are starving.

Newspapers find their way up to the shanty towns a week old. They are used as mattresses, as house insulation, as toilet paper. A few people can read the news.

A big news story for days concerns three plane loads of electrical appliances that arrived from France. One of the planes stopped off for refuelling at the airport of the eastern lowland city of Santa Cruz. The Santa Cruz customs men took a look at the appliances, found them to be machine guns, and impounded the plane. The weapons were distributed among the Santa Cruz police – it seemed a shame to let them go to waste.

It was a couple of days before President Siles Zuazo could convince the country that this was all above board, that the guns were part of a deal arranged personally between himself and President Mitterrand of France.

The instruction was sent out to allow the plane to continue to La Paz, but the Santa Cruz police like their new guns. They are better than anything they've ever seen before and they want to hang on to them. The wrangling goes on for days.

The machine guns were destined for the army, to help equip a special squad to combat the well-equipped armies of the cocaine business, in one of the periodic 'clean up' operations into the Chapare – the chief cocaine producing area. These jungle forays by the army to flush out the 'narco-traffickers' are generally ineffective because for some reason they are announced a couple of weeks in advance, and all that is found are empty cocaine factories, abandoned airstrips, and an occasional well-prepared ambush.

The Press deride the fight against cocaine as a sham, designed to counter international criticism of Bolivia's inability to control the drug trade, particularly, it is pointed out, criticism from creditor countries.

But people don't need to learn cynicism from the Press. It seems inherent.

'Nobody expects anything from the government except that it will take something away', says Anna, though in the light of past experience this is realism rather than cynicism.

Catholicism runs deep in Bolivia, and hoping perhaps to take advantage of a preoccupation with spiritual matters, the government chooses the start of Holy Week to announce its latest package of measures for economic recovery, that has been expected by everybody ever since the recent deal with the I.M.F.

In its own words, the measures will 'stabilise the economy, reduce inflation, and eliminate the black market for dollars.'

The measures are severe. All prices are raised. Mostly they are trebled – on everything: petrol, kerosene, public transport, electricity, rates, rents, all imported goods (manufacturing industry is virtually non-existent at present so this means everything), all basic foodstuffs – flour, cooking oil, sugar, bread, rice. The peso is devalued by three hundred per cent.

The immediate result of the measures is confusion and disbelief. Everything in the city closes up – shops, banks, factories, post offices, petrol stations. No buses run. No schools open. Nobody knows what the hell is going on. The country is paralysed. An economist could no doubt argue that paralysis is a form of stability.

The university students are the first to take to the streets in protest. They are joined by unions of the workers' cooperative C.O.B. The riot police stand guard in the roads leading to the presidential palace, outside the savings banks, outside the bread shops.

The protest march gathers momentum. All La Paz seems to be out in the streets. The city centre is blocked off, solid with people calling for a withdrawal of the 'starvation package', demanding the expulsion of the I.M.F. representative.

There has been no word of wage increases to accompany the trebling of prices. Many salaried workers with a family to support are living on the bread line already. Those with savings have now a third of what they had yesterday. Many people simply refuse to believe that the government is serious. There is nothing to do but register disapproval on the streets, to wait, to go home to bed, or to spend the night behind barricades of burning tyres, digging up cobblestones to throw at the riot police.

Anna decides to return to Sorata.

'Perhaps it will be better there', she says. 'The campesinos always have a hard life, they always get by.'

Many of the campesinos living away from the cities, virtually outside of the money economy, who never hear anything of the government from one coup to the next, who scratch out a living in the dust without its help, and are paid little attention by the government because they have nothing, are, initially at least, less affected by economic upheavals. It will all come back to them in the end of course. The cost of this temporary independence is perpetual poverty.

Anna visits the cemetery across the city, where the ashes of her mother sit in a pot in one of the tiny vaults stacked up in rows of tumbledown walls, grown over with creepers and spindly weeds. An old woman wrapped in a bundle of rags lives in the graveyard. She makes a living by sitting in the dust near the ashes of the recently deceased, chanting blessings when the relatives visit.

Anna has nothing to give her. She is broke. She has spent the last of her devalued pesos on a bunch of flowers.

I give something to the old woman, as I give something to Anna and her sister for the truck ride to Sorata that she queues for three hours for, as I give something to the beggars on the streets, to the woman with a baby a few hours old, born on the pavement – a few meagre charitable acts that will momentarily alleviate a little hunger, alleviate my conscience.

The only commercial transactions that take place for several days are those on the pavement markets. There is constant argument because prices rise hourly.

The government holds talks with representatives of C.O.B., to thrash out terms for the running of essential services, but is intent on pushing ahead with its economic recovery policies, undeterred by criticism that the austerity measures are merely cosmetic, that they take advantage of the poor, that they have failed anyway because at a stroke inflation has trebled, and speculation on the currency black market has intensified and continues apace under the noses of the authorities on Calle Camacho.

Illegal dealings are suspended momentarily however – when marching miners toss a few sticks of dynamite into the midst of pavement negotiations.

There is a shortage of cash in the economy because its value has been cut by a third. Printing companies in Germany and England are commissioned to print new high denomination notes – twenty and fifty thousand pesos. Meanwhile the government prints ten thousand and thirty thousand peso paper cheques to tide over the shortage.

The asphalt road leading to Cochabamba, that meets the dirt track over the mountains from the Altiplano, is an engineering master-piece. It winds for fifty miles around precipitous mountainsides, dropping six thousand feet to the Cochabamba valley. It has white and yellow lines painted on, crash barriers around the more perilous bends, and warning signs that read 'Geological Fault' before those stretches that have slid down, or been buried by the mountainsides.

I meet not one vehicle all the way down. A sports teacher accompanies me into the city of Cochabamba. He is not working today because the schools are on strike.

He tells me that the crack Leopards detachment of the army, accompanied by gringos from the C.I.A. and D.E.A., are setting out from Cochabamba tomorrow to flush out the 'narco-traffickers' from the Yungas region, and that the campesinos there are worried because the U.S. embassy in La Paz, in true Wild West spirit, has offered a hundred dollars to any soldier who brings in a 'narco' dead or alive. A hundred dollars is three months' wages, and they fear that the soldiers may become indiscriminate in whom they deem to be a 'narco'.

I take a tortuous route through the mountains between Cochabamba and Sucre, through gorges of tributaries of the Rio Grande, so narrow and deep that they only see the sun for a few hours. People pan for gold in the river and tributaries, and spend the nights in shelters dug into the riverside, with roofs of grass and pieces of sacking that somehow keep them alive through the nights that are so cold that even some of the waterfalls that plunge over the towering cliffs are silenced and frozen.

In the shacks that have sprung up with this desperate gold rush there is flour and maize and coca leaves for sale, and they'll measure you out an ounce of gold dust for three hundred and fifty dollars.

Sucre is an old Spanish colonial town. It is the official capital city of Bolivia, and a fashionable place to live. In the evenings the benches and trees and pretty fountains in the central plaza are colourfully floodlit, and families come out to stroll in the cool evening air, or ride around in jeeps and on mopeds that never leave the confines of town, because even though it is the official capital of Bolivia, all the roads in and out are rough dirt.

The beggars still curl up in doorways to sleep, and people have to queue for kerosene and bread and cooking oil and other essential foodstuffs.

From Sucre I intend to travel south east, through Paraguay and Brazil to Uruguay. This is all part of the journey homeward. In Uruguay I expect to collect the remainder of my original five thousand pounds fund, which should be enough for the air fare to England.

But there is no rush. Which is just as well because I have to spend a little time in Sucre waiting for my left knee to recover from the wayward journey across the high passes from Cochabamba. It has swollen up and refuses to bend.

The woman in one of the two bicycle shops in Sucre is surprised that none of her stock of bicycle tyres will fit my wheels. Twenty eight inch tyres are too big and the twenty seven inch tyres are too small. I will need two new ones for the journey to Paraguay.

'It's not a problem', she declares, 'We can reduce them for you.'

I don't know what she means by this 'reducing', but she shows me. She takes a twenty eight inch tyre and, with a pair of pliers, makes tiny twists in the wire running through the rim, until it fits tightly over the wheel.

The spring in the front brake broke on the way here. Both brakes are essential in the mountains, to share the braking on long descents when they are in use for hours on end. Even with both brakes, the wheel rims become excessively hot, which risks buckling, or bursting the tubes, and halts are necessary, preferably where streams cross the road, to allow them to cool. The woman in the bike shop has no spare springs.

'It's not a problem', she says, and I have no doubt that she is right. I show her the two pieces of broken spring, and she fashions a new one from a spoke. It works perfectly of course.

I am limping around the town when there is a tap on my shoulder.

'Hello Cris,' a familiar face greets me.

'Hello', I say, and pause, trying to remember the name. He looks like Olaf, the German I met six months ago in Chile.

'Olaf!'

No, it's not Olaf. It's Billy. Billy the German psychologist I met in the Spanish school in Guatemala. Since I last saw him he has been back to Germany, sold all his Mexican hammocks in the hot European summer, and come back to South America with the profits.

'Bolivia is in a mess', Billy says.

We discuss the mess. It is hard to gain an overall picture of what is happening in the country. The mess is not new, it is not always news, and when the newspapers are not on strike, for this and in some cases for political reasons, front page news is always the Pope, the war in Central America, Peruvian guerrillas, a state of siege in Columbia, genocide in Brazil, and everywhere else civil unrest, people demanding elections, and on the inside pages: further deals imminent with the World Bank, with the I.M.F., with the Organisation of American States, two Bolivian boys got their legs blown off by mines along the border with Chile, and Bolivia wants

Antofagasta back, come on folks, forget hyperinflation, malnutrition, desertification, *Hacia el Mar*, Ra Ra Ra.

I tell Billy I'm heading for Uruguay, to pick up some money, because I've seriously decided to go home, although I decided months ago now, which shows how serious I am.

Billy has come up from the eastern plains in a truck, and though it is just three hundred miles to Camiri – the next 'real town' – the journey took three days because the road over the mountains is a quagmire. Billy is expecting some mail in Sucre, so he is waiting for the post office to reopen. He has been here a week so far.

The man at the tourist office assures me that the road to Camiri is transitable, though from there, the road across the Chaco to Paraguay is difficult.

'It is deep sand, and full of tigers, and the only people who use it are contrabandists', he says.

Beyond the high ridge at Padilla, the road descends from high dry valleys of cacti and scrub into wet humid valleys, and ridge after ridge of thickly forested mountains, descending to the eastern plains.

The trees are full of squawking parrots, woodpeckers and kingfishers. Snakes bask in the road, and lizards lie around, gobbling up butterflies that collect in huge groups. Stick insects fling themselves acrobatically into the air, and land on their backs, stick legs akimbo.

There are a hundred varieties of ant – black ones, brown ones, orange and red ones, some an inch long, some that dig holes several inches across and a foot deep, into which they drag large insects, and anything else that they can move.

The vegetation encroaches on the road, the air hums with decomposition, but the soil is a thin layer of humus, and when the land is cleared it can quickly disappear. The road is sand, or when the road and a river follow the same course through steep gorges, deep trenches of sloppy mud. It is slow going.

There is little space at the side of the road to sleep at night, but occasionally, particularly around bends, the road has slipped down the mountainside – a few feet or yards – and a new road has been carved out above, leaving the old road hanging, disconnected. These vestiges are flat and out of the path of traffic – though traffic is limited to just a few trucks – and make ideal camping spots. The landscape is mountains and forest, and seems uninhabited but people always appear.

I'm sitting on just such a spot, eating some supper next to a smoky fire – smoky because all the dead wood is damp, which is fine because it keeps the mosquitos away – looking out at the mist collecting in the valley below, and listening to the sound of voices, wafting up from goodness only knows where, because since leaving Sucre I've lost track of the days and the distance I've come, trudging through measureless tracks of sludge in a world of humid green, when I make out a figure of a man with an axe over his shoulder, watching me from a distance.

'Good evening', I call out. He comes over.

He tells me that he has been chopping wood higher up the slope, to make a fence to keep the goats and pigs out of his maize patch. His axe head has 'Made in England' embossed in it. I tell him I come from England too. He says it is a good axe, and tells me how he moved into this valley only last year, from one of the high desert valleys north east of Sucre. The rain there failed to come for the second year running, the river dried up completely so nobody could grow crops, the animals died or were eaten, but the government trucked in tankers of drinking water, and distributed sacks of grain sent from Canada.

Many families like his move in times of drought to the lush slopes of the eastern sierras. Many families can no longer survive in the mining cities of the Altiplano because, with the fall in the price of tin on the world market, mines are no longer economic to run, and in the current climate of austerity many families move anyway, to the valleys of the Chapare where they are provided with land and young coca bushes by the cocaine industry, and guaranteed a regular income from the coca harvest.

Insects chirrup into the early hours, and the birds start singing long before dawn. When the sun rises, the whole valley below is hidden under a layer of mist, with a few islands of green poking up as if from a sea, into the bright sunshine.

There are a couple of huts directly below the piece of disconnected road that I didn't notice last night. Two men and a crowd of small children come up the slope as I pack up the tent.

'Why didn't you come to sleep with us last night?' one man asks.

A woman calls out from below for the children to come back for their breakfast, but they stay here with the two men. Then two women come up too, with hot maize cakes baked in banana leaves.

'Here gringo, there's some for you too'.

We all sit around eating, and presently a man comes crashing down a footpath from the trees above. He is carrying an enormous sack on his back. The sack is full of clothes that he hawks round from village to village selling. He spreads some out for us to see.

A man on a moped comes along next. He is a malaria doctor, armed with a rifle and a box of medicine. He sits down too, and brings out a bag of oranges. Then we bring out our bags of coca leaves and have a chew, except for the children and the doctor.

The doctor tells us that malaria is rife in the area, that many children die from it, though the biggest killer is dehydration through diarrhoea and dysentery. A hundred thousand babies die from this alone every year, but there is little he can do about it because people will go on shitting right next to the rivers. One of the men from the huts says that there was a cocaine factory near here but it has recently been abandoned.

'Everybody grows a few coca bushes around here', he says. 'The government pays some of the commercial growers to grow other crops. Many of them are not interested, and move to the Yungas where the 'narcos' pay them more. I don't know why there is such a fuss, and anyway, how are we supposed to work without coca? It's the first thing we do after breakfast – every day, everybody chews coca.'

'Coquear' is the verb 'to chew coca.' People who chew it are 'coqueros'. The millions of Indians who regularly chew the leaf give it as much thought as do the millions of Britons to the caffeinism of habitual tea drinking.

'Do they chew coca in England?' one of the men asks me.

I say no, coca doesn't grow in England. But some people take cocaine.

'Do they take it to work?' he asks.

I say no, they take it for fun, like alcohol.

'But what do you have to make you work?'

I say that we drink tea several times a day, which has much the same effect, which puts me in mind for drinking some, so I brew up a pot, and we all just sit around, not working, drinking tea and chewing coca, talking and admiring the view, and then the doctor sees the *charango* strapped to the bicycle, and insists on playing us his repertoire, and we all take it in turns to sing our songs, and the man with the sack of clothes even does a little dance in the middle of the road.

At the bottom of the valley is Muyupampa. I enter on foot, pushing the bike through deep sand. I seem to have been walking quite a lot recently.

In the course of my journey through the village, I am given a plate of potato stew, a fried egg roll, and offered the price of a truck ride to the next village by people who assume that I travel like this because I have no money. I say that I choose to travel like this because I like it, that I have money, but it doesn't stop them from pressing oranges and bread rolls on me for the journey.

A crowd of children escort me for a couple of miles out of the village, and show me the wreck of a truck that plunged over a cliff two weeks ago, where fifteen people died, 'Two of them gringos, just like you.'

They assure me that the road ahead is good and firm, though as always it is deep sand or sludge and I have to walk.

Camiri is called the Petrol Capital of Bolivia. Oil and gas is extracted nearby. Gas is exported by pipeline to Brazil and Argentina, but not to Paraguay which is nearer than either. Trade links between Bolivia and Paraguay have not prospered since the Chaco War fifty years ago, when Bolivia lost hundreds of square miles of territory to Paraguay, though at present nobody is getting much of anything in the way of foreign trade from Bolivia.

Camiri has concrete streets, street lamps, and an economic importance that requires travellers wishing to stay the night to register with the police.

It has taken me ten days to come from Sucre. The police recommend that if I'm heading for Paraguay I should take a gun because the route is full of tigers and smugglers.

The export of contraband fuel is at present one of the few thriving trades.

Y.P.F.B. – the Bolivian oil company – claims that the three hundred per cent devaluation of the peso has made it uneconomical to produce petrol for the domestic market, and that even with the threefold increase in the price of petrol it cannot afford to buy the imported technology on which it depends, which must be paid for in dollars, because the peso is unexchangeable outside the country, and it has to buy black market dollars at the inflated rate. In addition to this, the Y.P.F.B. workers are on an indefinite strike.

But while the Bolivian economy grinds to a halt, and the ancient, weary trucks of the country's minimal transport system queue at petrol stations, a steady trickle of fuel is smuggled across the border to Paraguay.

In the present climate it is the cause of national outrage. The Press carries photos of former Y.P.F.B. tankers on route across the Chaco, and suggests government and Y.P.F.B. complicity in the illegal trade.

The chief customs officer in charge of the vast, largely uninhabited region bordering with Paraguay, is sacked for turning a blind eye to the petrol contrabandists, and a number of other irregularities.

A track that leads to Paraguay leaves the main north–south low-land road at the village of Boyuibe. There is a customs control here, though the border is nearly a hundred miles away. The customs men try to dissuade me from proceeding.

'There is nothing out there,' one of them explains, 'just bush and silence. Nobody lives there, the road is very bad and there's no water.'

I say that I'm going anyway.

'What sort of gun do you carry?' he asks.

I say I have no gun.

'But there are many tigers. They hunt at night. They climb trees over the track, but you won't see them until they drop on you.'

'Wherever I go, people always warn me of tigers, but I've never seen one', I reply.

There are no tigers in South America, but people always refer to 'tigres' when they speak of big cats.

'They're not tigers,' says another man, 'they're pumas and jaguars. They leap out of trees and eat people', he continues, warming to the subject now, and goes on to document cases of mauling and death.

I ask about transport.

'There is none. Only contrabandists – very rare. Perhaps in a couple of weeks a truck may go through.'

The track into the Chaco soon deteriorates to a set of tyre tracks, a foot deep and a foot wide, through soft sand. The ridge in between is full of tall grass and flowers.

The vegetation on either side consists of tough bushes, small trees and cacti. Every plant, big and small, bears sharp spines, protection against animals and an adaptation to dry conditions. The Chaco is not a desert, but there is very little surface water because the terrain is so flat, and rain simply soaks down through the sandy soil.

Bushes and trees hang over the road, forming gloomy tunnels. Where I am able to ride I must constantly fend off the overhanging prickly branches. The breeze that rustles the topmost branches of trees never penetrates down into the humidity below. It is exhausting work.

Hundreds of butterflies of all colours and sizes follow me, smelling moisture and salt. When I stop they crowd around the tops of the water bottles, settle on my clothes and skin, curling and uncurling their long tongues.

It is magical to be covered in butterflies, but other insects are less welcome. A hundred varieties of creeping crawling creatures besiege me whenever I stop – familiar ants and beetles, and an army of unusual and extraordinarily shaped insects.

The flies are unbearable. Even when I am moving I have no chance of outrunning them. It does no good to swat at them because they make no attempt to fly off, and it just makes a thick black paste on which a thousand more come to feed. I pull them from my ears and wipe them from my face, and the sensation of them crawling all over my skin is so disgusting that I pull on slacks and a shirt and sweat it out in preference.

A bright red black and orange striped snake slithers slowly away as I pitch the tent in the road – in the middle of the road. Nobody will drive past tonight without stopping to offer a lift. I avoid the most obvious ant holes and hills, but lines of them are marching all over the place. A long line of moving leaves on closer inspection is revealed as a column of ants, four abreast, carrying pieces of leaf aloft in their jaws. The sound of their feet is audible as a hiss. The column extends for several hundred yards before disappearing down a hole.

I count six different types of mosquito, and tape up the splits in the netting over the door and back flap of the tent. I plug some of the holes in the groundsheet with bits of rag soaked in petrol.

Inside the tent it is bliss not to be covered with flies, and I doze off to sleep.

Something wakes me during the night – the sound of something rustling through the bushes towards the tent. A person? No, too slow and ponderous. A cow perhaps. Yes, that's it.

I always sleep with the doors and back flap rolled back, so I can see out. I peer through the mosquito netting. Blackness. Silence.

Suddenly a large shape moves past, glides almost, and circles around to the back of the tent. Looking through the back flap I can make out the outline of a large cat. I lie still, hardly daring to breathe. A deep throaty purr comes from outside, and then the sound of more noises from the bush. Now there are two of them prowling around, circling the tent, purring softly.

I don't dare shout at them because I am so scared that any sound I make is sure to betray my fear, and then they'll know it's O.K. to come in. Perhaps if I feign sleep they will think I am unconcerned, fearless, and go away. I snore gently, confidently. They stop prowling, come right up to the walls of the tent and sniff, loudly. I don't think they are fooled.

I must scare them away before they get too brave. What sound can I make that will not sound like a whimper of defeat? And what if I startle them so much that they are provoked to attack? They might just leap onto the tent. But the suspense is unbearable. I quietly select the large spanner and saucepan. This is it then.

I wait until they stop sniffing, and let rip, banging the pan with the spanner, and uttering a loud demonic shouting laugh.

Ho! Ho ! Ho!, clang clang clang!, Ha! Ha! Ha!

Then there is silence.

In the morning there are tracks of large paws, circling the tent, and two sets leading off down the road, one in each of the tyre tracks. But there is a deer too, with long legs and big ears, grazing on the flowers in the middle of the road just a little way off, so I guess the night visitors are long gone.

It is time to think about the flies again now. It is still unpleasant to be covered from head to toe, but I can ignore them for long stretches, just picking off the ones I recognise as deliverers of nasty bites or stings. The bright red crab-shaped ticks are the worst, burying their heads, jaws first, under the skin. Mostly they give a painful nip, but some manage to tunnel in unfelt, and I only notice them by chance.

I am quite keen to be out of here, but the going is slow. I have to walk for much of the way, and something I have eaten has made me sick.

At dusk it is time to think about tigers again. Ready made weapons are limited to a flimsy two inch penknife blade. I try out some stabbing techniques with a screwdriver on some mosquitos, which seem unimpressed, scatter some sturdy poles around outside, and haul a few stout staves inside the tent. Saucepan and spanner, proven deterrents, are of course placed close at hand, and a piece of cloth poked as a wick into the wine bottle of petrol gives some security as a last resort. The petrol fuels the stove I bought in Santiago.

The tent nylon is whipped and cracked startlingly several times in the night, but I hear no growling or prowling. There are paw tracks circling the tent when I emerge in the morning however.

Six young soldiers and an old sergeant are stationed at the army post at the border. They sleep in one small stuffy room. In the other room is a desk, a wind-up army telephone, a barrel of drinking water, and a map of Bolivia on the wall.

I give the sergeant three dollars and he gives me an exit stamp and a drink of cleanish water from the barrel.

'Paraguay is down there', he says, pointing down the sandy track. 'Good luck.'

An hour's walk brings me to a collection of brick huts. There are a dozen soldiers here, dressed in blue. This is Fort Rodrigues, the first army post in Paraguay.

The soldiers tell me that the main army post is Fort Garay, ten kilometers down the track. It takes me all day to reach. Fifty conscripts are stationed at Fort Garay, in a small barracks in a couple of acres of cleared land. A large mansion is under construction, and a large major and his wife live here.

'You have my permission to pitch your tent and remain the night', the major booms from the unfinished balcony. He has a liking for bawdy jokes and whisky.

It is two hundred miles to the town of Filadelfia, along the sandy track, but there are several army posts along the way.

In the morning I manage to struggle a mile or so through the deep sand in an hour, before giving up and turning back. I am quite sick and weak now.

I tell the major that I will remain here until I feel better or until a truck comes along. He says an army truck will come with supplies in a couple of weeks, and if I'm still here then I can get a lift, but he thinks that the petrol contrabandists will be coming through from Bolivia in a couple of days.

Meanwhile, I sleep in a bed in the barracks. There are showers and toilets, and piped water here. The soldiers are seventeen years old, doing their military service. Most of them opted to do it in the Chaco for a year. In the rest of the country military service lasts for eighteen months. They are all looking forward to returning to civilian life – to their families, farms, shops, garages, to start up businesses of their own. They are a friendly bunch of boys. Their faces are chubby, and glow from a diet of greasy meat. Their uniform is a blue overall, and a blanket with a hole cut in the middle, to wear as a poncho in cold weather. Their boots are ill fitting, and most prefer to go barefoot.

Army routine is strictly observed, but the relationship between the major, the sergeant and the conscripts seems relaxed. The place is run more like a scout camp than an army, except that the boys have to lug machine guns around wherever they go.

Reveille is at dawn. The boys line up and chant the army prayer. Then they each get a cup of *maté* before a couple of hours' work – cleaning the barracks, clearing the Chaco, sweeping around the big house and the exercise yard.

Next comes breakfast. The big oil drum that is the cooking pot is heaved over from the brick and thatch cookhouse that stands on its own in the clearing. I get issued with a tin bowl, and line up with the others.

Breakfast is the same as lunch and tea – meat stew. Sometimes there is a little rice, or noodles, floating around with the hunks of meat, but never any fresh vegetables or fruit. The major's wife is overseeing the construction of a vegetable garden. So far it is just a five ton mound of topsoil.

During the day work is done on the house. Some of the boys look after the fifty cattle that wander into the Chaco during the day and return to the corral at night. On some days there is drill.

As night falls, a drone can be heard all around the camp. Then the mosquitos invade. The boys sit out on the verandah, swatting mosquitos, drinking *maté*, playing guitars, embroidering their caps, and talking of what they will do when they leave the army.

Two battered petrol tankers with Y.P.F.B. markings half sanded off, rumble into the camp one morning. There are three Bolivians with each tanker. The major knows them all. A drum of petrol is syphoned off by way of an entry agreement, and in exchange for some meat.

They are taking the petrol to Filadelfia, and agree to take me along – if I don't mind riding on the roof for a couple of days. The roof racks are piled high with spare wheels and bundles tied up in tarpaulins. Two boys from the camp come along too, to get a few supplies – whisky for the major, and orange juice for his wife.

On top of a tanker is a comfortable place to see the Chaco – up above the bushes in the breeze, and free from flies that are kept away by the smell of petrol.

The first few miles take several hours because the tankers keep getting stuck in deep sand, and have to be towed out – backwards or forwards depending on which one gets stuck.

The tankers keep going through the night, everybody takes a turn at the wheel.

'Hey, gringo, do you want to drive?' someone calls up.

When there are punctures the men draw lots to see who will fix it. The rest stand around a fire, brewing coffee, chewing coca, drinking whisky and telling stories.

The track ahead is straight. Way in the distance a light can sometimes be seen, flickering. Nobody knows what it is. One of the drivers who comes this way a lot says that he often sees it. He thinks it is an optical illusion, a reflection perhaps of our own fire, or the tanker headlights, though it remains when they are turned off and we shield the fire. The two soldiers think it is the eyes of a tiger, or a fire of the Indians who live in the Chaco, who flag down vehicles pretending to hitch a ride and then hack the occupants to pieces and eat them. They keep hold of their rifles.

The next army post is called Mister Long. Mr Long was an

American who helped negotiate peace terms that ended the Chaco War fifty years ago. It was also called the Oil Company War, because Standard Oil supported Bolivia, and Shell supported Paraguay, in hostilities over a piece of land that, prior to the notion that lucrative concessions could be secured to exploit what were believed to be rich deposits, neither country showed much interest in. A few Guarani Indians were the only inhabitants of thousands of square miles.

Hundreds of thousands of people died in the conflict. Many Paraguayans simply died of thirst, because all supplies, including water, had to be brought to the front by truck along appalling tracks. Deep sand in the dry season, bogs during the rains. The work of those drivers passed into legend. They became national heroes. In the capital Asuncion, the '*Choferes del Chaco*' are commemorated with statues, and roads are named in their honour.

No oil was discovered in the disputed region. A couple of drums of petrol are syphoned off at Mister Long.

After two days we arrive at the army town of Mariscal Estigarribia. Ten per cent of the remaining petrol is syphoned from the tankers here. We wait under the shade of a tree, by a cafe near the transit checkpoint while our passports are stamped into the country.

The drivers know the woman who owns the cafe – they seem to know everybody along the route – and we eat a meal which they pay for with petrol.

Fifty miles beyond Mariscal is the town of Filadelfia, the centre of a German speaking Mennonite community. They farm the land around here, and run the factory, hotel and large general store in town.

The contrabandists sell the rest of the petrol to contacts here, though only after they have negotiated rooms in the hotel for the night in exchange for petrol. Each of them is paid one hundred dollars for the trip, which is good money here. They will return to Bolivia with the empty tankers in a few days' time, to pick up another load.

I leave the bicycle and most of my junk at the hotel in Filadelfia, and take the bus to Asuncion. From there I take more buses, on a lightning tour of Brazil, and on to Montevideo in Uruguay, where I pick up the money that will buy an air ticket home to England. I intend to fly from Bolivia.

18. Smugglers and armadillos

I am pleased to get back to Filadelfia, collect the bike and head back towards Bolivia. During the past two weeks, whizzing around on buses, I have felt bored for the first time in two years.

A convoy of four brand new Toyota trucks and a jeep is going my way, heading for Santa Cruz in Bolivia. A dozen Bolivians are with the vehicles, and two young lads with the military police who are hitching a ride to Mister Long.

I am offered a lift and I gratefully accept. I have equipped myself with a hefty knife, suitable for killing tigers, but the chance to avoid meeting them altogether, and days of trudging through deep sand, I cannot pass up.

Before reaching Mariscal, the trucks pull off the road, up a side track into the bush. The three men in the jeep who have bought the trucks drive on to the military post to arrange permission to take the trucks out of the country via the Chaco.

The trucks were bought in Asuncion for fifteen thousand dollars each. To buy them in Bolivia, or to import them, would cost a total of thirty thousand dollars because of import tariffs. For this reason the Bolivians are going to smuggle them across the border.

'What does Bolivia need?' asks Nelson. 'The country comes to a halt because there is no transportation. All the trucks are fifty years old and they always break down. Businesses cannot move their goods and they go bust. Only the gringo companies can afford to buy new trucks. I love my country. We all do. We can't stand by and watch it collapse. The government talks about economic recovery, but it does nothing. So we have to break the law to see something gets done.'

'The government is full of shit', adds Pancho. 'It has fucked the country right up.'

The owners of the trucks return in the jeep. They say it might be a couple of days before they can arrange permission for the trucks to pass. Meanwhile we will have to stay out of sight in the bush. They return to Mariscal, to sleep at the cafe.

A fine drizzle falls from a leaden sky. There is no wind. We sit around a fire, waiting, drinking coffee, talking. Nelson and Pancho are always discussing something.

Armadillos wander out of the thick Chaco vegetation. Pancho chases after them. They don't run away, but curl into a ball, and he picks them up and slings them into the back of one of the trucks.

'Let them be', says Nelson.

'But they are good to eat', says Pancho. He turns one onto its back, stabs it through its belly and tosses it onto the fire where it slowly uncurls as it cooks.

Pancho makes a living as a mechanic in Santa Cruz, and hiring himself out to drive contraband trucks across the borders with Paraguay and Brazil. He is full of stories. He tells Nelson about Brazil, how big it is. Nelson doesn't believe him. I say it's true. Some cities in Brazil have more inhabitants than the whole population of Bolivia.

'That's right', says Pancho, 'take Sao Paulo. They say sixteen million people live there. Half live in the slums and the other half work in industries. It's huge. Look at all the Brazilian goods we get in Bolivia. They all come from there. You'd think with all that industry, and all the timber they chop down in Amazonia that everybody would be driving around in their own cars. They don't. Brazil is all fucked up too. You think Bolivia has a big foreign debt? Brazil owes a hundred billion dollars. Their government is full of shit too.'

'It's not the government, it's the I.M.F. that is full of shit,' argues Nelson. 'Just like in Bolivia. The government has to do whatever it is told. Everybody knows that. It's the same in all of Latin America.'

'Pah!' exclaims Pancho, 'The I.M.F., the government, what's the difference? They're all full of shit. The countries may be broke, and people like you and me have to work to pay off the debt, but the governments do all right. Look at the man in charge of the Bank of Brazil. He owes a hundred billion dollars, and he's still got his own car and walks around in a five hundred dollar suit. Look at our government. The country is bankrupt. But do you see any government minister walking around without any shoes? It's all one big club. We pay for their cars and their five hundred dollar suits. They're all full of shit.'

We remain hidden here for two days. The two young Paraguayan military policemen are worried about tigers so I lend them my tent to sleep in. The only sound during the nights is the dainty clattering of armadillos in the back of the trucks.

The men in the jeep return on the third day to say it's O.K. to turn up with the trucks at Mariscal now. They will be permitted to pass on payment of an as yet undecided sum. This sum will depend among other factors, on how the trucks look, so we splatter the shiny new paintwork with mud and smear the shiny wheels with slime.

It is good to be moving again because we are tired of the drizzle and eating armadillos.

In Mariscal we park under the trees next to the cafe, and submit our passports to the army. Two more people will continue to Bolivia with us when we leave – an English guy called Ian and his Paraguayan wife. They have been here for several days hoping for a lift. At night, Ian has to sleep in the guard house of the transit checkpoint because he is under 'semi arrest'. He doesn't know exactly what 'semi arrest' is though. He had some trouble with some of the soldiers. They beat him with their rifles, though he says everybody has calmed down now.

The Bolivians while away the evening drinking in the back of one of the trucks. Nelson tells us about his father who fought in the Chaco War, about how he was taken prisoner, and escaped up the river Paraguay to Brazil in a home made raft.

The tales get taller as the whisky goes down. Pancho tells us about the mountain that sticks up out of the plain near Santa Cruz. There is an Inca burial site near the top, where gold is said to be hidden. Many have tried to find it – gringos too, but the mountain has a spell on it. Even on clear days, when people climb the mountain they find fog comes down and the ground is shaken by thunder and lightning. It is always the same, he says. They all get lost and end up fleeing back down in terror.

'You should come and look for the gold', he says to me. 'You can stay with me in Santa Cruz. If you don't find it I'll give you a job driving trucks across the border.'

The two military policemen are still worried about tigers, and pitch my tent in the cafe yard.

We pass through the following day to Fort Garay, where torchlight negotiations take place with the fat major. He takes three hundred dollars to allow each truck to pass. It has been raining heavily all day and the track has become a bog.

To avoid the border control of the Bolivian army we leave the main track here, and follow incredibly rough trails that have been turned into bogs by the steady downpour.

The trucks move mostly in a sideways fashion with the wheels constantly spinning. One or other of the vehicles frequently becomes stuck, and has to be towed out. Sometimes the towing vehicle becomes stuck too. In places the trail is so bad that we have to leave it completely and force a new trail to the side.

The smugglers are well prepared. They have axes and machetes, tow ropes, chains and spades, and pots of grease that they smear over the paintwork to reduce scratching from the overhanging trees and bushes that constantly claw at the sides and roofs of the trucks.

Pancho and Nelson continually argue about something. In places, deep pits have been dug across the trail by the Bolivian army to foil contrabandists, and a new trail has to be cut and slashed to the side. Nelson says that the army can at least dig good pits. Pancho says that the army can't dig shit.

The jeep and lead truck become stuck in a particularly bad stretch. It takes an hour to dig them out, and another hour to clear a new trail to the side. The rain pours down. It is pitch dark. The trucks have to be skidded up a bank to get around. The truck I am in comes through last. Pancho is at the wheel. At the crucial moment when the wheel must be turned, he is arguing with Nelson about whose turn it is to smoke the cigarette. Both his hands are in the air, gesticulating wildly, and we fly into the quagmire.

'Holy shit we're in the shit!', says Pancho, and continues to swear as he ploughs through, while Nelson and I get bounced around the cab. Somehow we reach firmer ground without being swallowed up, or turning over.

By daybreak we are nearly out of the Chaco. The Paraguayan licence plates, registration papers, and any other evidence of having come from Paraguay are thrown away. Bolivian licence plates are fixed on. We mount the railway track, cross over a large river on a narrow viaduct, and come out on the main road near a village called San Antonio, where the contrabandists turn north towards Santa Cruz. I thank them for the lift and turn south.

The river Pilcomayo outside the town of Villa Montes is a rich red brown. No one moves around unnecessarily through the streets because they have been turned to seas of sloppy red brown mud in the recent rain.

I take a room in the hotel. The water from the taps is tainted a light red brown colour. The woman who runs the hotel says that it is always like that, but it is O.K. to drink. She is cooking fish caught from the river. The fish are red brown. She has theories about all the world's troubles, and manages to expound them in response to any question. I ask her if many foreigners stay here.

'No, not many', she replies. 'There is nothing here for tourists. It is just a town in Bolivia where the people are poor. Tourists don't come for that. They want art, or they want to see how the Incas lived, they want pretty costumes and folk music, and to eat what are called 'national dishes' in restaurants in the cities. Some tourists come to see what Bolivia is really like, to meet the people, but when they see the poverty they turn away because it is unpleasant. Or they pretend that it does not exist. Or they give it noble virtues. What can they do? What do you do?' she asks me.

I say I don't do anything. Except that sometimes I make people smile because they think it's funny to see a gringo on a bicycle. I don't know what I can do and it makes me sad sometimes.

'They don't want your pity', she says. 'They get pity from other Bolivians, from the people in the cities. The people in the cities see the Indians and they are a race apart. They don't know what they want and they don't know what they think. It's the same with the tourists. Nobody understands one another.'

'Sometimes people do understand one another', I say. 'When I speak with people, they may be very poor, and we have little in common, but they understand what I am saying, and what I mean. They don't see me as a tourist or a rich foreigner from another country. They treat me as an individual, as just another person.'

'Oh yes, people can understand other people', the woman agrees, 'And the poor people can understand you because they have no time to do anything else.'

Perhaps this is the case. We who have time, forget that we are people, individuals. We think instead that we are nations, religions, soldiers, politicians, poets, painters, superiors, inferiors. We forget that we are human beings. We forget that everybody else is a human being. We imagine that we are something else, we imagine that we are all separate, and the result is always bloody conflict, brutality, misunderstanding and poverty, as we try to reunite the world, with our armies and our governments, with our poems and with our gods, that only contain the seed of further division, because they are born from our own divided selves.

To stay the night in Villa Montes I must register with the army. I hunt around for an immigration office, in order to get an entry stamp for my passport, but there isn't one.

'You have no entry stamp in your passport', says the sergeant at the town's army headquarters.

'That's correct', I reply. 'I have looked for the immigration office so that I can get one. I came from Paraguay and didn't pass any border controls.'

'Didn't you come along the road?' he asks. 'There are controls on all of the roads.'

'I got a lift in a truck. We must have taken a different route.'

'You are an illegal immigrant. There is no immigration office here, so you must go to the police.'

I visit the police post.

'No, sorry. We don't have any stamps here', the police tell me. They don't seem overly concerned about illegal immigrants.

The army sergeant turns up at the hotel later.

'Sorry to bother you', he says, 'But when you are ready, can you come to the army headquarters. The commandant would like to talk to you.'

'What was that about?' the woman who runs the hotel asks when he has gone. I say I have no entry stamp in my passport and the army thinks that I might be a smuggler.

'Hah!' She exclaims. 'Smugglers! Everywhere smugglers. The army says it is worried about smugglers. Petrol smugglers and drug smugglers. It's rubbish. Everyone is smuggling things past everyone else. Don't you worry about it.'

The commandant wants to know how I entered the country, who gave me a lift, what he was carrying in the truck, because he might not have been a farmer at all but a smuggler. He spreads a large scale map out on his desk, and I feel obliged to appear eager to help, and invent vague details and plain untruths as we pore over it, considering routes I might have come.

The Andes rise up in a wall to the west of Villa Montes, ridge after ridge, ever higher. It takes me five days to reach Tarija, with frequent stops to patch up the bike which is falling apart again. Frequent stops too at several military posts, to explain the shameful irregularity of having no entry stamp in my passport.

Tarija is the capital of the dry southern province, sufficiently large and administratively important to have several bicycle shops and an immigration department.

Inflation is running at over two thousand per cent now. Food is in short supply. By government decree, all wheat flour is to be used to make plain bread, not cakes or puddings. Mandarines however are in season. A hundred people sit with wicker baskets piled high with mandarines, in the streets around the market.

I ask a man dressed in a crumpled pin stripe suit if he can direct me to the immigration building. He says he will lead me there, but he does not know if it will be open today. The immigration department has been on strike recently, and what with this morning's attempted coup – who knows?

I say I had not heard about the coup.

'Oh yes. It happened this morning, but most of the army remained loyal to the government', the man tells me. 'The President has been kidnapped. He might be dead. Some people are saying that he has arranged it all himself as a stunt to gain support.'

We pass a shop where people are queueing up to buy slabs of cooking fat. A small blob lies smeared on the pavement, trampled and muddy. The man stoops down, scrapes it from the ground with his finger and puts it into his mouth without breaking his stride.

There is a small demonstration in the central plaza outside the municipal offices. 'Democracy not Coupism' read the banners.

At the immigration offices I get an entry stamp with no questions asked. Everybody is more concerned with what is, or is not happening in La Paz, and with who their new employer might be.

The President is released the following day, unharmed. The Popular Democratic Union party is still in government and the army pledges its continued support for the democratic process. Embassies in La Paz are full of ex high-ranking army officers – several from the special 'Leopards' anti drug squad – seeking asylum.

I leave Tarija along the dirt track that winds up into the high mountains to the west. It will lead me to La Paz, to the international airport, to England.

I'm still climbing after two days, but the pass is in sight now. I camp on a wide flat ledge overlooking a panorama of valleys and mountain ridges. I find myself thinking of England quite often these days, of my family and friends. Returning there is an adventure because it is distant and strange.

I am curious to see how the security of a life on the road in South America, of a here and now existence, among people who live in the present and who always have time to stop and talk, will stand up in England where it is all different. Or at least, where I imagine that it is all different, because I am indulging in my fears now.

This is what I imagine – that no one lives in the present there, because we are all too busy planning and fearing for the future, examining and analysing and regretting the past; too busy seeking exit from reality, through excitement, through our meditations and quietist pursuits, too busy devising our theories and philosophies that will guide us out of here, too busy running away down the road, any road, to somewhere else, anywhere else, so long as it is away from here, from now; too busy imagining what we will do when we get there, to this paradise, this dream world where we will exercise our free will, act and not just react to events that knock around our emotions and desires and attitudes like billiard balls, where we will be strong and powerful, and put into effect all the mechanisms and ideologies that we have invented with our science and our imagination, that will banish the poverty and disease and suffering and confusion that has been increasing while we have been busy, escaping down our little road, praying, writing books, fighting revolutions, fighting for peace and a better future, fighting because everybody else is fighting – to reach the grand illusion, that is always one step away, as we stumble forward, always and forever along the road to somewhere else. Obsessed with getting there, or, like me now, sitting on a ledge in a high place thinking about that obsession, we forget that we are already here. There is nowhere else to go. We are all right here, right now, and the ground beneath our feet is where we must make our stand.

Four men herd a group of llamas onto the ledge during the night. The surrounding rock forms a natural corral, and is frequently used by travellers journeying over the mountains.

They wrap themselves up in blankets and lie down in the dust, huddling together for warmth among the animals.

They are up before dawn, loading the llamas with the sacks of salt from Uyuni that they are taking to Tarija. The distant ridges of mountains glow with the colours of sunrise. The air is cold and clear and still.

They make a fire and sit around, drinking coffee and chewing coca. What do I have to trade? they want to know. Where am I going to? Do I want to swap the bicycle for a llama?

They set off down the road as the sun rises, joking with one another about where I am going, because the Spanish word for England – '*Inglaterra*' – sounds like '*En la Tierra*', which is what they thought I said, which means 'In the Earth.'

One of the men stamps his foot on the ground.

'It's a good place!' he calls out as they leave.

TRAVELLERS' TALES SERIES

Watching the Dragon
Letters from China
Charles and Jill Hadfield
ISBN 0 245 54390 2 / Hardboard / £8.95

A Winter in Tibet
Letters from Lhasa
Charles and Jill Hadfield
ISBN 0 245 54773 8 / Paperback / £5.95

Kevin and I in India
Frank Kusy
ISBN 0245 54417 8 / Paperback / £4.95

The Islands in Between
Travels in Indonesia
Annabel Sutton
ISBN 0 245 54829 7 / Paperback / £5.95

By Bicycle in Ireland
Martin Ryle
ISBN 0 245 54666 9 / Paperback / £4.95

Published by Impact Books,
112 Bolingbroke Grove, London SW11 1DA

TRAVEL TITLES FROM OLIVE PRESS

The Other Italy
David Price
ISBN 0 946889 01 5 / Paperback / £3.50

The Scent of India
Pier Paolo Pasolini
ISBN 0 946889 02 3 / Paperback / £4.95

Assignments in Africa
Per Wästberg
ISBN 0 946889 12 0 / Paperback / £5.95

Travels in Japan
David Price
ISBN 0 946889 14 7 / Paperback / £6.95

A Better Class of Blond
David Rees
ISBN 0 946889 04 X / Paperback / £4.50

Etruscan Places
D.H. Lawrence
ISBN 0 946889 13 9 / Paperback / £6.95

Sea and Sardinia
D.H. Lawrence
ISBN 0 946889 20 1 / Paperback / £6.95

Published by Olive Press,
112 Bolingbroke Grove, London SW11 1DA